WITHDRAWN Praise for *Rubble*

Named to the "Best of 2005" lists of
Time Out New York and *The Village Voice*

"Wonderfully illuminating . . . Byles has built a fabulous work from centuries of tearing down."
—*Entertainment Weekly,* A-, "Editor's Choice"

"Engaging." —*The Atlanta Journal-Constitution*

"Good fun." —*The Village Voice*

"A live-wire, multilevel study . . . the demolition of buildings inspires complex emotions—shock, horror, even awe—and those responses are well worth thinking about." —*Time Out New York*

"An ebullient and informative look at a trade that lurks in the shadows." —*Preservation* magazine

"Byles offers a colorful take on this strangely upbeat blue-collar milieu."

—*Kirkus Reviews*

"In this colorful thematic history of the demolition trade . . . Byles ably and pungently excavates the shadowy crannies of this under-appreciated art." —*Publishers Weekly*

"Urban design, it turns out, is as much about subtraction as addition. With matchless wit, Jeff Byles explores the American obsession with demolishing our architectural past. He's the poet laureate of those un-sung heroes: the 'unbuilders.'"

—Mike Davis, author of *Dead Cities*

RUBBLE

UNEARTHING
THE HISTORY OF
DEMOLITION

JEFF BYLES

 THREE RIVERS PRESS
NEW YORK

Grateful acknowledgment is made to the estate of Edgar A. Guest for permission to
reprint "Wreckers," published in *Living the Years* © 1949 by The Reilly & Lee Co.

Excerpts from "An Urban Convalescence" by James Merrill are from *Collected Poems*
by James Merrill and J. D. McClatchy and Stephen Yenser, editors, copyright © 2001
by the Literary Estate of James Merrill at Washington University. Used by permission
of Alfred A. Knopf, a division of Random House, Inc.

Illustration Credits: Page xiv: Julian Rosefeldt & Piero Steinle, *Detonation
Deutschland*, 1996, seven-channel video installation, loop 56 minutes, video still. Pages
39 and 51: Courtesy of The Skyscraper Museum. Page 60: New York Times Co./Getty
Images. Pages 74, 75, 81, 95, 225, 283, 288, and 290: Controlled Demolition, Inc. Page
107: From *Haussmann* by Michel Carmona, copyright © 2000 by Librairie Arthème
Fayard, English translation copyright © 2002 by Ivan R. Dee, Inc., by permission of
Ivan R. Dee, Publisher. Page 114: From *The City of Tomorrow and its Planning* by Le
Corbusier, translated by Frederick Etchells © 1987 by Dover Publications. Pages 119
and 125: © Photothèque des Musées de la Ville de Paris/Cliché Briant Remi. Page 136:
Edward Hausner/The New York Times. Page 148: © Norman McGrath. Page 157:
Photo by Peter Moore © Estate of Peter Moore/VAGA, NY, NY. Page 184: Courtesy
Deere & Company. Page 207: © Bettmann/Corbis. Pages 213, 231, and 248: © Camilo
José Vergara. Page 265: © Hulton-Deutsch Collection/Corbis. Page 273: © Reuters/
Corbis.

Library of Congress Cataloging-in-Publication Data

Byles, Jeff.
Rubble : unearthing the history of demolition / Jeff Byles.
1. Wrecking—History.   2. Construction industry—History. I.   Title.
TH447.B95 2005
690'.26'09—dc22   2005015288

ISBN-13: 978-0-307-34528-8
ISBN-10: 0-307-34528-9

Printed in the United States of America

Design by Leonard Henderson

10 9 8 7 6 5 4 3 2 1

First Paperback Edition

To my father

*I hear the ruin of all space, shattered glass
and toppling masonry, and time one livid
final flame. What's left us then?*

—JAMES JOYCE, *ULYSSES*

*Whether it's good or bad, it is sometimes
very pleasant, too, to smash things.*

—FYODOR DOSTOYEVSKY, *NOTES FROM THE UNDERGROUND*

ACKNOWLEDGMENTS

These pages have been profoundly enriched by the rubblemakers, implosionistas, and others who generously shared their life's work with me, especially the Loizeaux family, Jack McFarland, William Meyers, and Brent Blanchard. I offer my gratitude and respect to them all.

My adopted hard hat is off to the talented and fearless team at Harmony Books. I am grateful to Shaye Areheart for believing in this project, to my editor Kim Kanner Meisner for unstinting good cheer and finesse, and to copyeditor Carrie Andrews and designer Lenny Henderson, who have admirably rustled my prose into place.

For their eager response to oddball queries involving obscure wrecking lore, I thank Patricia Volk, Barbara Milton, Lance Brown, Michael Willis, Dan Pitera, Henry Sobell, and the staff of The Skyscraper Museum, in particular their dauntless leader, Carol Willis. The Skyscraper Museum also graciously provided photographic material, as did Barbara Moore, Norman McGrath, and Camilo José Vergara. Each of them has added immeasurably to this book.

In his editorial roles at the Village Voice and The Believer magazine, Ed Park commissioned some of my early ruminations on rubble, while doubling as writerly inciter and fomenter-at-large. Jeffrey Kastner and friends at Cabinet magazine also printed an early demolition essay. I am grateful for their support.

This book would not have been possible without the commitment and enthusiasm of my agent, Michelle Tessler. My colleagues in books, Lorraine Shanley and Constance Sayre, showed me the ropes of publishing, and I owe them bucketfuls of appreciation.

To friends and family who cheered me on during the debris-darkened hours, thank you. Among the faithful was Andy Merrifield, who as ever proved a remarkable comrade in words; Jon Raymond, too, propelled my quest early on and offered late, stealth assists.

My mother and father, Nancy and Charles Byles, have inspired this work more than they can ever know.

And to Denisha, my ready confidante from the first, skull-jangling implosion to the still-settling dust, I owe the wide, bewildering world.

CONTENTS

RUBBLE

A paean to impermanence: This melting house, a typical demolition in postwar Germany, was sacked in 1962 to make way for a Berlin highway.

INTRODUCTION

RETURNING FROM an epic study of historic preservation battles in major cities, from Paris to Cairo to Kyoto, architectural historian Anthony Tung flung down his luggage and staggered to the keyboard. He had made, he said, an unexpected discovery. Prepared to record the heroic salvation of world architectural treasures—Romans burnishing their temples; Muscovites on scaffolds, brandishing heaps of gold leaf—he was confronted instead with what he described as a riot of rubble-making on a global scale. "I learned that during the twentieth century," the shell-shocked scholar reported in 2001, "not only has modern civilization destroyed much of the architectural fabric inherited from previous generations, creating a widening chasm between us and our past, but, worse, on every continent we have adopted a culture of destruction that presages further loss."[1]

Whirling within this metropolis-munching juggernaut is a dynamo called *demolition*. Conceived as the "bastard child" of the construction and scrap trades, legitimated in America as a modern depredatory force with a defiant 1975 Las Vegas manifesto, and propelled to pop-culture status around the world as a de facto extreme sport, demolition has left a dynamite-and-acetylene imprint on our streetscapes and on our very souls.

Partyers gaily kiss off a stadium in Seattle. Vast public-housing slabs are annihilated in St. Louis. Sixty thousand dwellings are razed in rubble-strewn Detroit. A thirty-two-story office block, merely twelve years old, is summarily sacked in São Paulo. And the World Trade Center registers as perhaps the most iconic demolition—controlled or otherwise—in modern history. As devastating civic trauma, beguiling counterarchitecture, rousing urban spectacle, and sheer scuttling of place, demolition may well be the black art of our time.

This book is a cultural history of destruction. It's the story of how that illegitimate child grew up into a multibillion-dollar business and unbuilt an entire world. It excavates the eye-popping saga of what happens when buildings fall, when monuments drop off into memory, and when the "oxymoronic dance of destructive creativity"[2] of tearing down to build again holds us in its thrall. Call it an unbildungsroman—a narrative of growth and transcendence, but one writ backward, the celluloid on rewind, the genie wrenched back in the bottle. This is the story of a roiling, ripsnorting realm—"an existential Earth," as urban seer Mike Davis deemed it, "shaped by the creative energies of its catastrophes."[3]

Let the reels unspool. In 1996, two young architects from Munich wrought from buildings a *danse macabre*. In twenty minutes of stippled, faded film footage, they collected images of structures being razed—an accrual of absence in voluptuous slow motion—to make way for Germany's postwar building boom. Cooling towers sway. Foundries plummet. Smokestacks pirouette. Office blocks totter. Everything, in this paean to impermanence, ends beclouded in dust. A deeply haunting work when I saw it several years ago, *Detonation Deutschland,* conceived by Piero Steinle and Julian Rosefeldt, was projected on screens that engulfed the viewer in virtually wall-to-wall rubble. "When presented as an all-round panorama, what initially looks like a collection of materials from the archives of a television studio," a curator wrote of this montage, "exudes the ambivalent allure of a frightening yet fascinating *theatrum mundi.* At the very last moment of its existence, a piece of real estate, which seemed by definition to be immobile, becomes animated, as if rearing up like a huge animal."[4]

Dalí had nothing on this surreal estate, this occult choreography of collapse. Far more than mere eye candy, this study of slumping structures was an "archive in motion," an art critic noted, a whole patrimony sent packing. The grand march of progress, the architects suddenly revealed, had an arresting if oft-forgotten corollary—"a bombardment of mesmerizing beauty, inflected with violence, tragedy and human folly."[5]

Detonation Deutschland was my first taste of the alchemy of unbuilding. The Maspeth Holders would be my next.

At dawn one summer Sunday, I scurried over a stranger's rooftop in Brooklyn—coffee cup clutched in one hand, zoom lens cradled in the other—and stood slack-jawed with hundreds of onlookers who had stormed the quiet Greenpoint neighborhood for the implosion of two hulking natural gas tanks, known as the Maspeth Holders. By that time, my occasional research jaunts had dredged up two decades of *Demolition Age* magazine at the Library of Congress (headline: YEA, RAH, URBAN

RENEWAL![6]); scored video footage of the Dunes Hotel's Technicolor destruction in Las Vegas (commentator: "No one actually shed a tear over the Dunes' demise. After all, there is no crying in Vegas."[7]); and explored how the ruin of buildings evokes Edmund Burke's notion of the sublime: the psychic wallop of awe and danger he once called "tranquillity tinged with terror."[8]

If you'd come to scout tranquillity in Brooklyn that day, well, fuggedaboudit. The end of the Maspeth Holders was more like a funeral cortege gone carnivalesque—or just a good Irish wake. As news choppers circled like vultures overhead and fresh-faced crowds jostled against police barricades, in their last moments the decrepit holders radiated something like the blush of majesty. "The tanks seem to be growing more beautiful as the hour of their death approaches," a reporter noted, telling how days before the implosion, demolition crews had weakened the steel structures with dozens of narrow slits, piercing the murky volumes with light. "It's definitely art," a tank inspector marveled as sunlight spilled through the metal in thin, spangly shafts and gleamed like the arcs of some giant Calder mobile. "I'm used to the inside and the outside of this thing being separate," he added with a mystical air. "Now we're letting the outside in. Soon the inside will be the outside."[9] But with a sulfurous flash and a hollow report, explosives gored the four-hundred-foot-tall holders and crumpled them like tin cans. Whorls of rust-colored dust punched the air while pigeons pinwheeled above, stunned by the blast. Meanwhile, reporters swarmed local residents, who had campaigned fruitlessly to rescue the half-century-old neighborhood icons from oblivion. "I feel like my heart was just ripped out," one resident stammered. "My son said he felt like he just witnessed an execution."[10] In the event, the havoc was captured most fittingly by a twenty-one-year-old lad who had turned out for the blast with his art student pals. He roundly declared: "The four of us are here to see a postmodern spectacle."[11] Outside a local bakery, departing gawkers were obliged to tuck into a twin-towered confection: the Maspeth Holders in sugar-and-flour miniature, topped with red-and-white checkered frosting.

Two months later, I was working as a writer-in-residence for the World Views program, which offered artists studio space atop the World Trade Center. Perched on the ninety-second floor of the north tower, I and my sixteen colleagues exulted in the site's dizzying verticality, which I had deemed a "barnstormer's-eye view" of the city. The phrase now seems uncanny. On September 11, 2001, I stood near Sixth Avenue and watched both towers collapse, taking with them one of my studio mates, the sculptor Michael Richards, who had been on the ninety-second floor that morning. My nightstand at the time held Eric Darton's history of the World Trade Center, *Divided We Stand*, and beneath it a long out-of-print children's title on demolition called *Tear Down to Build Up*. ("It is a scene of order and confusion at the same time," the latter says with spooky aplomb, "wonderful to watch!"[12]) When that dreadful vellum of smoke and dust finally settled, demolition had become my leitmotif, and rubble my métier.

There was no cake, of course, after the Twin Towers crumbled, and the Irish wakes proved all too welteringly real. As contractors divvied up the acreage at Ground Zero and, after a time, the Augean "scoop-and-dump" brigades began to toil (the diesel excavators, William Langewiesche memorably wrote, "roamed through the smoke and debris on Caterpillar tracks and in the hands of their operators became living things, the insatiable king dinosaurs in a world of ruin"[13]), I delved into the literature of destruction. Whether it was Heracleitus (who supposedly said, "The most beautiful world is like a heap of rubble, tossed down in confusion") or dear old Rose Macaulay ("To be fascinated by ruins has always, it would seem, been a human tendency"[14]) or the earth artist Robert Smithson ("After all," he quipped, "wreckage is often more interesting than structure"[15]), I aimed to understand rubble as some sort of going concern. New Yorkers soon began searching on similar wavelengths, gently telegraphing thoughts from Ground Zero of "beauty in a moonscape of tragedy."[16] In time, as my forays took me farther afield, I found that Gothamites held no particular monopoly on Dresdenlike ruins.

Demolition was minting moonscapes all over.

[1]

ERASE-ATECTURE

Y OU HATE TO wake up to the sound of chainsaws or bulldozers," one Los Angeles resident groused not long ago about his losing battle with the newfangled "erase-atecture."[1] Tough luck, buddy. Like it or not, the buzz and rumble of house-hungry machinery has become a permanent fixture of the American landscape. In 2001, the city of sunshine and noir doled out 1,211 demolition permits for destruction as diverse as the Gilmore Bank (a '50s relic ditched to build a shiny happy shopping mall) and the "Pink Palace" of Holmby Hills (former lair of Jayne Mansfield), prompting the *Los Angeles Times* to tut-tut: "Snakes shed scales. Roses drop petals. And Los Angeles levels buildings—about three per day."[2] Indeed, what the paper called a "new sort of ghost town" of now-spectral structures is growing more jam-packed by the minute, with the city's wealthiest neighborhoods doing most of the damage as they make way for McMansions. "We just smash it up and separate what we can," one Canoga Park contractor said and shrugged when asked about the down-and-dirty particulars. A savvy L.A. salvage firm, on the other hand, was having a field day amid the ruins, doing such booming business that they'd managed to amass one hefty pile of porcelain. "We probably have about three hundred toilets," said Jerry Hernandez of Santa Fe Wrecking. "We go as far back as about the 1890s."[3]

The nutty story in La-La Land is only symptomatic of a demolition derby stretching from one upmarket end of the nation to the other. "A disturbing pattern of demolitions is approaching epidemic proportions in historic neighborhoods across America," complained the National Trust for Historic Preservation in 2002.[4] Behold the teardown, or the junking of an existing house in order to build a vastly larger one on the same site. From Boston to Beverly Hills, the quaintest bungalows, Cape Cods, Colonials, and ranches are getting munched away in tactical real estate maneuvers known as "bash-and-builds" and "scrape-offs," clearing the plot for gentry-friendly "starter castles" and perilous "snout houses"—the latter so called for their forward-thrusting garages, which are deemed so gangrenous they're banned from older neighborhoods in Portland, Oregon. Blame it all on soaring real estate prices and the supersizing of the American house (the average newly built home has 2,305 square feet, up 53 percent from 1970, despite the shrinking of the average American family by 15 percent over that period), a formidable double-whammy whose side effect happens to be massive profit margins for brazen speculative developers. "A house is most likely a goner," the experts confirmed, "if the property it's on is worth far more than the structure."[5] The mechanics of the teardown are bracingly simple. You plunk down $400,000 for a lousy 1,500-square-foot house on a prize lot. Then, it's just $3,500 for a quick bulldozer blitz, and a day or two later, voilà—tabula rasa is all yours. There isn't even any shame in it these days. "Builders used to be afraid to be the first person in a neighborhood to tear a house down," a New Jersey developer cheerfully explained. "But now they're looking around and saying they don't mind taking the risk."[6] No, siree. Formerly quiet, leafy neighborhoods everywhere are now gripped in mano-a-bulldozer combat as neighbors battle developers, preservationists report: "Teardowns, in short, have reached crisis proportions."[7]

In places like Stamford, Connecticut, it's creative destruction at its finest, and don't go running next door when the wrecking crew rumbles down the street. "For the most part, people are pretty apathetic about these things," said the head of the Stamford zoning board.[8] And demolition dust is knee-deep in Illinois, where Chicago's Hinsdale suburb has seen more than twelve hundred homes razed in the past two decades—a boggling 20 percent of its housing stock.[9] But nothing quite touches Bergen County, New Jersey, where the number of demolitions jumped 82 percent between 1995 and 1999, plowing under everything from $200,000 ragtag bungalows to $800,000 turn-of-the-last-century Victorians. "The logo of this town shouldn't be a monument to the Revolutionary War," growled a disgruntled councilman in historic Fort Lee. "It should be a bulldozer."[10]

Don't blame the bulldozers, of course, which just follow the builders, who supposedly follow the "Rule of Three," which says that wrecking a structure will be profitable if new construction on the plot will fetch three times what the developer paid for it. And when the councilmen grumble, there's always the next hamlet over: "Developers are like ants. If you put the cover on the Bundt cake on the picnic table, they'll just move to the potato salad," said one Chicago architect, a developer himself.[11] Indeed, any house in a prime location that falls into the doomed category of the "not-keeper" and happens to come on the market, as one real estate agent gently explained, is ripe for the picking: "the builders buy it, bulldoze the house, dig a hole and go."[12] Fully a third of all home sales in some areas are now made to buyers like Larry Bruno, a thirty-two-year-old mortgage banker who had just snapped up a four-bedroom 1970 Colonial on western Long Island for $1.175 million—only to replace it with a six-bedroom "modern Colonial" replete with pool and basketball court. "Our realtor said that in Woodbury and Syosset there was no land left to buy, that we'd have to tear a house down," he calmly told a reporter in 2004. "I said, 'Fine, find me something old to demolish and we'll build our dream house.' "[13] That was music to the ears of the bullish Long Island Builders Institute, which was actively promoting the joys of sacking a house for a mere $20,000 and indulging one's taste for luxury living. It's all bang-up business if you're in the wrecking game, of course, but there are a lot of sensitive types who happen to drive bulldozers. Over in the Hamptons, George Mathys, owner of George's Roll Off and Demolition Service on Long Island, wrecked eighteen large homes one year. "Probably 50 percent of them were totally livable," he confided. "It makes me sad because I would love to live in a lot of them myself."[14]

Leave it to those Angelenos to have invented another leisure pursuit for developers—"scorched-earth land-banking"—whereby at least two thousand housing units have been sacked in the last decade by real estate high rollers holding out for the economic tide to turn. "While awaiting redevelopment to come their way, they were permitted, criminally, to demolish entire neighborhoods in the Crown Hill and Temple-Beaudry areas," fumed Mike Davis. "It was to their advantage to 'bank' land in desolation rather than take the risk of tenant organization or future relocation costs."[15] And so if L.A.'s got rubble overload, pity poor Philadelphia, where on March 13, 2003, Mayor John Street clambered behind the wheel of a backhoe and rammed a wrecking claw into a brick wall, ceremonially gouging the first of 318 vacant South Philadelphia homes. "So commenced Philadelphia's $295 million, five-year plan to raze 14,000 abandoned redbrick rowhouses and dilapidated Victorian mansions. The hope is that the swaths of vacant land will attract private developers."[16] And how. Detroit has vanquished sixteen thousand buildings over the last decade, while St. Louis razed 43 million square feet of abandoned properties in a desperate quest for urban resuscitation. Chicago? SQUANDERED HERITAGE, blares the headline.[17] In Vegas, they merely jest: IS 'LAS VEGAS LANDMARK' AN OXYMORON?[18] All told, more than 360,000 houses a year are razed in the United States, with a projected 4 million due to bite the dust over the next decade.[19] "We're living in a society," said David Goldfarb, president of New York City's Historic Districts Council, stating the glaringly obvious, "that wants to tear things down and throw everything away."[20]

It's not just Americans who've gone gaga over the bulldozer—demolition is hitting the prime time in the United Kingdom as well. "We want the Government to introduce grants for destruction," George Ferguson, president of the Royal Institute of British Architects, wrote not long ago, proposing a dastardly new historic building category: Grade X. Buildings awarded this dubious honor, Ferguson explained, would qualify for demolition or alteration grants, with preference given to those goners whose destruction would help spruce up a whole neighborhood.

He went on, barely restraining his flat-smashing zeal (and lifting an eyebrow or two among his peers): "I live for the day that some radical urban 'dentistry' is carried out and the most painful examples are extracted."[21] Ferguson perhaps got more than he bargained for when he touched off a massively pent-up wave of wrecking fervor around the British Isles. DOWN WITH EYESORES, affirmed London's *Financial Times* in an editorial, noting that a cull of the worst offenders "would make room for more appealing replacements and allow the rediscovery of historical gems that have been swamped by architectural monstrosities."[22] Liverpudlians, for their part, were all fired up to cast their votes for the ugliest building in Liverpool after the city council there was said to be drawing up a "hit list" of hideous structures that marred the city's World Heritage status,[23] and Scotland's design community was rounding up its most hated for the henchman as well.

And then all hell really burst loose. Inaugurating an "architectural ugliness pageant,"[24] Britain's Channel 4 announced it would air a four-part reality television series in 2005 called—yes—*Demolition*, in which citizen-viewers nominate Britain's ugliest buildings, and experts winnow the list to one unlucky winner that will suffer a predictable fate: "After the nation's nastiest structure is named and shamed, it will be dynamited or bulldozed live on TV."[25] (A replacement will then supposedly rise in its place—its construction being fodder for another reality series, of course.) This "real-time architectural snuff film," as it was called—some even went so far as to brand it "cultural vigilantism"[26]—was tipped to be "an even greater ratings grabber"[27] than the BBC's famed *Restoration* series, in which millions voted for their favorite endangered historic building, which was then lovingly fixed up. (The Royal Institute of British Architects, hot on its "Grade X" campaign, was wholeheartedly backing the new show: "Vile buildings are an affront to our senses," reiterated the ever-feisty Ferguson. "What I seek is public intolerance of the worst and demand for the best."[28]) The program's producers were casting it in an emancipatory light, noting that bad buildings blight people's lives and vowing that their interest was all in "kick-starting a nationwide debate about the value of architecture and empowering people to feel they can improve the quality of the built environment."[29] Not to be outdone by its home-turf rival, the BBC was gearing up its own show *Raze It!,* which critics promptly knocked as "a cheap and cheerful daytime version in which contestants must demolish hated landmarks by themselves with sledgehammers, while linked together chain-gang style."[30]

All this precipitated a minibout of soul-searching from Britain's more cerebral quarters. "Here's a neat idea for a new television series," scoffed critic Deyan Sudjic. "Let's get the public to nominate the six vilest books in the English language and in the grand finale, they get to burn them live on camera."[31] Taking sharp issue with what producers hyped as "a spectacular celebratory demolition of one of the nation's nastiest eyesores," Sudjic drubbed the whole notion as "wretchedly ill-conceived TV programming"; he added, "After the appalling vision of the Twin Towers reduced to rubble or the tsunamis in the Indian Ocean, how can anybody find even a hint of the celebratory in watching a building [being] erased from the world?"[32] To suggest that dynamite is the postmodern planner's best friend, he said, was the trope of the dodgy politician grasping for a photo-friendly fix. But the fight for architectural clemency was an uphill battle. In cities around the United Kingdom, the media rushed to piece together all manner of hit lists, such as the "Seven Horrors of Aberdeen" in Scotland, which, still preparing to blast its biggest eyesores, had begun pondering proposals for tax incentives to encourage demolition and had even topped Ferguson's zeal by suggesting that buildings be slapped with ratings from the dreaded X all the way to ultranaughty XXX, depending on how truly vile "the nasty" was deemed.

Reacting across the pond, consciences were jarred as if demolition were some heinous new precept instead of a sterling link in the creative-destruction nexus. "Architecture is the only art form that society condones destroying," lectured the *Wall Street Journal,* hoping to dissuade American television producers from grabbing their rubble-cams and fanning the populist flames. "The fate of buildings matters too much to be decided by the mob and turned into an entertainment spectacle—like a public hanging."[33] (This, too, may be an uphill battle, given the predilection of the media for all manner of collapsed, tornado-squashed, and otherwise destroyed structures. "Twelve years ago," the head honcho of the American Institute of Architects recently recalled, "frustrated over the meager press coverage of architecture, I was informed by a CBS News executive that architecture seldom becomes newsworthy except when it fails."[34]) The *Journal*'s point may be well taken, but try telling it to the citizens of Cumbernauld, a bleak 1950s town of fifty-two thousand not far from Glasgow and a distinguished honoree of the 2001 Carbuncle Award for the most dismal place in Scotland ("a rabbit warren on stilts," the judges declared). When Cumbernauldians got wind of Channel 4's lurid offer, they were among the first to jam the station's phone lines, bowling over even jaded producers with their unbridled zeal. Clamoring for "dynamite and bulldozer to deliver them oblivion," the soul-sapped residents took the show's premise to its logical conclusion. "It seems they wanted the entire town to be razed for the planners to start again," said a flabbergasted station rep. "This is a little further than we want to go for the programme."[35]

To be sure, there's a well-known penchant for *Ruinenlust* in England—lust for ruins, that is, as Rose Macaulay was wont to call it—where even architects hanker for a good structural sucker punch on occasion. Foremost among them, aside from our friend Ferguson, is the ebullient, eccentric Cedric Price, fondly tagged as "the only architect to be a fully-qualified member of the National Institute of Demolition Contractors."[36] One of the big architectural bruisers of the twentieth century, Price famously demanded the destruction of his Inter-Action Centre in north London, rebuffing preservationists who, so he thought, fecklessly wanted to preserve his arts center, which had "come with instructions for its demolition." (Built in 1971 and subsequently fallen into disuse, it was duly razed in 2000.) "Cathedrals, too, he thought had stayed too long and should be flattened," one admirer wrote. "Cedric liked to compare design with cooking, and seemed to be taken in by the analogy because he so enjoyed the notion of buildings being eaten like a meal by users and then excreted when the nourishment had been taken out of them."[37] Price, who died in 2003, called his culinary constructions a kind of "calculated uncertainty"—animated by their willful ephemerality—and, when he wasn't pasting up manuals showing how his buildings could be wrecked and the material recycled, liked to say that when structures lose their purpose they should be shucked off "like a worn-out pair of Hush Puppies."[38]

Goaded on by Price, other titans of the trade have now uttered the unutterable, making the wrecking ball the new mascot
of the architectural avant-garde. De-building, unbuilding, not
building—it's all the new rage. "How many of these buildings
deserve eternal life?" Dutch architect Rem Koolhaas cavalierly
wondered when begged by French officials to spiff up the
scabrous urban fabric around the Parisian precinct of La
Défense. *Mais oui,* counseled Koolhaas, historic or sentimental
sites could be salvaged. "But when we looked at these buildings—their materials not intended to last forever, their programs
merely articulations of a momentary financial legitimacy—it became difficult to consider them part of Europe in a historical
sense," he later mused. "They were not conceived with claims of
permanence; they are a kind of provisional—short-term—
architecture."[39] In homage to Price's knack for torturing uptight
colleagues, Koolhaas has pegged the demolitionist as the profession's patron saint. Today's architectural output, after 30 years
at the most, simply expires, he noted, "all within a single generation. Modern building is literally written off."[40]

As Frederick Gutheim wrote in *Architectural Record* in 1949,
"From the time a building is completed, its destruction be-
gins."[41] A scuff here, a dent there, soon the facade's in pieces,
and the roof caves in, and the dump trucks pull up to the curb.
Koolhaas, by the way, wasn't far off the mark. The average
American building lasts thirty-five years.[42]

In other words, there's a whole lotta wrecking goin' on, and
all indicators show that this scoop-and-dump bonanza won't go
bust anytime soon. "Many trends indicate," a recent report
chirped, "that building demolition and renovation will continu-

ally increase as a portion of the overall U.S. construction industry."[43] According to the 2002 U.S. Economic Census, which con-
tains the most current data available, there are 2,097 wrecking
and demolition contractors in the United States doing business
worth $3.1 billion with an annual payroll of $944 million and
almost thirty thousand employees. Over the last decade, moreover, business has been booming. Between 1992 and 1997, the
number of demolition contractors grew nearly 60 percent, the
value of work soared 107 percent, payroll doubled, and the industry added more than five thousand workers.

One good thing about capitalism: Crisis comes with the territory, and, sooner or later, it'll always take a contractor to mop
up the mess. Bulldozers may as well be on continuous standby to
slough off the architectural damage from what economist Joseph
Schumpeter in 1942 dubbed "the perennial gale of creative destruction,"[44] a maelstrom of industrial mutation "that incessantly revolutionizes the economic structure *from within,*
incessantly destroying the old one, incessantly creating a new
one."[45] This havocking free market spawns a spatial showdown
with plenty of fodder for the unbuilding brigades. Just take
brownfields, for example. Those are the frequently rotting tracts
of once-thriving industrial properties that litter the outskirts and
waterfronts of cities everywhere. Defunct factories, shuttered re-
fineries, abandoned slag dumps—it's the polluted detritus of a
disappeared way of life. Heavy industry having decamped to
more cost-effective climes, brownfields are now ripe for the
wrecking ball, and the cycle grinds on. It's "a perpetual struggle," said geographer David Harvey, "in which capital builds a
physical landscape appropriate to its own condition at a particular moment in time, only to have to destroy it, usually in the

course of crises, at a subsequent point in time."[46] Or, as they like to say in the destruction industry: Explosives are not a discretionary purchase.

As it does in capitalism, a perpetual struggle rages at the heart of demolition. It's a trade always hunkered down at the front lines between the built and the unbuilt, the past and the future, even the living and the dead. The annals of wrecking abound with richly dialectical allusions, whether it be the ever–au courant Marx ("All that is solid melts into air" is the thinking wrecker's credo bar none[47]) or the bug-eyed Sturm und Drang of Goethe's *Faust* (in which "the demonic lust for destruction turns out to be creative"[48]) and there's even sashaying Shiva, that Hindu god of cosmic dissolution whose dance of doom paves the way for rebirth. Perhaps it's deference to these cosmic currents that gives rise to a sixth sense among experts such as Anna Chong, president of the wrecking firm Engineered Demolition, who has blasted her way from Saudi Arabia to Calgary, Canada. Chong, who was raised in Micronesia and is a martial-arts black belt who speaks five languages, has been known to sprinkle holy water around dynamite-packed buildings before their detonation. "We know God's really in control of these things," Chong's former partner, explosives expert Eric Kelly, once explained. "Because of the work we do, we're probably more spiritual than a lot of people."[49] (Respect for the spirit world, anyway, is essential when working in Japan or Korea, where the numeral *four* is associated with death. "We won't demolish a structure on the fourth of the month," Chong explained, "and we often avoid loading explosives on the fourth floor of a building."[50]) In 1994, Chong's firm took down what may be the largest structure ever imploded—the Sears Merchandise Center in Philadelphia, spanning 2.7 million square feet. That massive complex, which opened in 1920 (wowing the public with its "Industrial Gothic" decor), was felled with more than twelve thousand pounds of dynamite, enough to sound like a .357 magnum fired from ten paces away. "It literally can move a mountain," Kelly told the press, which was certainly a feat of biblical proportions.[51] But with all due respect, it wasn't exactly God who pulled the trigger that day. It was the ghost of Joseph Schumpeter. The Sears Merchandise Center was leveled for a Home Depot.

"It's always about money," a Chicago city planner sighed not long ago. "It's either about too much money in some neighborhoods and you have tear-downs. Or there's not enough money."[52] Yes, the perennial gale is bitter in the Windy City, which recently played host to the "demolition ceremony" for the former headquarters of the *Chicago Sun-Times,* a site Donald Trump—the Incessant Destroyer incarnate—commandeered for a ninety-two-story hotel and condo tower. The scene was a classic wrecking kickoff, full of awkward machines and fluttering toupees and plenty of empty pomp. "Mr. Trump arrived at noon and gave a speech," wrote a grumpy New York correspondent, "then walked to the front of the building. He signaled to the hard hats, and a mechanical claw started ripping out the entryway. People clapped. The protesters—Chicagoans appalled that a New Yorker would dare to vandalize their city in broad daylight for TV crews—never came, probably because they don't exist."[53]

Chicago, it's worth noting, is one of those forlorn metropolises ravaged by that "unlikely combination of tear-down trends that are wreaking havoc nationwide."[54] You've got traditional teardowns on the one hand, and on the other, city-sponsored bulldozers plowing whole blocks of houses into weedy pasture as part of Chicago's "fast-track" demolition program. Since 1993, the city has rubbled more than seven thousand buildings deemed unsafe or that are haunts for junkies and thieves, a procedure some have likened to clear-cutting a forest. "I call that urban planning by subtraction," retorted one irked resident. "We have gangs in buildings so we get rid of buildings. They're turning the South Side back into the prairie."[55] A *Chicago Tribune* study found that one in five demolished Chicago homes was wrecked via "stealth demolition"—hacked down under the radar, without a demolition permit—all courtesy of a thriving "demolition machine," which "is likely to keep smashing and crushing buildings, hauling away profit as well as wreckage."[56] Likened to the city's famed Union Stockyards, where pigs and cattle were slaughtered with such brio that "everything but the squeal" made a profit, the demolition machine shears off ornaments and terra-cotta sculptures—once part of the so-called "public patrimony"—and sends them across the lands into the living rooms of wealthy collectors. No surprise, wink-wink, that Chicago's city aldermen were reaping tens of thousands of dollars in campaign contributions, according to the *Tribune,* from hordes of "architects, construction companies, contractors, developers, drywallers, engineers, lawyers, pipe fitters, real estate agents, unions," and—you guessed it—"wreckers."[57]

Back at the Trump site, however, as crews rapidly dispatched the squat, seven-story *Sun-Times* block, the only alarms ringing were the cell phones of the city's architectural elite, who were crowing to one another about how the disappeared building allowed a glorious glimpse of the city's massive IBM tower across the way, which had been all but blotted from the skyline by the *Sun-Times* bunker. "Never before," gasped an awestruck television reporter, "have we seen famed architect Mies Van Der Rohe's last and largest American building in full view." (The revelation stunned even non-architects. "I didn't even really know it was there," a bystander blurted into the camera.[58]) The fast-rising Trump property would, of course, soon plunge Mies's masterpiece back into its penumbra, as the Donald commenced bickering with city officials over the height of his structure's spire.

About the constant churn of creative destruction, John Kenneth Galbraith got it right: "The greater the wealth, the thicker will be the dirt."[59]

Time to cue up another reel. Midway through a briskly paced video montage called *The Art of Demolition*—a ten-minute romp documenting more than seventy-five toppled high-rise towers, imploded stadiums, and fetchingly felled bridges—the jump cuts give way to a long, low-angle shot of a tall chimney framed against cloud-scudded skies of depthless blue. Read: bucolic grandeur. Craggy low mountains crouch on the horizon (we're outside Tulsa, maybe, or greater Billings), and the slender stack is a brilliant stroke of white with bold black stripes etching its upper half. Already, a fusillade of smoke spills from the chimney's base as the dynamite kicks in, and a Homeric fall is upon us: A gallant first tilt, then a broadening arc, then it's all pure, luscious geometry as the chimney top scribes a perfect curve through the air. Ramrod straight to the end, the column at last smacks the earth in a shower of dust and debris. Never has a smokestack been so lyrical. These nine seconds of video vérité get very near to nobility.

Smuggled in between clips of a severed, plunging drawbridge and a couple of rearing natural gas tanks, these are perhaps not the most bankable few frames from *The Art of Demolition,* an in-house curriculum vitae produced by the Loizeaux family of Phoenix, Maryland, one of the world's roving explosive demolition teams. Yet that bolt of smokestackian sublimity carries the shock of a manifesto. Away from the excavators, the economists, and the developers, it's possible again to feel that exhilarating thrill of destruction. While the dynamite and detonating cord play out their magic, what you're seeing is the supercharging of space. "At last each particle of space is meaningful," as surrealist author Louis Aragon wrote in another lifetime, "like a syllable of some dismantled word."[60]

[2]

FIREBALLS AND
SKULL CRACKERS

IN THE WEE HOURS of Sunday, September 2, 1666, one of the most ravaging fires in history crackled to life at the home of Thomas Farriner, a London baker whose shop on Pudding Lane turned out ship's biscuit for the Royal Navy. The flames, fanned by a brutal easterly gale, engulfed a city that was already parched from a ten-month drought. The scene, one witness wrote, was paroxysmal: "The noise and cracking and thunder of the impetuous flames, the shrieking of women and children, the hurry of people, the fall of towers, houses, and churches, was like a hideous storm; and the air all about so hot and inflamed, that at the last one was not able to approach it, so that they were forced to stand still, and let the flames burn on, which they did, for near two miles in length and one in breadth."[1] The devastation spawned yellowish clouds of smoke, said another, that "ascendeth up to heaven, like the smoke of a great furnace."[2] The sun seeped through, bloodred. The dreadful roar of blistering glass and fracturing stone was "pierced by explosive detonations as superheated casks of brandy, black powder and a thousand other combustibles succumbed to the flames."[3]

Shortly after seven o'clock that morning, Samuel Pepys, the remarkable diarist and civil servant with a rough-and-ready grasp of firefighting tactics, clambered into a boat and had himself ferried along the Thames to deliver the news to King Charles II. Giving house-wrecking a famous cameo role as a crisis-management tool, Pepys boldly declared "that unless his Majesty did command houses to be pulled down, nothing could stop the fire."[4] It was said to be the only good advice the king got that day. The Great Fire of London devoured 13,200 houses—a hundred every hour, by one count—blackening more than four hundred acres and snatching the rooftops from one hundred thousand people. Pepys was not the first person who thought of flattening houses to save a city, but thanks to him, demolition put in one of its first impressive appearances on the world-historical stage.

As the conflagration kindled, razing the as-yet unscathed homes of prominent citizens was hardly uppermost on the mind of London's lord mayor, a man named Sir Thomas Bludworth, who was dimly viewed around town as "delighting more in drinking and dancing than is necessary for such a magistrate." Bludworth arrived on the scene, took in the first bits of the blaze, and was supposed to have said: "Pish. A woman might piss it out."[5] Before long, however, what Pepys called the "cracking of houses at their ruin"[6] could be heard throughout the city as the searing wind shoved the fires westward. It was an apocalyptic panorama, with pitch dripping from weatherboarding and embers dropping out of the sky, and, Bludworth's proclamation to the contrary, it soon transpired that the "eastern face of every building now streamed with smoke, and the air was so dense with it that people groped their way blindly through the streets."[7] By this time, a handful of self-deputized wreckers—most of them seamen and soldiers—had joined the fray, wielding axes, crowbars, ropes, and chains as they toiled to chop firebreaks into the city. As early as 1612, it had been common recourse to yank down burning houses to stop fires from spreading. This was said to be expertly accomplished with fire hooks, large iron grapnels fixed to poles, reaching to thirty feet in length. As one description explained, the method was fiercely effective: "The hook was thrown over the ridge-beam of a burning building, there being iron rings at the end of the pole and part way up, to which cords were attached, and were dragged by companies of men or horses till the fragile timber-built house came clattering down."[8] Some builders, planning for every contingency, had even installed iron rings under the rafters expressly for the fire hooks.

By the time of the great London blaze, however, any such conveniences proved beside the point. The wrecking work was arduous, and aside from the physical strain, those in the line of fire had to worry about being sued by irate homeowners demanding compensation. (Bludworth himself was heard muttering over and over, "When the houses have been brought down, who shall pay the charge of rebuilding them?"[9]) Moreover, as the tumbling houses sent dust swirling into the already thick plumes of smoke, it was clear that stronger measures were needed. The firebreaks were made, but the "flames were either upon them before the breaks had been completed, or else seized on the timbers and laths among the rubble left mounded in the street and burned unhindered across the gap."[10] Bludworth, who had finally sprung into action, cried to Pepys amid the mayhem: "Lord, what can I do? I am spent! People will not obey me. I have been pulling down houses. But the fire overtakes us faster then [sic] we can do it."[11] With that, he scampered off into ignominy. (Pepys, meanwhile, famously hustled home and buried his wine and Parmesan cheese in the garden to save them from the advancing flames.)

As the fire wore on, reinforcements arrived to spell the exhausted sailors and civilians at their wrecking work, and the authorities came to their senses. Since the very first day of the fire, seamen had clamored for the use of gunpowder to blast open firebreaks—a measure thought rather "too desperate a remedy," until, when Tuesday rolled around, residents awoke to find that more than half of their city had been charred beyond recognition. The blasting of houses was speedily ordered, "with entirely satisfactory results." Seamen lugged a full barrel of powder to the ground floor of each house in a row to be demolished, linked them together by a thin powder trail, and ignited the blasts in series. It was almost too easy: "The force of the explosion lifted each timber structure a yard or so; the straining frames broke, and the building collapsed flat on the ground where it had stood, with but trifling danger to bystanders." Any flames sparked by the blasts were tidily stamped out. Pepys himself admired the efficiency of the work but observed that "at first it did frighten the people more than anything else."[12]

The blasts may have been nerve-racking, but it should be noted that demolition by powder keg wasn't exactly unheard of. Blowing up houses with gunpowder had been a subject of intense interest in London since 1605, when Catholic agitators loaded thirty-six barrels of the stuff under the House of Lords.

What become known as the Gunpowder Plot to blow the structure up—and knock out King James I along with it—was foiled
when the mercenary Guy Fawkes, a low-level conspirator in the
scheme, was caught skulking about in the powder-packed cellar
at midnight before the planned detonation on November 5. The
date is still riotously commemorated in England with bonfire-
fueled festivities.

In the years following the London fire, anyway, city authorities were far less timid about ordering the wholesale demolition
of houses in times of crisis. Sailors were on virtual standby with
their barrels of naval powder—"and this they were able to sup-
plement by purchase from the store of a local grocer"[13]—should
their services be required. And sure enough, little more than a
decade had passed before houses erupted in flames at the Pump
Court of London's Middle Temple, threatening to destroy the elegant complex of lawyers' chambers. "The Thames being
frozen," one witness reported, "there was great scarcity of
water, it being so bitter a frost, the water hung in icicles at the
eves of the houses." Quick-thinking tipplers dashed into a
nearby cellar, where casks of beer were laid up, and firemen deployed the primitive fire engines of the day to douse the flames
with ale. "The engine plaid away many barrels of beer to stop
the fire," but the brew was soon tapped out. Sailors were called
in, and their blasts speedily snuffed the flames. Clearly the technique had not been perfected, however, for the explosions put
many in the infirmary, including the unlucky Earl of Faversham,
whose skull was nearly split.[14]

Demolition continued to play a salvational role in fires on down
through history. Little had changed by the time of New York's

great blaze on December 16, 1835, when a similar turn of events played out across lower Manhattan. The fire, thought to have been kick-started by an exploding gas pipe in a five-story structure at 25 Merchant Street, was puny by London standards, torching only 674 buildings over 17 blocks. Still, the blaze battened on the densely packed district of warehouses, banks, newspaper plants, and churches and was called the most devastating conflagration to have ever besieged the city. The temperature that night dipped seventeen degrees below zero, snow had been falling steadily for twenty-four hours, the Hudson River was frozen solid, and the East River nearly so. "The thin streams that came from the hydrants would not throw more than thirty feet," one account said, "and they were so feeble that the wind blew them back against the firemen who held the hose pipes, quickly coating the men with ice."[15] The infernal glow of the flames that night was seen from a hundred miles away; on the ground, it revealed a looting binge of such merry abandon, it was later estimated that "ten thousand bottles of champagne alone had been consumed by the mobs which swarmed about the streets, stealing and fighting."[16] A peculiar story survives from this blaze about the Dutch Reformed Church on Garden Street. As it began to go up in flames, the church organ broke out in a funeral dirge: "The solemn strains soared high above the roar of the flames and the shouts of the firemen, stopping suddenly in the middle of a bar when the building collapsed. The identity of the musician was never learned."[17]

By four the next morning, Mayor Cornelius W. Lawrence was persuaded that "only the most heroic measures could save the entire city from destruction." The sale of powder was banned in New York, and only a few pounds could be scrounged up at the army post on Governor's Island. Eventually a barge found its way to the naval magazine at Red Hook—now part of Brooklyn—and the explosives landed at dawn under guard of eighty marines and a dozen sailors. "The demolition of the buildings was begun immediately, but it was not until noon that the necessary break was made at Coenties Slip by the destruction of a building occupied by a firm of wholesale grocers. The southward progress of the conflagration was then checked, and what remained of New York had been saved."[18]

At every great blaze through the centuries, it seemed, wreckers were vigorously improving their techniques. During Chicago's epic fire of 1871, the mere sound of detonations was enough to buoy the spirits of bystanders. "Everybody was asking everybody else to pull down buildings. There were no hooks, no ropes, no axes," as *Chicago Tribune* editor Horace White described the hopeless scene. Then a great fusillade rang out. "The reverberations of the powder, whoever was handling it, gave us all heart again. Think of a people feeling encouraged by the fact that somebody was blowing up houses in the midst of the city, and that a shower of bricks was very likely to come down on their heads!"[19] After the fire, ever-chipper Chicagoans were even more gladdened by the demolition. City elders surveyed the impressive ruins—eighteen thousand buildings up in smoke—and declared the blaze a wholesale blessing. "Specifically, by having wiped out all the small-time landlords who still held downtown property, the fire did in a couple of days what would have taken many years for land speculators to accomplish," scholar Ross Miller reported. Indeed, at Plymouth Church, on the first Sunday following the debacle, Henry Ward Beecher sermonized that the city "could not afford to do without the Chicago Fire."[20] Salvation instantly materialized in the form of frenzied real estate operators and architects, who skittered around reconstructing the rubbled avenues, although in the rush to rebuild, much of the work turned out to be discreditably slapdash. Not until several decades later did saner minds prevail and kick off the real urban redemption afforded by the city's ruin, when the great Daniel Burnham and others drafted the master plan—showcasing signature public spaces such as lakefront Grant Park—that is the glory of Chicago today.

Those who thrilled to the blasts during the Chicago fire would have gone bonkers in old San Francisco, where explosives were liberally used to beat back flames after the earthquake of 1906. Whole blocks were blasted to bits as artillery specialists snuck into buildings under showers of sparks, working maniacally to level structures already burning away. No one would even take a stab at estimating the quantities of charges deployed at the time, "but it must have been tremendous," avowed General Frederick Funston, the army's man on the spot, "as there were times when the explosions were so continuous as to resemble a bombardment." Funston reported that meager stockpiles of explosives had to be bolstered by tugboat trips to the California Powder Company at Pinole across the bay, the tug returning each time freighted with its fearsome load. "While frame and old brick buildings were reduced to piles of rubbish by these explosions," Funston observed, "the modern steel and concrete structures remained as impervious to the heaviest charges as they had been to the earthquake."[21] The stolid structures, it turned out, had rebuffed a relatively new armament in the fire-wrecker's arsenal. This was something called *dynamite*.

Alfred Nobel—the patron saint of creative destruction who patented dynamite in 1867—was a meek semirecluse with a gloomy countenance and a dark, brooding beard. He was, he wrote, "a misanthrope, but exceedingly benevolent." Summed up for good measure, he was "very cranky, and a superidealist." This saturnine Swede would launch the high-explosives industry and make his name synonymous with the cause of peace. A tinkerer at home everywhere among his test tubes and nowhere in the world, Alfred Nobel "felt that his work was misunderstood on a massive scale."[22] He had a demolitionist's temperament to the core.

In 1862, Nobel first successfully detonated a compound called *nitroglycerin*—by igniting it with a charge of gunpowder in a water-filled ditch in St. Petersburg—and with it inaugurated a new era in the world of wrecking. Nitroglycerin, a high explosive that's been an implosionist's little helper for more than a century, was going nowhere fast when Nobel got his hands on it. The stuff had been invented by the thirty-five-year-old Italian chemist Ascanio Sobrero, who was toiling in Turin amid a pan-European frenzy over new forms of explosives, when in 1846 he stirred up a mixture of nitric and sulfuric acid with a sweet, syrupy alcohol called *glycerin*. Sobrero, tantalized by his discovery, tasted a bit of the stuff, but its future as a cocktail mixer was grim. "A trace of it placed on the tongue, but not swallowed," he reported the following year, "gave rise to a most violent, pulsating headache accompanied by great weakness of the limbs."[23] Calling his serum "pyroglycerin" (the "pyro" soon swapped for a prefix more palatable to public opinion), Sobrero kept fiddling with the liquid but soon ran into trouble. His invention proved notoriously fickle, especially when transported, being wont to detonate at the slightest provocation. Sobrero was so beguiled by it that for a time he couldn't even learn its chemical composition.

Many shattered beakers and shrapnelled limbs later, Sobrero abandoned efforts to tame nitroglycerin, resigning himself to ponder its properties as a poison.

Enter Nobel, whose father Immanuel was a crackerjack inventor (his sea mines were admired by the Russian navy) who had got wind of nitroglycerin's peculiar promise. The younger Nobel was hoping to bottle the genie when, in 1862, at his brother Ludvig's engineering shop in St. Petersburg, he corked a glass tube full of the explosive liquid and snugged it inside a second tube packed with gunpowder. Lit with a fuse, the powder detonated the nitroglycerin, a basic principle that would prove remarkably useful in the obliteration of buildings. One structure in particular would sadly prove a test case. On September 3, 1864, as the Nobels refined their experiments, Alfred's younger brother Emil, home on vacation from college, had been tinkering with nitroglycerin in the family's one-story lab in the Swedish village of Heleneborg, outside of Stockholm. The town was jolted awake that morning when a blast devastated the place, killing five people, including Emil, in the first recorded fatal accident due to nitroglycerin. Alfred and his father stoically told investigators that young Emil had botched an experiment. Sorry about that, they said. "Nitroglycerin, they insisted, was harmless if it was properly handled; indeed, with its unprecedented explosive force, it could prove to be of immense value to humanity."[24]

Humanity would have to wait. The authorities soon exiled Nobel to work on a tiny floating platform in the middle of Lake Mälaren, where he ably filled the orders that began pouring in for his powerful new product. Almost as soon as his global marketing campaign geared up, however, more accidents ensued, among them a sensational blast in New York in 1865 (it was a wild morning eye-opener for patrons of the bar at the Wyoming Hotel, where a wayward box of the material had been stashed), another the next year in San Francisco (fifteen people killed), again at a port in Panama (where a seventeen-hundred-ton freighter packed with seventy cases of the stuff exploded and sank, leaving fifty people dead), a blast at Nobel's own factory near Hamburg (another lab down the tubes), plus wicked fireballs in Norway and Australia.

Nobel scurried back to rebuild his demolished German operation, and in 1866 found that a porous, clayish substance called *kieselguhr*—which he dug up from the sandy dunes around the factory—when mixed with nitroglycerin would make an impressively stable dough he called *dynamite*. You could burn a box of it on a pile of wood, even drop it from a height of sixty feet, but nothing save for an explosive detonation—via a blasting cap, Nobel's other great invention—would ignite the miracle product he proudly deemed "my safety powder." Factories sprouted across Europe, and dynamite became known as "the fastest-growing business in history."[25] By 1870, during the Franco-Prussian War, the Prussians pressed Nobel's new concoction into service to blast away barricades, and soon enough structures of all sorts were being downed around the globe. (The Hungarians are currently feted in the explosive demolition world for dynamiting a two-hundred-foot-tall chimney in Budapest in 1883.[26]) Never one to rest on his laurels, in 1875, Nobel swirled nitroglycerin together with a couple of other additives and brewed up blasting gelatin. Fearsome stuff, it packs a bigger punch than nitroglycerin but is as safe as dynamite and reigns as "the most valuable explosive ever used for peaceful purposes."[27]

But the dynamite magnate grew increasingly glum about his

reputation as the go-to guy for destruction—the "Merchant of Death," a French newspaper branded him in 1888[28]—and his restless mind fixed upon peace, a subject he'd worried over ever since his youth. In his final will of 1895, he established the famous awards, among them the Nobel Peace Prize, financed by a $9 million fortune he would leave after his death in 1896 in a villa in San Remo, Italy, unattended by either family or friends. Nobel had finally surpassed himself. Humanity would get its due.

The same year Alfred Nobel was preparing his bequest to those who have "conferred the greatest benefit on mankind," a different sort of destruction was being pressed into service in the name of humanity: one of the pioneering slum-clearance projects of the modern era in New York City. BOUGHT A HOUSE FOR $1.50 was the *New York Times*'s snickering headline on June 7, 1895, a day after ninety-nine tenements at the notorious Mulberry Bend district on the Lower East Side were auctioned for salvage by the city, which was obliterating them for a public park. "The 'Bend' has been one of the darkest spots in the old Sixth Ward," the paper explained, choicely noting that the site had been "the scene of almost continual riot and disorder," in particular, "many murders and atrocious assaults committed by the rum-frenzied denizens of the rookeries." It appeared that a few such souls had turned up for the auction—"a motley crowd," the *Times* said—the regular salvage dealers having skipped the occasion altogether, since "the materials in the buildings were so old and so filthy that they were not in any sense desirable." As the bidding opened, the first house went for a heady $110 (it was thought that "the purchaser will probably not realize one-half of that"), but the second house fetched just $3.50, and only a few of the mainly brick structures topped $10, with one going for $1.50, rock-bottom even by 1895 standards. The lucky winners were obligated to wreck the buildings and haul off the rubble (keeping anything they may deem valuable) within one month's time, but there was a catch: Some of the houses came with tenants included, owing many months' back rent. This sum the new owners were entitled to pocket if they could, it being explained that tenants—exclusively Italians—had been notified long ago that they'd be getting the boot. While some purchasers gave the residents a few days to vacate, others wasted no time getting cracking: "One man who had purchased a three-story tenement, with a store on the ground floor, for $2.75, entered into possession at once, and began to demolish the structure. The keeper of the store protested, and there was a lively row, which required the services of two policemen to quell." It was not until after the sale that "the ignorant tenants" realized their time was up, the paper testily concluded.[29]

As the global epicenter of creative destruction—flaunt it if you got it—New York looms large in the prehistory of wrecking. And no Gotham destroyer loomed larger than Jacob Volk.

He was a housewrecker out of "Herculean mythology."[30] The Lithuania-born son of a Delancey Street butcher, reared on New York City's Lower East Side, this dandy of devastation "pulled down the best places, and was proud of it. He never passed a tall building without an appraising glance and a sigh." As soon as he had scraped up $300, he fetched a horse and wagon, bought crowbars and sledges, and commenced crumbling twenty-five hundred buildings over a thirty-year swath of ruin. A born batterer, who took credit for the wrecking ball, he was remembered as a roué, a wise man, a show-off, and a pro.

His Park Avenue offices were poshly appointed, and upon his death in 1929, the essayist E. B. White called him "the greatest wrecker of all time."[31]

"Destructionist" was the heading over Jacob Volk's obituary.

A compact, burly man with a heavy jaw and a booming voice, Volk strode over busted balustrades and littered limestone like an admiral on his bridge. As pneumatic guns salvoed and steam shovels sallied, he'd bark through a megaphone at his hundred-odd crew. They jumped, said a witness, like sailors in thrall of some sagacious sea captain, "for though the work of each man was fraught with danger, one of the great characteristics of Mr. Jacob Volk is that he never sends a man where he would not go himself."[32] He kept a blackjack on his desk, a totem of rough-and-tumble days. Beside it stood a whiskey bottle. A wrecker's wrecker, Volk was.

When he took housewrecking by storm, it was said in 1917 that Volk knew he was "invading a field of service which up to that time was never followed by a Jew."[33] Anti-Semitism in the building trades cost him a few contracts, but no matter. Business boomed. "Among other good Russian qualities," wrote White, "he had a great genius for speed—which of late has been the most important factor in the wrecking game, where contracts always contain time clauses. The wrecker must back his experience against the strength of walls; it's a gamble." The odds could pay handsomely. When Volk dispatched the Cotton Exchange well ahead of schedule, he scored a $30,000 bonus. At the Chemical National Bank, on the other hand, he smacked up against a column of solid concrete running the full height of the building. (As White explained, "Ordinary tools were of no avail; the indomitable Jake finally leveled it by sheer force of character.") The Jacob Volk Wrecking and Shoring Company was cowed by one thing only: builders who had chutzpah. Volk hated Stanford White and Richard Morris Hunt, his obituary said, referring to the storied architects of the day: "They meant architectural permanence, structural intricacy." When Volk wrecked W. K. Vanderbilt's château in Manhattan (it was Hunt's sumptuous design), he vowed to destroy it in twenty days. Walls bulged twice as thick as advertised; gables and balconies had to be begged to fall. Thirty-five days later, Volk took a loss. Around that time, he had been finishing his own home in Bensonhurst, Brooklyn, and was asked why he didn't salvage the Vanderbilt loot—the carved Caen stone fireplace, the tiled Moorish billiards room—for his pleasure palace. "Listen," Volk said, "am I a piker? You won't see second-hand stuff in my house."[34]

The sign on Volk's wagons read: THE MOST DESTRUCTIVE FORCE IN WALL STREET.

In 1910, he vanquished the twenty-two-story Gillender Building in lower Manhattan, loosing two hundred fifty men upon the tallest building that had ever been razed. The press was titillated by the brazenness of the act, calling it "the first time that such a high-class office building, representing the best type of modern fireproof construction, has been torn down to make way for a still more elaborate structure."[35] The Gillender, only twelve years old, had been the tallest office structure in the world upon its completion in 1897, thrusting 306 feet into the sky at the corner of Nassau and Wall Streets—a site deemed "the most famous intersection in business history," what with the stock exchange across the street. The Bankers' Trust Company, which had acquired the building and leased an adjacent lot, wanted the Gillender gone to build a $4 million edifice tagged as "the most magnificent office building in the city."[36] The $50,000 demolition contract called for the Gillender to be banished in forty-five days, with a $500-per-day penalty for breaking the deadline.

Volk was prodigious. He had wrecked, he said, more than nine hundred buildings. He knew which end of the crowbar was up. He got to work. A protective scaffolding arose over adjoining streets. A shaft was chopped clear through the center of the building so rubble could be dumped to the lower floors. Then chutes shot debris out to a loading platform below. Plumbing was ripped out. Partition walls were sundered. Swarms of masons and mechanics crushed cornices and stripped away stone. To save time, Volk used pneumatic guns to blast away brickwork that backed stone on the structure's facade. ("If it cannot be managed with the air guns," he jauntily declared, "we shall use dynamite."[37]) When the building had been stripped to its naked steel frame, the men would knock heads off the rivets and drive them out with drift pins. Derricks were rigged up. Power winches groaning, they plucked large steel beams away and lowered them to idling trucks. The building rapidly dwindled. The hundred-man night shift carted it all away.

"This will be the most rapid housewrecking feat ever performed either in the United States or any other part of the world," Volk boasted. But speed had its costs. "If we had been allowed ten days' time to clean the buildings, we could have made fully $7,000 by the sale of the fittings," Volk admitted. "But as it was such a rush, everything had to go by the run and be consigned to the dump heap."[38] Almost exactly forty-five days later, no trace of the Gillender remained. Years later, Volk boasted of the job that he "made a considerable profit from tearing down the first steel building."[39]

Jacob Volk was always searching for a faster way of work-

The Gillender Building on Wall Street was only twelve years old when Jacob Volk brazenly loosed two hundred fifty men upon it in 1910.

ing. Thus he hit upon what he called the "upside-down method of housewrecking." Until the mid-1920s, the usual way was to start from the top of a building and proceed arduously floor by floor to the bottom, prying up bricks and woodwork and sending material down through wooden chutes built along the sides of buildings and into hoppers, under which trucks would be loaded. Trucks had to idle as long as a half hour under the chutes before they had a full load. Volk decided to first gut the lower floors of a structure, then chop a shaft through the building and dump the debris clear to the bottom, where it would be scooped up by power shovels and loaded into trucks. Steam shovels could load a seven-yard truck in three minutes.

"Jake got another idea," his granddaughter, Patricia Volk, later wrote. "Ramming had been used for razing since Mesopotamia. But ramming wasn't effective on New York's multistoried buildings. How do you ram a skyscraper? On the other hand, what if you could ram *in the air?*"[40]

And with that, she said, the wrecking ball was born. It's not clear precisely when this invention rammed its way into history (other wreckers, over the years, have also taken credit for the tactic), but Jake's earliest "wrecking balls" were probably heavy lengths of flat or square iron, or any other bludgeon-like material ready to hand. We do know that the true wrecking ball was wowing sidewalk superintendents at least as early as 1936, when Jake's brother Albert Volk (who learned his wrecking chops at Jake's side) was hoisting a three-thousand-pound iron "cannon ball" from a ninety-foot crane and whacking a five-story brick building in New York's theater district. Albert had apparently deployed the ball for some time by that date, perfecting what he called the "Dempsey Method." Instead of bashing a wall down in one fell swoop—landing a messy tangle of steel, timbers, and masonry on the ground—the crane operator would smack the top of the wall smartly with the ball, but not hard enough to heave it over. Just as renowned pugilist Jack Dempsey plied opponents with body punches, softening them up for the final knockout blow, the wrecking ball batted away to make manageable chunks of masonry drop and shatter. The debris was then mopped up by a "gasoline shovel," a lumbering, backhoe-like beast with a bucket attached to a lifting arm.[41]

The Jacob Volk Wrecking and Shoring Company eventually commanded a fleet of motor trucks from its splendid Park Avenue suite, where, in his later years, Volk would turn up at noontime and eat a caviar sandwich, munching away in his shirtsleeves. Volk died of pneumonia on March 15, 1929. He was just over fifty years old, belonged to forty-eight fraternal and philanthropic societies, and left an estate worth $254,000, a head-spinning sum worth millions in today's dollars. Jake never got a chance to wreck the Woolworth building, but he coveted that 792 feet of terra-cotta and steel. It would have been only fitting for Jake to fell the famous cathedral of commerce. "With all his prosperity," his obituary concluded, "he remained a true East Sider in his talk and his way of thinking. He had, however, trod the crumbling ruins of too many haughty dwellings ever to feel selfconscious or out of place, no matter where he was. Jake knew that everything that goes up comes down."[42]

Quite probably it was Jacob Volk—the satisfied little smasher—who drove urban aficionados to bitchy deprecation. "The busiest man in our midst, in these days, is the stalwart, heavy handed house wrecker," the print collector William Loring Andrews said in a speech to fellow city enthusiasts in 1913.

"Nothing stays his pick-ax, his crow-bar and his shovel in their iconoclastic work of wiping piles of brick and mortar off the map of the city, and when his work of destruction is accomplished, he surveys the scene of ruin and devastation he has wrought with as much pride and complacency, as the builder before him experienced in the erection of the edifice."[43] But as the wrecking business blossomed, it was Jacob's older brother Albert who would come to epitomize the impenitent wrecker.

Albert Abba Volk arrived in New York from Lithuania as a four-year-old and soon ran into trouble. Ousted from two public schools, he quit a third school to work for a hymn writer at the age of thirteen. "Five weeks later," a newsman noted, "he was discharged for suggesting a rhyme to go with 'Jesus with faltering feet.' He has forgotten the rhyme but believes he was discharged because the writer felt the shipping clerk should stick to his packages."[44] The pubescent poet, after a roundabout career path that included a stint managing a Puerto Rican cigar plant, at length joined Jacob's housewrecking enterprise, where he helped keep the books and write up estimates. Eventually the two brothers quarreled bitterly, and by 1915 Albert had struck out on his own.

Business went briskly for a time. Work poured in, and secondhand brick was going for $50 a load, because builders preferred the used stock to foreign bricks, which were marred by haphazard coloring and sizes. Five years later, however, the economic tide had turned. "There was a time when we would clean and sell the brick as we took it off the wall," Albert explained, "but now it is cheaper for us to dump the brick in the cellar as fast as we can pull down the walls, and then shovel it out by steam." By then it cost $20 a load to clean secondhand brick, which would bring in just $25 when resold. When speed counted on a job, it was better business for wreckers "to tear out the building on the site and use the brick they get in filling up the Long Island swamps."[45]

The economics of wrecking kept getting worse, with alarm bells ringing across the construction industry. "Increasing cost of destruction," industry watchers reported in no uncertain terms, "is keeping up the cost of construction."[46] Not only that, but "the increase in the cost of house-wrecking has immeasurably outdone that of any other kind of building work," said the Dow Building Reports. In other words, until about 1925, wrecking contractors were willing to pay handsomely for the privilege of pulling down a building, figuring a profit on the salvageable material they contained. Even if bricks were by then a lost cause, plumbing fixtures, pipes, steel beams, marble, and granite were also sometimes salvaged, and timber was often reused on the jobsite itself as the "bridge" erected around the building to save passersby from a conk on the head. Even plate glass "can frequently be sold and therefore care is taken to keep it unbroken; it is removed from the building almost immediately after the wrecker takes over the structure."[47] But by 1928 the economics had reversed, and harried wreckers were demanding hefty sums to clear away old buildings.

For one thing, rising wages were driving up the costs of salvage operations, destroying a sophisticated salvage economy that "formerly returned to profitable use an enormous quantity of second-hand material," as Albert Volk explained. Roving "wood merchants," for example, would once hover around the old buildings, their carts at the ready, snapping up broken timbers and bits of trim for $10 a load. They would trundle their spoils to basement shops where "woodchucks" would break it into kindling, then sell it by the bagful as firewood to tenement dwellers. But by 1928, "such labor provoking material is scorned. The wood must now be hauled by the wrecking contractor at a cost of $15 a load to swamp lands and there be burned, creating one of the largest wrecking costs." (Plus, on new construction jobs, nobody wanted to keep a carpenter around at $14 a day to hassle with used timbers and boards.) Even plate glass once fetched $800 a load, and old granite, which had been profitably recut for buildings, now went for tombstones—if you were lucky. Albert also blamed insurance hikes due to rising accident rates, as "the increased use of heavy machinery for wrecking entails a larger and more serious casualty list." The transformation of the wrecking business had other repercussions. Builders could no longer count on the up-front cash that wreckers would pay them in advance as salvage fees and so had to find other means to make down payments on their building sites. As for the lowly wreckers, they were left to "become a creditor class and suffer along with other harassed subconstructors while waiting for payments long due, but slowly paid."[48]

At that time, "barmen," or skilled housewreckers, were making $1.05 an hour, and twenty-seven hundred of them went on strike that year in New York City to gain a fifteen-cent raise. In some quarters, this was considered an extravagance. Several years later, when the National Recovery Administration was looking into fair competition after the Depression, uniform wage scales of seventy-five cents per hour were proposed. "I pointed out that in Alabama we were paying 75 cents per day," one wrecker recalled. "I said that they would ruin the entire industry if they forced the same wage scale on us as in the north. Our economy couldn't take it. I think that we compromised on 60 cents per hour."[49] Though done for a pittance, the work, said the leader of the House Wreckers Union, "is extremely dangerous and the casualty list high."[50]

Barmen were so named for their use of the classic wrecking bar, a five-foot-long shaft of rounded steel with a tapered point on one end and a bent, heel-like wedge on the other. This trusty sidearm of the old-school wreckers' arsenal was advertised in Sears, Roebuck catalogs at least as early as the 1920s and was for decades without peer in its ability to pry up floorboards, peel away paneling, and yank lath off walls ("a fairly ingenious design," one longtime wrecker observed, "which you will not find on the shelves of the local hardware store"[51]). Using the bar and a handful of sometimes custom-forged tools—among them the wrecking adze, a long-handled prying device with a narrow, flat blade on the end—barmen and "adzemen" would whittle a structure away, often with a delicate touch as they gathered up the salvageable spoils of the trade. In the halcyon wrecking days, demolition was truly construction in reverse: A structure would be stripped of its fixtures and appliances; its wood trim and flooring pried up, studiously denailed, and tied in bundles; plaster pulled down; then lath popped off of each wall and ceiling; non-load-bearing studs uprooted; and finally bricks lopped away and cleaned by fiendish characters (sometimes called *Klondikers*) known to knock the mortar off five thousand bricks a day. Laborious, yes. Wasteful, no. It was an elegant way to wreck.

But as building materials evolved, wrecking strategies regressed.

Prior to the late 1920s, structures built of brick or stone were typically held together with lime mortar, a binder used since antiquity that is soft and pliable, and thus much cherished by wreckers. Two or three hefty workers could sink their bars into the lime-mortared joints of massive granite or marble walls and pluck them apart with one jolly heave. "Lime mortar was the best binder known in the good old days," one wrecker dreamily reminisced. "Bricks will shake out of lime mortar like peanuts from their shells, are easily cleaned and are sold at second hand." Newer masonry was slathered not in blissful lime but in varying mixtures of Portland cement, an industrial-strength superglue that drove wreckers to despair. Stuck to the curtain walls of steel-frame buildings, the bricks congealed into a dreadful mess. They had to be bludgeoned away and barged out to sea—"great masonry chunks to be dumped as so much dead waste."[52]

Even older structures could make life miserable, as the Albert A. Volk House Wrecking & Excavating Company learned when it rammed up against 80 Broadway in 1929. This stalwart Romanesque structure, designed by architect George B. Post and completed in 1890 for the Union Trust Company, was built to last. Albert's wreckers were stopped dead in their boots by bastionlike walls ten feet through, "with brick and cement so firmly welded together ordinary methods of wrecking have been unavailing." Albert's usual plan of attack—the "plug and feather" approach, in which a steel plug was wedged between two iron guards, or "feathers," and driven into the wall to pop loose pieces of masonry—proved sluggish. They tried the "growler" tactic, drilling into the wall from above and prying off large hunks, but this, too, was fruitless. Finally, compressed air was called in, with holes drilled into the bricks and blasted with fifteen hundred pounds of pressure per square inch, all to no avail. Hasty consultations were arranged with Columbia University experts, and various unorthodox measures were pondered, including hydraulic pressure of three thousand pounds per square inch; dousing the walls with freezing water (if it worked for marble quarries in Vermont, the logic went, it could work on Wall Street); and even quicklime, which reacts tempestuously when mixed with water. "Some of these methods," a news item reassuringly noted, "are to be used in an effort to keep the demolition work, now three-quarters finished, well ahead of schedule."[53]

Albert Volk, busy that year, was rushing off to wreck the old Hotel Majestic in the Central Park West area, where onlookers were dismayed to find wreckers smashing marble bathroom fixtures with sledgehammers and punching out windowpanes with poles in another sign of the wrecking times. The assault upon the hotel, which was considered "one of the finest apartment hosteries in the country" when it opened in 1894, symbolized two ugly conditions confronting the modern builder: "One is the fact that the better the building the more costly it is to demolish; the second is that nothing, in the construction world at least, approaches the worthlessness of a building which has served its time and must come down." The hotel cost $2 million to build, but it was estimated that salvage would yield less than 10 percent of the wrecking expense. "To recut the rosewood, mahogany and black walnut used in the interiors of the old Glow Room and the Rose Rooms of the Hotel Majestic, among the sights of the city when the hotel was new, would have cost more than to use new materials," explained construction honcho Irwin S. Chanin, who had plans for a new tower on the site. "It is going out of the Majestic as badly splintered firewood." Because of carrying charges, Chanin continued, "the technique of building demolition has become tremendously important in the past few years."[54]

It had apparently just dawned upon builders that their lavish investments would one day be bashed into bits. Indeed, the Dow Service Daily Building Reports indicated that real estate tycoons "may have to include in the calculations of operating expense and yield the approximate cost of tearing the building down again, perhaps only twenty years hence." Mortgage, tax, and interest costs had soared so fearsomely, the report said, that you now had to shell out $200,000 to wreck a structure that a decade earlier cost only $420,000 to build. For his part, Albert attested to the rapid devaluation of old bathtubs, again sacrificed for speed. "We used to get from $15 to $25 a tub," he said, "while now, under the penalty and bonus system rapidly coming into vogue in handling demolition jobs, we smash these tubs up and they sail out through the Narrows on Father Knickerbocker's trash-carrying scows to find a well-earned rest at the bottom of the sea."[55]

Every wrecker abominates a cash penalty, so Albert Volk had been improving upon his brother's demolition shortcuts and had now devised his "slot system," which he was perfecting on the Hotel Majestic job. The system sounded much like Jacob's "upside-down method," with a pit opened at the bottom of the structure and floors of hallways chopped open, one level above the next, creating slots running the height of the building. Everything but steel was chucked down the slots "as rapidly as it [was] dislodged,"[56] to be scooped out by steam shovel. Unfortunately for Albert, men began tumbling into the slots as well, and the following year, in 1930, two hundred housewreckers went on strike to protest what became known as the "break through" method. The House Wreckers Union blamed the practice for twenty deaths in the prior year, and soon the papers blared: CITY URGED TO CURB HOUSEWRECKING PERIL.[57] Albert, somewhat beside the point, kept insisting that the method was "scientific, saving one-half to one-third the time in demolishing buildings";[58] he claimed that the deaths were unrelated accidents. Seventy percent of the city's wrecking contractors nonetheless signed pledges that they'd shun the new method (including the Jacob Volk Company, which was still doing business, minus Jacob). Albert, undaunted, derided the whole affair as "a smoke screen" for a conspiracy between the Second-Hand Brick Dealers' Association and nefarious unions plotting "to prevent the use of steam shovels for loading bricks and rubbish and prolong the jobs by the use of man labor pushing wheelbarrows."[59]

Albert must have licked that labor skirmish, for the "new wrecking technique" was hailed as a veritable stroke of genius the next year, when he assaulted "the highest building yet to fall before the pinch-bar and steam shovel": the twenty-four-story Hanover National Bank building on Nassau Street, next to the site of the Gillender Building, which Jacob had wrecked years earlier. A pitiless pile buttressed by mammoth slabs of stone, the bank "was built to stand for possibly 250 years," a newsman reckoned. "Now, at the early age of 25, it strongly resists death."[60] Albert babbled endlessly in an interview on the subject, offering the most detailed run-through yet of his new routine. Starting at the bottom, the housewreckers liberated the cellar of bulky or valuable objects, including boilers and furnaces (in a bank building, the vaults were vanquished with acetylene torches). Then, floor by floor, they made their ascent, sorting the scrap-worthy steam and water piping, and heaping up piles of wood. Holes were hacked through floors and ceilings to open the dreaded man-eating maw. Thus the mayhem began. Using tempered-steel pinch bars—crowbars with one end bent over for leverage—the barmen nudged bricks from their moorings and chucked them down the shaft. Massive, thirteen-ton stones were battered with twenty-four-pound mauls, hustled along by the incessant roar of the growlers, those industrial-strength drills. When the masonry had been hurled downstairs, structural steel workers nipped at beams with acetylene torches; then derricks lowered the beams, stacks of wood, and bundled pipe to waiting trucks. A floor per day went down that hole. Eventually the mound in the cellar bulged so much it posed a problem: a five-story-high hillock of smashed-up stone, wood, pipe, steel, and gunk. Then the steam shovels hissed and glowered, loading trucks bound straight for the dump. Growlers would grate away at a lingering stone wall, while, as a final flourish, "a little dynamite, judiciously placed" loosens another.[61] A photograph of the Hanover Bank takedown shows stout men in overalls, blurred in midwhirl upon a stone precipice. Bits of rope and riveted steel are littered in sunlight. A sledgehammer's askew. The scene radiates speed and cunning and careworn magnificence. A wrecker with a dangling cigarette, in effortless, workaday panache, completes the tableau.

Albert Volk hit the pantheon of pummelers as "one of the leading housewreckers in the country" when he died in 1950.[62] In later years, the wrecker indulged his penchant for poetry with what readers groaningly came to know as his "epistolary crusades." These were long-winded letters to the editor, sent off to

Topped by thirteen-ton slabs of stone, the Hanover National Bank building strongly resisted death. Albert Volk's brawny barmen vanquished it in 1931.

dozens of newspapers, pondering the nuances of industrial peace or the deviltries of democracy. ("The French laissez-faire is in the anarchistic spirit," he declared. "We call it individualism."[63]) America's go-getter ethos, in any case, proved more than providential for this one-time immigrant wiseguy who scotched skyscrapers for a living. "I can't help laughing to myself," Albert once said, snickering at his strolls around town in sartorial splendor. "Me and my silk hat. I came here in the steerage and I have attained Fifth Avenue. I get a big laugh out of that."[64]

Wreckers strutting around in top hats, needless to say, were not exactly barging onto big-city society pages. For all Fifth Avenue

cared, destructionists in general ranked among the more indus-
trious noble savages. "It is a risky business, housewrecking, even
riskier than construction, but, probably because his work is less
spectacular and seems simpler, the housewrecker gets little of the
credit he deserves for his daring and skill," a reporter commented in 1931. "If the riveter must sometimes pound into place
the very steel girder on which he is standing, the housewrecker
cuts it from under himself; yet the riveter has a popular and well-
deserved reputation as a daredevil, while the housewrecker's
work is considered almost uneventful. The riveter's job is constructive; he is 'a poet in steel.' The housewrecker is 'the morti-
cian of the building trades.' Few seem to appreciate the
constructive value of destruction."[65]

Even morticians got a better break at the turn of the last century. Before the 1890s, when the term *housewrecker* was in common use, the wrecker was all too easily mixed up with the petty
thief, both being called *house-breakers*. (In 1898, the *Daily
News* of London had to clarify: "The house-breaker—the man
of the pick, not the jemmy—is hard at work.") Things had
hardly improved thirty years later, when the wrecker was gently
lampooned in a cartoon from the *New Yorker* magazine. Relishing the lumpen laborer's tragicomic potential, the scene shows a
cigar-smoking developer sauntering in front of a twenty-story
Beaux Arts behemoth. He gestures at the hulking building as
two hapless tradesmen, grasping pickaxes and hammers, dis-
mount from their wheezing jalopy. They gape at the edifice, perfectly befuddled. "All right, boys," the boss says nonchalantly,
"down she comes."[66] Probing the limited repertoire of demolitionists—the dupe, the cretin, and the dupe—became a kind of
pet project for the magazine in the 1930s as Volk and other con-

tractors laid waste to large chunks of the city, leveling a hundred or more houses at a pop for massive projects such as Rockefeller Center. "Architecture must be a heart-breaking art anyway," the *New Yorker* pouted. "Paint a picture, write a book, and you possess your creation forever, even if it's no good. But design a building and you have it for twenty years and then a wrecker takes charge of the situation. We're so sorry for architects we're practically in tears."[67]

Choking back the sobs, an assistant at the magazine scurried out and boldly chatted up a housewrecker, extracting a few tales of lucre unearthed on the job. Only three times in thirty sweaty years did this unidentified contractor (who was probably Albert Volk) catch a lucky break. In 1909, the much-loved Arena Restaurant went down, and the owners, the Muschenheim brothers, were known to have popped a good-luck silver dollar into the woodwork whenever they made alterations. "The wrecking company didn't get much work done the first few days," the story went, since "the men were too busy roaming about the building, hunting out silver dollars and prying them loose. They found twenty in all." A few years later, it was time to wreck the old Assay Office, a hallowed site where gold and silver had been refined into bullion for more than half a century. Albert Volk, whose crew took on this enticing gig, meticulously swept the place for stray gold nuggets, then yanked up the floorboards in the furnace rooms and burned them (the ashes were mined for gold particles). Finally, Volk's foreman was hoisted up in a boatswain's chair, a hundred feet off the ground, where he attacked the elbow of a smokestack. Though traps had been built into the chimneys, which were routinely cleaned, and their contents returned to the furnaces for refinement, a couple of horizontal runs of iron flue had apparently gone untouched. The foreman grabbed a bushel or two of soot, which was aglitter with flecks of pure gold—$10,000 worth, if Albert could be believed. (Perhaps feeling that they owed it to the city, Volk's men carefully took down the Assay Office's Tuckahoe marble facade, numbering each stone, and the reconstructed building front can still be seen today in the American Wing of the Metropolitan Museum of Art.) The last great haul, as it happens, did go up in smoke. When tearing down a hundred-fifty-year-old school, wreckers stumbled upon massive, hand-hewn oak timbers, mortised and pegged together in boggling perfection. Hardly a nail turned up in the entire edifice. "Country-house builders would pay a lot for such materials nowadays," the article related, "but at that time nobody had gone in for antique effects, so the timbers were just taken out and burned."[68]

Even the *New Yorker*'s smirking staffers, however, were trumped by the decade's pithiest wrecking tale. That came from an obscure Public Works Administration report on the sundering of six hundred structures to make way for a Williamsburg, Brooklyn, housing project in 1935. The wrecker waltzed onstage, arranged his squirrelly band of barmen and rogues, and summoned up a whole fantasia of filth. "Steam shovels and picks played a tune to rival that of the pipes of the Pied Piper of Hamlin," as one wag recounted. "From every dank basement and crumbling wall rats fled in droves. Backyards disgorged an assortment of rusted cans, trash, filth and litter that would have discouraged the most voracious goat."[69]

The razzing of E. B. White–era wreckers reads like tender tribute next to the blows that history would later deal them. Back in those bygone days of lusty, brick-by-brick embattlement, the old-school barmen—strutting atop parapets, brawny limbs akimbo, with pickaxes poised against spire and sky—could even boast an epic grandeur. Morticians, hell. These men of the pick were some kind of spark-belching, granite-gobbling Goliaths, whomping whole blocks to the ground with gut-thumping bolts of brimstone and tarnation. Even Goliaths were too lumbering for their bosses' stopwatches, and they went bumping on down the rubbish chute as drills, jackhammers, and other new, payroll-obliterating machines thundered onto the scene. By the time the wrecking ball got into full swing (it wasn't until the 1940s that cast-iron balls were being widely advertised, and as late as 1960, long after Jacob Volk, the wrecking ball was still called "quite a newcomer to the business"[70]), the grandeur had all gravitated to the machinery itself. In 1954, for example, wreckers were laying waste to a triangular office building at Manhattan's Columbus Circle with a twenty-five-hundred-pound ball stretching twenty-four inches in girth. "Repeatedly the wrecking ball, or, as they call it in wrecking circles, 'the skull cracker,' hurtled through space to smash into the billboard and the walls of 7 Columbus Circle," a reporter wrote. The menacing hunk of metal, it turned out, boasted an august provenance. "It helped clear the sites for both the United Nations and Stuyvesant Town," yammered H. B. Mack, president of Wreckers & Excavators, Inc., whose spiel got him kudos as "a kind of Boswell of the ball."[71] There's honor in that, by God. But it isn't ledge-dangling bravura. Soon enough the tough guys of yore had blipped into "heavy-handed plastic surgeons," as one sneering trope had it, "armed with pile drivers, iron wrecking balls, steam shovels and cranes" as they blithely knocked off another urban face-lift.[72] Pundits totted up the score: Skull Cracker, 1; Romance, zilch. The heroic age of demolition was dead.

The vanishing era's swan song—clangorous as ever—found a few grace notes one day as crews were crunching up New York's old Center Theatre and stumbled across a grand piano parked on the second mezzanine (it had foundered unnoticed in jagged drifts of debris). A dashing wrecker-about-town named Harry Avirom, who had "lost his voice from inhaling bits of the theatre he [had] been tearing down since June 1, found expression on the piano," a witness recounted. "He sat down on a fire extinguisher, pushed back his white demolition helmet and began to play among the drills and hammers for a claque of workmen." When his crack serenade of standards and torch songs was over—toothy grins all around on the gang of wreckers who paused for a postrecital photo—the piano lid was slammed shut, and the instrument was trundled off to tempt a buyer from Cleveland. Then, from the bowels of the theater, the next act came chuffing along. "On stage, or where it used to be, a new performer was making a debut. Known to the profession as a 'skidshovel,' it began to contribute to the kind of 'Hellzapoppin' show under way."[73] This new cast member, the skidshovel, was a tractor-like machine equipped with a large bucket on the front end for scooping and dumping materials. Effectively a minibulldozer, it was a fierce performer indeed. (This lighthearted scene was still great fun next to the Wagnerian ruin of the old Metropolitan Opera in 1967. "Inside the 84-year-old house," a report said, "dust hung ominously in the air. All was silent except for an occasional thunder provided by the wreckers on the roof. The atmosphere was that of the 'Death of Gods' scene in Götterdämmerung."[74]) But despite the jolly mood at the

Center Theatre, it was clear that Avirom had pounded the ivories in one last hoarse hurrah for barmen getting scrapped by their own beastly efficient machines.

The demise of hand wrecking—about the only wrecking there was until the 1930s—got kicked off in earnest when the clamshell-type bucket, dangled from a crane, became the go-to demolition accoutrement. The clamshell, still widely used for material-moving tasks, is a metal bucket with two opposing, jawlike pieces that swing open and shut like a clam. Though it could be delicately lowered to a structure and used to nibble or chomp away as needed—grasping chunks of building in its teeth and ferrying the load off to be dumped in a waiting truck—the clamshell was eventually just thunked down on buildings like a proto–wrecking ball, with heady results. "One cannot help wonder who was the first operator to let one fall on a house," a historian burbled, "and thereby start a whole new method of building wrecking!"[75] But in congested urban areas unfit for flailing balls and buckets, the jackhammer was the bludgeon of choice, and by the 1960s would-be barmen had brushed up their résumés: Typically attacking in pairs, one wrecker would jack-hammer at a wall, while the other pried until it toppled. The jackhammer proved so successful that the wrecking ball was sel-dom seen in compact city centers, because "a two-ton weight smashing into concrete can have unpredictably lethal effects."[76] So the old ball and chain—though championed even today by loyalists as the fastest way to demolish a tall building—began a long, losing battle to various air-driven (and, later, hydraulic) contraptions such as the hobknocker, a primitive tool that was then just coming on the scene. This pneumatic "superjackham-mer" was bolted onto Caterpillar treads and could be cranked

around a building's interior to pretty much blast away at anything. Unfortunately, its hammer blows tended to smack out the
floor from underneath the operator, and the hobknocker soon
ran into other trouble as well: "Part of the controversy surrounding its use concerns its dangers, but the main issue is that it
does to the man with the jackhammer precisely what he did to
the man with the pick."[77] Amen, brother. Obsolescence, for sure,
was no idle worry. In the late 1930s, New York membership in
the House Wreckers Union peaked at twenty-five hundred—
swollen by massive projects such as junking the World's Fair—
but withered to 320 by 1978. Broader economic trends are
partly to blame, but, anyway, with power tools like that, who
needs muscle?

Midcentury demolition was soon one diesel-belching curtain
call after another, with the wrecking ball occasionally starring in
ever-bolder scenarios. The boisterous New York restaurateur
Bernard "Toots" Shor used the ball to smashing promotional effect when his establishment at 51 West Fifty-first Street was demolished on August 4, 1959. Shor was known about town as a
beloved saloonkeeper and "den mother" to legions of sports
icons and celebrities such as Joe DiMaggio, Yogi Berra, and
Ernest Hemingway, who would crowd around his circular bar
and subject themselves to his caustic humor. Toots Shor's "was
almost surely the most widely known saloon on earth," sports
columnist Red Smith later recalled, so it was a moment for the
history books when the structure was wrecked along with thirty
other buildings on the block to make way for a planned forty-
eight-story hotel (the owners abandoned the project after clearance had been completed, and an office tower was eventually
put on the site).[78] Shor, whose restaurant had stood on the spot

for twenty years, had previously made headlines when he refused to budge in an earlier redevelopment effort, forcing architects to design a building neatly around the perimeter of his restaurant. This time, however, the impresario was coaxed out of his lair for a whopping $1.5 million, and following a black-tie closing party attended by 300 revelers (crying in their beers, no doubt) it was time for the fun to begin. Just after 8 A.M. on the fateful morning, Shor got behind the controls of a crane and swung the one-and-a-half-ton iron wrecking ball—painted to look like a baseball, in honor of his sporting milieu—against the wall of the doomed saloon, then cheekily posed with his handiwork. Wrecking's poetic justice prevailed when Shor rebuilt his restaurant a block away—on the site of another club where, decades earlier, he had toiled as a bouncer.

The wrecking ball as baseball took another star turn a few years later, when our helmeted pianist Harry Avirom razed New York's old Polo Grounds, the original home of the New York Giants, who had decamped for San Francisco. (Demolition men cavorted in fetching Giants outfits as the first walls began to crumble.) "One thing I'll say for this place, no collapse action here, very well built," Avirom averred of the stout structure. "Very well built. It could have lasted forever," he muttered as old seats from the ballpark were hauled off by weepy season-ticket holders for three bucks a pop. Soon the wreckers were deluged by rabid fans who flocked to the site, phoned in pleas, and mailed desperate missives in a quest for holy ball field relics. A Manhattanite transplanted to California begged for "anything, anything at all from my former home away from home," while an Iowa resident pined for a brick, and a guy in Yonkers said he'd be content with "just an envelope of dirt." The job scored

Sports bar impresario Toots Shor took a ceremonial swing with this one-and-a-half-ton iron wrecking ball to raze what was called the most widely known saloon on earth.

Avirom's firm so much free air time that a baseball was immediately adopted as the company logo (the new slogan: "On the Ball"). Himself apparently a major-leaguer manqué, Avirom one day roamed around the debris-strewn grounds, warming to the cosmic import of it all. "We slug harder than the Giants ever did in this park, slug harder than the Mets ever did," he exhorted his fellow wreckers. "When we hit the ball we knock the walls down, get it?" As ticket stubs from long-gone games skittered about the infield and whorls of steel deepened on home plate, Avirom found the scene entirely apropos. "Wrecking is some business, let me tell you," he said. "Slug. Bang. Slam. Hardship. Gotta make the right moves. Gotta take calculated risks. Yeah, yeah, something like baseball you could say."[79]

The high point of these stunts, no doubt, was the frenzy-whipping arrival of the S-58 helicopter. "Sidewalk superintendents have something new to look forward to—airborne demolition," announced the press in 1962 as a thousand-pound ball, slung from the heavy-duty chopper, sailed toward a two-hundred-foot-tall grain storage pier in the Hudson River. "The S-58 swayed and joggled until the demolition ball began swinging in a wide arc, looking no larger than a basketball, to bash repeatedly high against the pier's north wall," an account said, adding that the hour-long spectacle "proved that helicopters can increase the safety, effectiveness, and economy of wrecking operations on tall buildings." Yes, and demolition experts—apparently gone slaphappy at this departure from grueling routine—were seeing the dawn of a whole new era of sky-ball wrecking that would have a miraculous downward effect on their insurance premiums. "The main consideration is safety," a contractor explained. "There is always the chance with a

300-foot crane that the ball will whiplash and tip the crane over, destroying equipment and lives."[80]

If sky-ball wrecking was so much safer, it's too bad all those obsolete barmen couldn't have been retrained as S-58 pilots, because the wrecker's health and welfare in those dotty days was somewhat cavalierly looked after. "Wreckers, if they can, prefer to avoid the subject of accidents, and the picture is not a pretty one," the *New York Times Magazine* reported in 1964. The construction sector had the highest death rate of any major American industry—only miners were worse off—and housewreckers were hard-pressed to find life insurance at reasonable rates. Go figure: "Cut feet [and] crushed fingers and toes are unpleasantly common, and wrecking contractors buy barrels of first-aid equipment."[81] That same year, *Architectural Forum* took note that members of the House Wreckers Union, Local 95, made $4.85 an hour, with working conditions so abysmal that, as the union's contract specified, "each iron-worker must get two quarts of milk each day—they believe it is beneficial in offsetting possible ill effects from breathing the toxic gases from acetylene torches."[82] In fact, these kamikaze-like "burners," who spent their days torching structural steel, guzzled milk as a protection against lead poisoning (calcium is known to reduce lead absorption), as they were habitually exposed to lungfuls of flaming, lead-based paint.

Nor were those the only occupational hazards. "A lot of the guys in wrecking are physical types," a demolition laborer explained to the *Times Magazine*. "You know, they don't read as much poetry as they should. They're good guys, but sometimes when they get mad they don't write to the newspaper—they slug

you. And then the police come. If you're interested in this sort of
thing, it's too bad you weren't around for the Raymond Street
Jail job. I could have introduced you to six guys who would have
taken you through their old cells. That was the happiest wrecking they ever did."[83] Alas, a dozen years later, contractors were
trooping back to the slammer after an eighteen-month under-
cover operation, looking into "a long history of allegations of
corruption in the demolition industry" in New York City, turned
up bribery charges against six city demolition inspectors and
seventeen contractors (plus a dozen cases of illegal dumping).
Bribes were going for 2 percent of the contract price; inspectors
toiled just four hours a day and pocketed an extra $15,000 each
year (this in 1977 dollars). As one scammer remarked to a wired
confidant, "We are like a house of cards. If one of us falls, we
all fall."

Demolition honchos—not without reason—have long
fended off perceptions that their trade is pestilentially ridden
with vice, and even Albert Volk, back in the 1920s, was a bit
player in one of the big racketeering scandals of his day—a
nasty showdown in the building industry that "terrorized several
hundred thousand workers of the city, and brought to their
knees some of the largest construction companies in the United
States."[84] The graft was so bald it boggles the imagination. In
testimony at city hall, numerous housewreckers shuffled forth to
offer up unsavory details about an industry rife with "rake-
offs," or bribes, running into the tens of thousands of dollars; of
housewreckers driven to bankruptcy; and of one Robert P.
Brindell as a "despot, ruling and ruining labor and capital." The
blustering Brindell—known to associates as simply "the Judge"—
was president of the New York Building Trades Council, which

commanded 115,000 union employees at the time. The Judge, it turned out, extorted large sums from wreckers in exchange for green-lighting their contracts, even though they had already hired union labor at union rates. The crux of the matter was that the wreckers' trade group, the five-year-old Building Demolishing Contractors Association, was on the skids because many of its sixty-seven wrecking companies were forced to hire only workers paying dues to Brindell's council. Problem was, wreckers had to take out cards in Brindell's organization for $50 a pop and were expected to fork over $10 a week to the council out of their $44 wage. If veteran wreckers didn't comply with the Judge's whims, employers were ordered to give them the boot and instead hire shambling characters who looked "as if they were picked up in the park."[85] Albert Volk himself coughed up $6,026 to Brindell, at a time when Volk was doing $600,000 a year in business. (Small wonder the two men were later called "enemies for a long time."[86])

Perversely enough, the first time wreckers banded their motley interests into a bona fide confederation, it was to assault anticompetitive behavior—not from Brindell-style bandits, but from the federal government and its abominated Office of Price Administration, which had plagued the industry with price controls on used lumber. Wreckers were bent out of shape because the salvageable wood they scored from busted-up buildings could be sold only at sharply capped prices as part of the government's drive to snuff inflation during World War II. (The price ceiling for one thousand board feet of used lumber was $12. On the open market, the same amount would fetch $80.) This was sufficiently miffing that on August 26, 1946, representatives of thirty-one firms hunkered down at a powwow in Chicago, a meeting deemed "the first attempt to weld the members of the wrecking industry together on a nationwide basis" amid a bursting "new feeling of pride" and a "new sense of professionalism." Thus was born the short-lived National Association of Wrecking Contractors, which promptly pulled out its brass knuckles: New York attorneys were promised a $50,000 contingency fee if they could get price controls deep-sixed in thirty days. According to an industry account, the attorneys missed their deadline—but only by ten days—and a little more than a month later, controls on used lumber were toast. Its mission apparently accomplished, five years later, the wreckers' association officially disbanded.[87]

It was a rare moment of pluck for a browbeaten profession, dissed by the feds and taken for dupes, criminals, and flunkies by everyone else. Everyone, that is, except a few half-delusional groupies, given to odd flights of poetry and boosterish raptures that must have bulged demolition helmets half to bursting with pride. "Thus do the great cranes of the building wreckers crawl across the face of our country, their tracks making a literal path of civilization," as one blissed-out acolyte wrote in 1960. "America has come full circle. Where the dinosaurs roamed at will the cranes rumble on, looking very much like these first inhabitants, bent on their work of constructive, creative demolition."[88] Wandering brontosauruses were hard to beat, but suddenly unencumbered real estate was probably the next best thing. Neighbors of a wrecking site, a journalist discovered in 1964, had briefly laid eyes on the equivalent of urban manna. "The wrecker has provided them with a beauty no architect could equal—a vista, light, a view," he wrote. "They discuss banding together, petitioning the city to make the plot into a park for children and mothers and pigeons, with a fountain in the shape of a jackhammer. But all they will do is talk: by the time they act, the enemy will have arrived—the construction worker—who, with aluminum and glass, will seal out the sky."[89] Honored as galumphing Jurassic beasts and lauded as liberators of urban verdure, all that remained for the ascendant wrecker was to make the *New York Times*'s cut of around-town "Living and Leisure" activities for readers whose tastes ran to the sublime. And so with the 1940 razing of an elevated railway—the Ninth Avenue El in Manhattan—citizens were urged to revel in wrecking's brow-singeing glory. Be forewarned, said the *Times,* that the El running almost the length of Manhattan "is not suitable for hikers except possibly Boy Scouts with overnight kits," but once properly outfitted, hardy venturers could survey the eye-popping pyrotechnics at hand. "At what seem to be entirely arbitrary intervals," our correspondent giddily explained, "workmen attack some part of the structure and golden waterfalls of sparks cascade to the ground." And the wrecker's half-finished work, strung out along the avenue, could be ogled as a lovely de Chiricoesque tableau: "Here and there the remains of an El station stand precariously, roofless and skeletal, with the wind blowing through the peaked roofs and the jigsaw work."[90]

It's an artful image, vainglorious, even. But the prevailing vision of the thuggish wrecker had already been set in roman type. In 1949, a *Detroit Free Press* newspaper columnist named Edgar A. Guest challenged the industry with a poem. Guest, a one-time police reporter who started as a *Free Press* copyboy in 1895, eventually bloomed as a prolific versifier whose daily dose of poetry, called "Breakfast Table Chat," was syndicated in three hundred newspapers at the height of its fame. The English-born "poet of the people" was adored for verses such as "The Joy of a Dog" and "Song of Consolation for Poor Golfers," to say nothing of the inimitable "My Aunt's Bonnet." Edgar Guest wrote what was probably the single most influential piece of writing ever published about demolition. Titled simply "Wreck-ers," it says:

> I watched them tearing a building down
> A gang of men in a busy town.
>
> With a ho-heave-ho and a lusty yell
> They swung a beam, and the side wall fell.
>
> I asked the foreman: "Are these men skilled,
> And the men you'd hire if you had to build?"
>
> He gave a laugh and said, "No, indeed!
> Just common labor is all I need.
>
> "I can easily wreck in a day or two
> What builders have taken a year to do."
>
> And I thought to myself as I went my way
> Which of these roles have I tried to play?
>
> Am I a builder who works with care
> Measuring life by the rule and square?
>
> Am I shaping my deeds to a well-made plan
> Patiently doing the best I can?

Or am I a wrecker, who walks the town
Content with the labor of tearing down?[91]

Guest's devastating parable would haunt those in the industry who wanted to convince the world that wreckers could be just as dazzlingly original as builders. Around the time that "Wreckers" was published, a new breed of destructionist was setting out to prove the poet wrong, and, along with fellow mavericks in the modern explosive demolition field, turn wrecking into a first-class trade with its own creative ethos—and a raucous, spine-tingling adventure.

[3]

FRAGMENTATION AT A PRICE

REVELERS LOOKED ON from their $125-per-plate, violin-serenaded breakfast (a Sunday-morning "demolition party" at a nearby high-rise) and clinked champagne flutes as Seattle's Kingdome stadium was dynamited at the turn of the millennium in a tempest of dust and debris. News reports pegged the event as "a vandal's fantasy attracting gawkers from around the planet," but for Mark Loizeaux, the job was less a concrete-and-confetti spectacle than an engineer's Zen koan. "I just looked at it and asked myself, 'What does the Kingdome want to do?' " he said, explaining how he'd turn the world's largest concrete dome to a heap of rubble in just seventeen seconds. "Basically, it's gravity, the power of the planet that brings the structure back to grade." He added, "The Kingdome is coming down. It wants to come down."[1] It's wanted to do that, Mark said, since the day it was built.

Meet Mark Loizeaux, master unbuilder.

What Jacques Derrida is to literature, Loizeaux is to demolition: He's the philosopher king of deconstruction.

"I think of a building as a person," Loizeaux has said about his craft. "I have to find out all I can about it, searching in every corner for any secrets it might have, and then prepare my plan of attack. That building is fighting me, and I've got to bring her to her knees the first time."[2] Loizeaux's battle plan remains formidably elegant, the $E = MC^2$ of demolition. "Every nail that was carried up in the pocket of some construction worker is potential energy that's at our disposal," Loizeaux explained. "God gives us gravity and we just harness it to bring the building back down."[3] The Loizeaux family, whose company, Controlled Demolition Incorporated, has consigned thousands of structures around the world to oblivion, is based in the town of Phoenix, Maryland. It's an odd toponym. Loizeaux's buildings never rise from their ashes. Not the Sands Hotel in Las Vegas, not the Beirut Hilton Hotel, not even a Russian military base in Skrunda, Latvia, blasted to bits for President Clinton's Partnership for Peace project.

The company's early motto: "Fragmentation at a Price."

Part matador, part sage, and part connoisseur of collapse, Mark Loizeaux was born the son of a forester who began blowing up tree stumps for extra cash and was thrown into a demolition career at the age of twenty as one of the youngest licensed blasters in the United States; he emerged, despite one near-fatal accident, as the man who has most profoundly shaped his country's faith in the redemptive power of demolition. "The Murrah Building bombing was so senseless," Mark's father, "Daddy" Jack Loizeaux, once said, explaining how his company was chosen to implode the remains of the Oklahoma City structure after Timothy McVeigh blew the building's front half off with a bomb-packed Ryder truck in 1995. "It caught the conscience of 200 million Americans," Jack said. "But while we were there, we couldn't think emotionally about it. It wasn't a higher calling, exactly, but we knew we could do a service. There was a collective sigh of relief when we pushed the button and that building came down. It was a catharsis, really. It let the healing begin."[4]

Controlled Demolition works for the Department of Housing and Urban Development (blasting decrepit housing projects), the Department of Energy (scotching nuclear sites), the Department of State (toasting weapons of mass destruction in central Europe), the Department of Justice (pitching in on criminal investigations), and the Department of Defense (don't ask, don't tell). They've been adoringly showcased on so many television documentaries that their rivals glumly call the Discovery Channel the "Loizeaux Channel." They've been called the "Flying Wallendas of tearing down buildings,"[5] and "the implosion world's equivalent of the von Trapp family."[6] But when Mark, his younger brother Doug, and then twenty-seven-year-old daughter, Stacey, landed in Seattle to pull down the twenty-four-year-old Kingdome on March 26, 2000, it was still no run-of-the-mill structural smackdown.

Completed in 1976 for $67 million, the Kingdome spanned over 7.5 acres and was girded by a steel-reinforced tension ring ratcheted to 8.8 million pounds of force. It was a marvel of engineering hailed as "the most impressive concrete-roof structure in the world," and the dome's curmudgeonly engineer, Jack Christiansen, was apoplectic that they were wrecking the masterpiece he designed to last a millennium. "I'll defy anybody to tell me it's not a beautiful roof," Christiansen said. And don't expect him to furnish any torsional tips, either. "They're not going to get one bit of help from me," he added. "I feel terrible. Sick. Mad as hell, actually."[7]

The dome's energetic defenders marshaled their forces, and you had to credit their embattled eloquence. "I can't think of a place on Earth that has a space and a structure like the King-dome, and they seek to destroy it," said one such partisan. "Well, there was one other moment like this—the Warsaw Opera House was bombed in World War II. The Luftwaffe was proud to take credit for that."[8] For his part, the semiretired Christiansen remained flabbergasted. "I can't understand how a conclusion was reached to demolish the building," he muttered before angrily withdrawing from all public debate on the matter. "Somebody seemed to think that the Kingdome is a very ordi-nary thing you throw away if the numbers don't come out a cer-tain way."[9]

The numbers, if you're a professional sports maven, are not very forgiving. As the dome neared the quarter-century mark, some said, the hunk of mounded concrete looked "dated and cheap as an old Volkswagen bus."[10] In 1997, Washington voters agreed and gave the thumbs-up for a bid by billionaire Paul Allen to buy the Seattle Seahawks and install them in a sparkling new $430 million outdoor football stadium on the site. Con-trolled Demolition was given the $750,000 implosion contract for what would be, altogether, a $9 million demolition. The only question now was how to bring her down.

"The problem here was to create a sequential collapse of a building with a 660-foot clear span,"[11] Mark explained. Slicing the top of the twenty-five-thousand-ton dome into sections like a pie allowed the pieces to drop in separate chunks, thereby cut-ting down on the hefty vibrations kicked off when the whole shebang hit the ground. Surrounding columns and forty vaulted ribs would be pulverized with staggered explosions, precisely orchestrated with over a thousand timing delays to gently lower the beast back to earth. And it all had to take into account the tremendous stresses of the post-tensioning ring, with its cables taut around the dome's base "like a rubber band around a bouquet of flowers."[12] Over three months of preparations, crews drilled 5,905 holes into the moribund dome and packed them with 4,728 pounds of high-velocity gelatin explosives. The columns were wrapped with mesh to buffer the flying debris. As Mark described the finer points of the operation on NBC's *Today* show, cohost Matt Lauer tried to get a grip: "It's been compared to me to be like a soufflé falling," he said, "not that a lot of people have ever watched a soufflé fall . . ."[13] It was all so boggling that even eighty-five-year-old Jack Loizeaux admitted he was stumped. "The Kingdome—that's one thing I would not have touched with a 10-foot pole," he said, happy to leave the job to his kids. "It's just so big and it's so different from anything we've done."[14]

With two dozen choppers and planes buzzing overhead in a beautiful blue sky on that fateful morning, as the revelers hoisted their bubbly and somewhere Jack Christiansen cursed and caviled, Controlled Demolition crewman Thom Doud punched the magic button, and twenty-one miles of orange detonating cord lit up in a brilliant flash a split second before the main charges blasted away. "It was just steel, concrete and dynamite," said a witness, "but together it performed like nature at its angriest: lightninglike flashes followed by thunderous cracks, then ground-shaking collisions and a blinding dust storm."[15] The blast created the equivalent of a magnitude 2.3 earthquake, but the debris pile poked up a mere twenty-three feet high, so compact and origami-like that, as Loizeaux later preened, it looked "like a pressed flower."[16] Crews found five broken windows on neighboring buildings, but even philosopher kings have their limits.

"We're just contractors," Mark said. "We aren't gods."[17]

John "Jack" Darby Loizeaux is doubtless the only person on the planet who's been called "a dentist of urban decay, a Mozart of dynamite, a guru of gravity," as a woozy interviewer once scribbled, adding for good measure: "Like Joshua, he blows, and the walls come tumbling down." A handsome, trim man with neat gray hair and a trademark curling beard "of Hapsburgian

Serenaded by violins, Seattle's Kingdome stadium bit the dust on March 26, 2000, with the help of more than four thousand pounds of high-velocity gelatin explosives.

The blast carried the jolt of a magnitude 2.3 earthquake. The verdict:
The fetchingly felled structure looked just like a pressed flower.

distinction,"[18] Mark's father was a dead ringer for a college lec-
turer rather than a congenital building basher. Some say the
wrecking business is a close kin of funeral parlors—local companies, family owned, both absorbed in "the passing of the
great, the obscure and sometimes the infamous"[19]—but this was
not at all Jack's style. "We're not the judge who passed sentence," as he preferred to say. "We're just the guillotiners."[20]

Jack Loizeaux was the seventh son of a seventh son. Born in
Towson, Maryland, to Alfred Samuel Loizeaux, chief engineer
for the Baltimore Gas and Electric Co., Jack had precocious tu-
torials in the potency of dynamite. Alfred, as the story goes, put-
tered around the family orchard with a few sticks of the stuff
ready to hand, firm in the conviction that if he blasted open

planting holes for his trees, the dynamite would deposit nutrient-rich nitrogen in the soil, provide ample drainage, and be easier on the back to boot. One summer, young Jack closely observed a trunk-to-trunk matchup between an ordinary tree and some in nitrogenated soil. "The tree we planted in the hand-turned earth grew about an inch the next year," he recalled. "The ones we planted in the dynamite holes grew a foot."[21]

Jack's wild-eyed initiation into the power of explosives, however, came in 1938 when he was loading holes as a forestry student at the University of Georgia in Athens. The wayward Oconee River was washing out the forestry department's seedling nursery, and the school wanted to reroute the channel around its precious seedlings. One day during a surveying class, he helped a DuPont engineer, a fabled Mr. Johnson, load dynamite into the holes the students had drilled. When it came time for the blast, Jack recalled in an interview with *Playboy* magazine in 1974, Mr. Johnson turned to him and said, "How would you like to shoot it?" "Wow," Jack stammered. "I was just a kid. I pressed that plunger and we threw *hundreds* of *thousands* of tons of loam and mud and it just went skyward and when it was all over and the mud settled, the old lazy river came straight as an arrow for about 200 yards. It just fascinated me. The tremendous power that was at my finger tips. I couldn't sleep for a week."[22]

Before fully indulging his newfound obsession, Jack took a forestry degree in 1940 and signed on with Baltimore's forestry department. Following a stint as a wood technology specialist during World War II—he was chief inspector for wood products used in bomber production at the Glenn L. Martin Co. in Middle River, Maryland—he launched his own tree-care company,

Burnbrae Tree Service (so named for his residence on Burnbrae Road in Towson). Taking on hefty city contracts on the scale of twenty thousand trees at a pop, the bustling service soon grew to a hundred employees. All Jack needed now was an excuse to hoard dynamite, which promptly presented itself. Behold the American elm, devastated by Dutch elm disease after 1930, dying in such profusion that cities everywhere were littered with rotting stumps. As dynamite had been used for stump blasting in England as early as the 1870s—and caught on in the United States after 1890—Jack quickly took to sawing off the blighted elms, drilling the stumps, and blasting the suckers to splinters.

Soon Baltimore builders would come skulking around, luring him off to a boulder in need of banishment or a foundation footing to be thwacked, and for a quick $100 he'd take on the job. Never entirely forgetting Mr. Johnson, of course, Jack had taken classes in engineering and geology at Johns Hopkins University and had hung out with engineers from DuPont, which was based not far away in Wilmington, Delaware. In 1947, the fateful call came in, and Jack was off to wreck his first structure. As he told the story to *Playboy:* "DuPont called me and said a colonel at Aberdeen Proving Ground thought he'd be cute and there were three smokestacks to come down and he shot one and he's broken windows for many miles, so he's in hot water. So I went out there. He'd taken three cases—50-pound cases. One hundred fifty pounds of explosives—and he'd had his men scaffold the stack and his engineers had lowered the cases into the stack at different elevations. Well he blew it. So I went out there with six pounds of explosives for each stack and I dumped the other two."[23] Jack notched the stacks at their bases. They toppled just like trees.

Gravitating inexorably toward the black magic, Jack jumped into rock removal and foundation blasting under the name Burnbrae Drilling & Blasting, then devoted himself to stack work, bounded off to Chile to blast a deepwater port, and in 1957 landed his first big break in Washington, D.C.: the implosion of three eight-story apartment buildings on the Foggy Bottom site where the U.S. State Department now stands, making way for what was charmingly described at the time as "another massive, untrimmed behemoth with about as much esthetic appeal as a concrete bunker."[24] Though in its report on the momentous blast, *Engineering News-Record* took pains to commend the "top-notch team" behind the effort and singled out Jack's "sure-fire dynamiting plan" for special praise, the fact is that Loizeaux's first building implosion was a mortifying occasion. Things went smoothly at first. The reinforced-concrete structure, stout enough that it had earlier rebuffed a wrecking ball, was stripped to its naked concrete frame, its basement columns weakened, blast holes drilled in its columns, and a test blast blown in the building's bowels. One stick of dynamite proved about right to blitz each beefy column, and Jack sketched out seven timing delays that would sequence the blasts from the inner core columns out to the perimeter walls, causing the building to sag in on itself and drop straight down (a classic implosion plan that would prove remarkably serviceable in later years).

Apparently, Mr. Johnson was suffering from bad juju that day, because as soon as the first round was fired, the building sank all of three feet but halted disconcertingly upright, with nary a scratch on its exterior walls. These walls, the *News-Record* reported, "were supporting the building so sturdily that the severed interior columns, on later blasts, dropped almost vertically and rested on their battered stumps." Scratching their heads, the "dumbfounded blasters" packed "a fairly heavy charge" into the structure, which sank another depressing three feet. A third blast, meanwhile, merely "bulged the building walls," while a fourth nudged the building a bit more, for a total of seven feet in all, and even pulled a dogleg front wall back into place. The structure looked as solid as ever. "You can't believe it even when you see it," the blasters moaned, having watched the building "rebound into an upright position after repeated explosions."[25] The recalcitrant beast went down on the fifth try, with a modest round of charges knocking out the first-floor columns and perimeter walls. Having learned his lesson, Loizeaux attacked the subsequent two buildings with blasts in both the basement and first-floor columns—and they mercifully gave way without a hitch.

Fifteen years later, Jack Loizeaux hit the cover of *Engineering News-Record* as the wrecker who "pioneered the use of explosives to demolish just about everything built by man."[26] In 1960 he shuttered his tree-care company and changed the name of his blasting firm to Controlled Demolition, Inc. (known to the industry as CDI), which he founded with his wife Freddie, a licensed blaster herself when she wasn't heading up the Maryland PTA. The demolition world took note the following year, it was said, when Jack "dynamited 300 feet of curbing in six hours without damaging the adjoining pavement,"[27] and soon this dynamic duo—plus sons Mark and Doug, joined eventually by Mark's daughter, Stacey—became evangelists in the good fight for explosive demolition.

Evangelism, in Jack's case, was no mere professional duty. Jack Loizeaux was so devoutly religious that he'd never juice up a blasting cap without a nod to the great unbuilder in the sky. "I give the good Lord a lot of the credit," he would say. "He's turned the gravity on."[28] Jack's father Alfred, born in Vinton, Iowa, was known as a hymn writer who edited the monthly Christian magazine *Help and Food,* and Jack schooled his family in the style of the Plymouth Brethren—"a somber, Quakerish sect," as one chronicler noted—whose precepts gave Loizeaux's line of work a spiritual twist. Demolition played out for Jack as "a kind of parable in which the moral tenets of his faith find their concrete, earthly expression"; corroded steel columns in a crippled building could be read as metaphors for a person's character, and letting the least structural rot take root could put you straight on the road to the scrap mill.[29] Gravity, meanwhile, was a kind of divine dispensation, a God-given gift to the chosen wrecking contractors. "Gravity is everywhere. It's free to everyone," Jack explained. "It's an awesome power that's available out there if you know how to control it."[30] Whatever his doctrinal program, the man's stirring testimony to his faith was beyond dispute. "Loizeaux," Richard Rhodes noted in 1974, "whose chosen work is reducing the American past to pieces of rubble conveniently sized for loading into dump trucks, has made more than one audience weep for its lost innocence."[31]

Jack's pyrotechnics in the pulpit were notably undimmed nearly a quarter-century later, when he and his sons—and virtually the whole city of Pittsburgh—called on the Lord's good graces when they imploded the 500 Wood Street building in 1997. Built in 1905 as the Farmers Deposit National Bank and brawnily braced against the wind, the twenty-six-story tower was the tallest steel-framed building ever imploded when the Loizeauxs toppled it on May 25. It loomed a precious few hundred feet away from $20 million worth of irreplaceable Tiffany glass, the pride of First Presbyterian Church. Not only that, but neighboring Trinity Cathedral, dating to 1872, on that very Sunday morning was feting the 125th anniversary of the laying of its present cathedral's cornerstone. Those ceremonies bumped the implosion hour from morning to afternoon, with unintended liturgical effects. "It'll give us lots of sermon material," said Trinity's dean.[32]

CHURCH ASKS GOD TO GUARD THE GLASS was the *Post-Gazette*'s breezy headline as worshippers at the two institutions furiously prayed for their temples during the preblast Sunday

Guru of gravity: Jack Loizeaux couldn't sleep for a week after his wild-eyed initiation into the power of dynamite.

services; some parishioners were even prepping to hold a prayer vigil inside the Gothic cathedral all through the ordeal, but that plan was politely vetoed due to safety restrictions. Eighty-two-year-old Jack Loizeaux mounted the pulpit of First Presbyterian Church, assuring jittery congregants that he thought of the Lord as his chief executive officer. "We set off more big bangs, my sons and I, than anybody on earth in peacetime," he preached, adding that he was not shy about appealing to a higher power. "If you did what we did, you'd pray a lot too."[33]

At 3:50 P.M., following a twenty-minute delay due to a muck-making downpour the previous night, a prayer crackled over the demolition crew's radio—"May we have a safe job in Jesus' name, amen."[34]—and 595 pounds of explosives detonated in hundreds of blasts spaced milliseconds apart, heaving the tower forward at a 7.5-degree angle and plunging it straight down into "a mini-slag heap of twisted steel and dust."[35] Not a single pane of Tiffany glass was scratched during the fifteen-second shot, though windows were unfortunately shattered at nearby stores, including a Lerner Shops that had its entire front facade pummeled. "I personally did not expect to take out that much glass at Lerner's," said CDI demolitionist Jim Santoro with a trace of chagrin, noting the curious special effects to be found in the carnage. Older windows split in shards "like a guillotine," Santoro said, while newer panes were shot through with circular holes, and any made of safety glass simply fractured as designed. None of the store owners would speak to a reporter about the destruction, however, with one of them only commenting as he hosed down his shop that "Santoro is a very nice guy."[36] (Indeed, Santoro, before coming to work for Controlled Demolition, ran a mental hospital in upstate New York, "an activity that seems to have prepared him well for dealing with the many different types of people one meets on construction sites worldwide."[37])

While the shot was nonetheless deemed "a good kill" by project manager Jim Parasella,[38] reactions around town elicited quasi-Biblical reportage. Correspondents tracked "a huge and smelly cloud of dust that crept closer and closer" like some plague of locusts straight out of Exodus, while a staff member for the American Institute of Architects, eyeing the pitch-black dust devil from the luxurious seventeenth-floor ballroom of the Westin William Penn, could only conjure up visions of the infernal. "It's diabolical," she stammered. "It's like Hades." Others just relished the catharsis. "It was great," one satisfied customer told a TV camera. "I loved it. I have been waiting a long time for them to blow that up." Apparently relieved that gravity had once again held up its end of the bargain, Mark and Doug sauntered around their thirty-foot-high heap of rubble and did that little Fred Astaire trick of rolling their hard hats down their arms. And bringing it all back down to the realm of the ultramundane was a CNN anchor who, signing off the segment, reassured viewers everywhere: "And you know that every time there's an implosion of a building we'll bring it to you, yes, we will, because it's neat."[39]

That CNN would devour footage of every nifty implosion it could scrounge up is due in some part to Freddie Hill, a natural genius at coaxing headlines from falling buildings. Jack had met Freddie at the University of Georgia—the glamorous couple were the talk of the quad—and the two were married in 1940 on the Fourth of July (a date Freddie deemed an omen). She would

cook dinner in the thirty-one-foot travel trailer the couple sometimes towed to extended jobs on the East Coast, but her prime
contribution to the evangelical cause was a knack for publicity.
Implosions are Sunday-morning rites for a reason. Sure, there
are fewer gawkers and less traffic tooling around to tangle up a
shot, but in the days before torquing towers became a staple of
cable television, Freddie exploited that motive force governing
demolition: not gravity but the Slow News Day. If you phoned
up the magazines and newspapers and laid a juicy photo op at
their feet, you were guaranteed to have front-page coverage
come Monday. And if you were a developer hankering after
some exposure, this was like free money. Implosions, real estate
mavens quickly learned, carried an attractive fringe benefit over
the wrecking ball. Implosions gave you buzz.

"My mom doesn't get nearly the credit she should have for a
bright spot of communications in an industry that was dark by
nature," Mark told me one day when I visited the family's forty-
five-acre estate in Phoenix, Maryland, outside of Baltimore, a
woodsy compound of houses on a tranquil stretch of land pro-
tected from development on two sides. In Freddie's day, he recalled, implosion contractors weren't necessarily getting the
red-carpet treatment from city officials beckoning them to detonate a few hundred pounds of high explosives in the central
business district. What Freddie understood—and what her son
Doug, who holds a communications degree, has cultivated since
Freddie's death in 1992—was that implosion was about marketing almost more than anything else. "That's what I realized a
long time ago," Doug told me. "It's a selling job. And you have
to be gentle. We're here for a short time. And again, all of that
thought process goes into promoting what we want to promote,

and what we're trying to get away from is that it's a violent thing. If you watch a close shot of an explosion in one of the columns, it's violent. But overall, it's graphically beautiful, it's like a ballet." The more emotionally vulnerable of the two brothers, Doug's open sensitivity to frequently gut-wrenching wrecking scenes only seems to heighten his rapport with terrified civilians, edgy fellow contractors, and even his own family. "When I was younger, I'd go off in a corner and vomit before a blast," he once said. "That helped me to get through, and in a strange way it helped Dad, too. Seeing someone else who is very nervous helps him somehow."[40]

In her flair for marketing, Freddie—a proud member of the Public Relations Society of America—is often credited with having popularized the word *implosion* to describe explosive demolitions. Jack once recalled that during the razing of the King Cotton Hotel in Greensboro, North Carolina, in the early 1970s, a reporter asked Freddie about how the building was going to explode. "It's not an *ex*plosion," she replied, "it's an *im*plosion." The term is a misnomer, since implosion denotes something that bursts inward, like a vacuum-filled vessel being crushed from the force of external pressure. (In the case of buildings, our old friend gravity does the job, not external pressure.) Misnomer or not, the term captured a powerful mystique. "We don't implode a building—an implosion is the creation of a vacuum," as Mark told me. "We don't do that. But it provokes thought. It generates a mental image. We live in a world of euphemisms. It makes life more palatable. We're trying to take something that is innately dangerous and innately scary and make it acceptable and package it."

To be schoolmarmish about it, you could just as well call an implosion the "sequential elimination of vertical structural supports." But that might only get you about two seconds on CNN. Better to package it with a little zing, something at which the Loizeauxs have continued to excel, to the occasional consternation of their competitors. "Structures, like people, have a life expectancy," Mark once explained in a typical trope. "They get tired. They get old. You might call what we do 'building euthanasia,' if you want to be positive about it."[41] Others have riffed on this death-by-lethal-injection theme, calling implosion "choreographed construction suicide—a death that is neat, tidy and frighteningly quick."[42] Then there's the surgery motif, a little passé now but potent enough back in the vintage slum-clearance days. "We like to think we have a skill something like that of a surgeon," as Mark put it in 1972, weighing the connotations. "We do the work, and leave the cleaning up to others. My father has been called 'an artist with dynamite,' but I prefer the surgeon metaphor."[43] One of the Loizeauxs' often quoted lines, delivered to many a journalist and network correspondent, may have originated during the implosion of a convent in Melbourne, Australia. The nuns were up in arms, quite understandably, Doug recalled, at the despoliation of the place where most of them had spent the majority of their adult lives. "And I don't know if a nun coined this expression or if it came up on another job," Doug went on, crediting the Mother Superior with the phrase: "It's better to have it bow out quickly than to be pummeled with a crane for weeks on end."

One of Doug's most wrenching public-relations efforts took place at the scene of the Alfred P. Murrah Federal Building in Oklahoma City, after the forty-eight-hundred-pound truck bomb piloted by Timothy McVeigh mauled the nine-story structure on April 19, 1995, killing 168 people. Many will never forget the indelible image of the half-shattered Murrah—"an open wound of flapping cables, toppled furniture and shattered lives"[44]—with the bodies of several credit union employees still buried in the rubble, lodged in too precarious a position to be safely extricated. Called in by officials to survey the tattered structure, the Loizeauxs found the Murrah far more severely damaged than previously thought, nixing any hope for low-key, traditional demolition. Their recommendation: to implode the building by "coaxing" and "cajoling" it into another progressive collapse. On May 11, the General Services Administration gave Controlled Demolition a $215,250 contract to bring the rest of the ruined building down. Though barraging the city with a second explosion was a repulsive idea in some quarters, Doug patiently advocated for implosion's slate-clearing powers. "People just don't need to see this anymore," he said at the time. "It's a monument to terrorism."[45]

His powers of persuasion hit the mark. "Gosh, I wish they could use a hammer and knock it down a piece at a time," related a local pastor. "But that is not realistic. We don't want to hear another blast, but in the real world, this is the only way to do it." Even the families of victims were ready to put the Murrah out of its misery. "We're tired of seeing it on TV. We're tired of hearing it on the radio and we're tired of reading about it in our newspapers," said Paul Howell, whose twenty-seven-year-old daughter, Karen, perished in the blast. "I think I'll feel a lot of relief when it's finally down and we can get back to life. I think it will do a heck of a lot of good for all of us in Oklahoma City." Having met with relatives of the two victims known to be in the rubble, Doug proposed covering their location with a black tarp spray-painted bright orange so that workers excavating the site would know where to search by hand for their remains. Meanwhile, panicked FBI officials had asked wreckers to shovel up sensitive documents from half-destroyed government offices; the feds were worried the building would tumble and launch their files over downtown Oklahoma City. And then after painstaking preparatory work had commenced, crews waited two days to allow defense lawyers for the bombing suspects to scour the structure for evidence. Not to mention the matter of bringing down the Murrah while preserving an adjacent building's underground parking garage, which the authorities had hoped could be salvaged. Coping with these contingencies, the veteran of many a disaster scene struggled to keep reality in check. Said Doug: "I still can't believe the magnitude of destruction here."[46]

There was no applause and nary a cheer on May 23, 1995, at 7:02 A.M., when a ferocious round of charges gutted the Murrah's east end, then its west flank, and finally kicked over an elevator shaft from the south. "Despite a warning siren," said one report, "the collapse was sudden and surprisingly violent, physically jolting many in the crowd, which had been kept two blocks away." As many spectators quietly wept, for some the blow served as a kind of gruesome revelation. "It was awful," said forty-four-year-old Carol Cook, who had made a pilgrimage from Tulsa to bear witness to the blast. "You could actually feel the repercussions, which makes me think the bomb itself must have just been indescribable." For others, it was a defiant time to move on. "You really wanted to kick the rubble and say: 'There, it's over. You're outta here,' " Oklahoma Governor Frank Keating said after surveying the scene. "There was almost a feeling of exhilaration." In perhaps the event's most telling detail, the Murrah's implosion allowed a surreal state of normalcy to come flooding back to town. Moments after the blast, it was reported, the city decisively turned the page when a worker pasted over a billboard that for weeks had lifted spirits with the message: "Oklahoma City . . . Our Hearts and Prayers Are with You." The new billboard advertised breakfast at McDonald's.[47]

Implosion is a brutally simple concept. If you put a bolt in your pocket and trudge up twenty flights of stairs, stick that bolt through a hole, and throw a nut on it, you've stored energy in the building. The energy comes from the calories you burned lugging your nut up twenty flights of stairs. That stored energy is ready to bring the building down to grade. The implosionist's task is to unleash that energy in an artfully conceived collapse, coaxing the building to fall wherever the wrecker wants it. Implosion, the Loizeauxs have said (using yet another trope), resembles the art of a judo champ who downs an opponent by kicking out the foe's leg and then twisting the adversary's off-balance body to the mat. As any martial-arts maven knows, you must take advantage of the natural balance and resistance of a foe's body—the rigidity of the rib cage, say, or a good solid femur. Similarly, demolitionists use the lingering stiffness of columns and beams of a collapsing building—selectively taking out some elements, leaving others where they lie—to guide the structure down. A doddering tower with weakened concrete may thus need to be shored up or partially rebuilt, even to the point of pouring new concrete, before it can be blasted away. Then, once the key legs are kicked out, the groaning weight of all those bolts heaves the structure down to earth.

Blasting out a building's legs, of course, is the province of Alfred Nobel's dynamite—or, nowadays, any of the dynamite-like explosive concoctions on the market with varying densities, velocities, pulverizing properties, and price points. Svelte, simple to use, and packing plenty of punch, the classic dynamite stick—à la Wile E. Coyote—is one-and-a-quarter inches in diameter and eight inches long. It can be bumped around, snapped in half at will, and pounded into the predrilled holes of concrete columns with abandon. Building movement is controlled by placement of the sticks in their holes: Dynamite placed forward in a hole will blow out the front half of the column and leave the back hooked together just like a hinge, pitching the building forward (not unlike the trees Jack started out felling). A charge at the back of the hole will blast out the rear of the column and tilt the sucker backward. And a charge smack in the middle eliminates the column, moving the building straight down. To detonate the charges, as in Nobel's day, the dynamite will still need a wallop from a blasting cap. The series is then wired together with detonating cord, a high-explosive-filled line toasting at twenty-one thousand feet per second (that's zippy enough to smolder from New York to Los Angeles in under fifteen minutes), and strung along in any order a wrecker can devise. Finally, it's all plugged into a little battery pack called a *capacitor discharge blasting machine* (aka the "Scorpion" or simply the "Hellbox") that shoots six hundred volts of electricity down the line to get things started, and the building's ready to rumble.

It's worth noting that among its attractive qualities for the discerning wrecker, dynamite is dirt cheap compared to clawing at buildings by hand. This was a much-bruited selling point among the product's boosters as early as 1923, when an agricultural blaster named Arthur Fencott blew down two hundred-foot-tall brick chimneys at a lumber mill in Lakewood, Ohio, at a total cost for labor and explosives of only $100, a sum, said the *Explosives Engineer,* that formed "an interesting and significant contrast with the thousand-dollar contract awarded only a few years ago for similar work to be done on a smaller stack by hand labor." The "efficiency and economy" of the whole operation even wowed the general public, "since many Cleveland theatres are exhibiting pictures of the razing."[48] (The journal's editors could hardly control themselves. DYNAMITE—A CONSTRUCTOR OF CIVILIZATION, they sighed in a different issue that same year.[49]) In the early days, dynamite was so cheap and ready-to-hand that when wreckers like Loizeaux were imploding buildings in the '50s, he'd pick up a case of the stuff over the counter at the hardware store, toss it in his truck, and speed off to blasts. (No more, of course. To keep up with today's slightly more draconian protocols, the Loizeauxs employ a full-time staffer who does nothing but track the firm's explosives.) Cost is still a prime selling point for explosive demolition (it can shave 20 percent off the bill compared to a traditional wrecking job), and Controlled Demolition prominently boasts that their handiwork has "saved property owners and contractors hundreds of millions of dollars worldwide."

Dreamy as it is, there's more than just dynamite in Dr. Demo's kit bag. For drop-kicking all manner of solid steel columns, trusses, girders, and beams, there are linear-shaped charges, which are usually V-shaped copper tubes packed with plastic explosive. The idea behind these handy devils was devised in the late nineteenth century by chemist Charles E. Munroe, who figured out that if you place the open end of the *V* against a surface and ignite the explosive, twin shock waves are unleashed from each slope of the charge. When these two wave fronts converge upon some poor hapless hunk of metal, the upshot is a high-velocity plasma jet traveling at twenty-seven thousand feet per second that, as they say in the business, cuts through steel like a buzz saw through butter. And there's a whole pharmacy of acronymed explosives such as HMX (high melting point explosive), RDX (rapid detonation explosive), and PETN (pentaerythritol tetranitrate, one of the baddest in the book) to hazard every destructive eventuality.

You might think wreckers would wax as rhapsodic about explosives as self-confessed pyromaniac Richard Rhodes did in his lead sentence about the Loizeauxs in 1974: "Dynamite," he began, "the big red-paper-wrapped sticks lying in their box ominous and yet exhilarating, fuel for fantasies of some ultimate Fourth of July, giant firecrackers packed with brown paste that looks like plastic wood—*is* plastic wood, but the binder that holds the sawdust is nitroglycerin."[50] But as Rhodes went on to note (after his palpitations slowed down a little bit), the Loizeauxs were fanatical about using the least possible amount of explosives to get the job done—"They'd take down the Empire State Building with Black Cats and ladyfingers if they could figure out a way to do it," he chuckled[51]—and the company shies away from hiring ex-military types with a gusto for blowing things up, for the simple reason that they may like it too much. Better that an aspiring destructionist cringe in terror at the thought of using plasma jets to buzz saw a tubular truss or three. Overload a building with explosives, and you end up "launching" the thing, raining debris down, busting windows, and wreaking general havoc upon neighboring structures—and paying for the damage.

The consequences can get much grimmer, no doubt. In one of the industry's black eyes, on September 12, 1993, at what was deemed Europe's largest building implosion in Glasgow, Scotland, two 190-foot-tall apartment towers called the Queen Elizabeth Square flats in the city's Gorbals district came down. Flying debris shot nearly four hundred feet into the spectator zone, causing the death of sixty-one-year-old Helen Tinney and injuring three others. "There were pieces, big and small, coming down all over the place," one spectator said of the scene.[52] Even though the wreckers—one British firm and one based in South Africa—used a massive 2.5 tons of explosives, one three-story-high section still didn't fully collapse and was "hanging rather precariously" over a shopping center.[53] All in all, what "had promised to be Glasgow's greatest ever free spectacle" was a rout, made all the more distressing by the headline two days later, which said: TOWER BLOCK FIRM INSISTS FATAL BLAST WAS A SUCCESS. As a wrecking honcho told reporters: "It is very sad that the people of Glasgow and Scotland have somehow misinterpreted that because of the fatality of the woman it was not a success." The operation, he said, was a remarkable technical feat.[54]

Implosions may be conceptually a cinch, but don't try this at home, folks. "The techniques for razing a building by implosion have never made their way into any engineering school," the Loizeauxs wrote in a 1995 treatise on the subject.[55] "Each building has its own personality," they went on, "manifested not only in its design but also in the 60-year-old sardine cans and scraps of prewar newspaper that turn up once we start knocking out walls and drilling holes in the support columns to insert the dynamite."[56] (Buildings can be different, it turns out, even when their structures are identical. "Believe me," said Mark, "taking down a building touching another building full of lawyers is completely different from taking down a building that is full of just people.") In any case, that proprietary process of choosing where to place your charges and which columns to fire in sequence—otherwise known as the loading and delay plan—is a closely guarded, often highly intuitive, and battle-tested form of knowledge. "It's the secret sauce," as Mark's daughter Stacey put it, "to what we do."[57]

Every wrecker has his or her own approach to discovering the hidden secrets of a building, but things can get downright weird when you start assaying the "natural frequencies of structures" (how they respond to vibration waves) or a building's "natural failure mode" (its own stress points that a wrecker can leverage to bring it down), and my all-time favorite piece of wrecking nomenclature, the "symphony of failure." This idea, as Mark described it to me, illustrates how an implosionist marshals the death of a building like a brilliant conductor might lead the New York Philharmonic. Once you know where the stored energy is in your structure, you need to know how and when to release it so that you get a symphony of failure humming, a kind of massive, upwelling, Mahleresque movement that sets all the various different parts of the structure in tune with one another, then unleashes a pealing harmonic response that will bring the whole thing down in concert. "A lot of people take down a structure—the stairwell goes north, the rest of the structure goes south," Mark said simply. "Well, they didn't have a harmonious failure mode." It may sound loony, but many wreckers are uncommonly attuned to the peculiar sounds of failure. "Buildings speak to us when they are being wrecked," industry veteran Jack McFarland explained in a more literal sense. "When portions of a building are stressed and on the verge of failure, they give an isolated crack or we see or hear a few pebbles drop or grains of sand. When we hear these sounds, we know that a failure or collapse is imminent. The trained operator can often lead that collapse as he chooses."[58] This isn't wrecking. It's structural telepathy. "If we can empathize with the structure, if we can get to know it," as Doug once put it, "then that building is as good as down."[59]

Mark Loizeaux's studies in structural symphonics started early. Born in 1947, he was fiddling with his own blasting patterns by the time he was twelve, and he graduated from the University of Tennessee with work in architectural engineering (though his degree was in business administration). "Studied to be a builder, and now I'm in the business of tearing down," he told a reporter

Jack Loizeaux and his son, Mark, share a special demolition moment.

in 1972. "But this has to be done, too. I wouldn't be in anything else."[60] Mark's academic career was put on hold for two years when he dropped out of college to take over the company's explosive work—getting his blasting license at an uncommonly youthful age of twenty—after Jack's back was broken when a car skidded into him as he was helping a motorist stuck in the snow. Lifelong exposure to his family's blast-punctuated brand of gospel has left a peculiar imprint on the implosionist's psyche. Mark's manner, wrote one perceptive reporter, "is very similar to that of a convinced Marxist or neurobiologist or horse-player who believes that he has found the secret fix, the hidden lever that moves the world. He is a man whose entire being is energized by one big idea."[61]

Yet there's also a poignancy to Mark's story. In 1973 (around the time Mark and Doug were described as "two clean-cut, fresh-faced young guys in white hard hats"[62]) the company had been blasting concrete blocks at the Jacksonville International Airport. Mark and the pilot of the company's private propjet were burning fifty-seven sticks of unused dynamite after a flawless demolition job. Following the usual routine at the time, he unrolled the dynamite tubes, loosely spread the powder over a remote patch of the site, and sparked it. The powder should have flamed out quietly. But in a freak explosion that remains unexplained to this day, the dynamite detonated and flung Loizeaux thirty feet into the air. Another man was instantly killed. Mark would find himself badly scarred and suffer a loss of hearing in one ear. Demolition as a kind of Loizeaux worldview seems profoundly informed by the family's brush with mortality. "What we do is finite," Mark told me. "It's a lot like going to LBJ's funeral. There's only one. Life is short," he added. "We are seizers. We seize."

Spend time with the Loizeauxs, and demolition begins to seem like an eminently logical solution to just about any psychosocial problem. "When we go out and take down three or four 17- or 18-story buildings, what are we doing?" Mark asked me rhetorically about the countless public housing blocks he's flattened. "We're improving the chances of young people to succeed. We are improving the community. We are effecting social change. What we did was create a much grander opportunity for vision. What we did was create a clean canvas. And let someone else be the artist. That's why my dad was once described as Jack Loizeaux, 'the dentist of urban decay.' "

Mark's loyalty to the cause and an unbudgeable sense of self that some read as arrogance ("He's just so French," an acquaintance once huffed, having heard the family name and taken Mark for a haughty Parisian) puts me in mind of Howard Roark, the heroic architect in Ayn Rand's 1943 novel *The Fountainhead*. In the climactic moment of the book, Roark dynamites his own government housing project called Cortlandt Homes, after the design is shamelessly watered down by other meddling architects. Roark's love interest, Dominique Francon, wonderfully describes the blast: "In the flash when walls rose outward and a building opened like a sunburst, she thought of him there, somewhere beyond, the builder who had to destroy, who knew every crucial point of that structure, who had made the delicate balance of stress and support; she thought of him selecting these key spots, placing the blast, a doctor turned murderer, expertly cracking heart, brain and lungs at once."[63] Roark calmly stands by the plunger as the police arrive and is carted off to jail. "Even as the dynamite which swept a building away," a prosecutor sputters at his trial, painting Roark as a common criminal, "his motive blasted all sense of humanity out of this man's soul. We are dealing, gentlemen of the jury, with the most vicious explosive on earth—the egotist!"[64] Opting for ego over spinelessness, the jury acquits him.

The Loizeaux family does not want for Roarkian egotism. Jack adamantly refused to dilute the company, choosing instead to limit the firm's work to only the most intriguing structural adventures (among unfulfilled goals upon his death in 2000: "to fell a whole-block building in New York City"[65]). One such exploit of Jack's concerned the Navy's Texas Tower No. 2, a massive radar base erected on three legs sunk in the ocean floor one hundred sixty miles east of Boston. "It was quite a moment when we set the timing device to detonate 21,000 lb of flow-gel and then tried to get out of there fast by boat," he recalled. "The area was being lashed by gales from passing Hurricane Hazel, and the swells were 30 to 40 ft from crest to crest. One does a lot of praying while being lowered in a tiny boat by electric motors. We were going down 100 ft to the heaving ocean surface. We could hear the time clock ticking away the minutes with 16 tons of explosives ready to detonate." Unfortunately, Jack never saw the blast. The boat's terrified pilot gunned the engine once the wreckers clambered aboard, and the tower disappeared into the fog.[66] The firm still gets some unusual kicks thanks to government work, which has recently dispatched the Loizeauxs to Europe to dismantle all manner of Soviet missiles—FROG-7s, Scuds, SS-23s—destroyed under the 1987 Intermediate-Range Nuclear Forces Treaty between the Soviet and U.S. governments. "Every time we take out a missile I feel good," Mark told me. "Getting rid of these is not only a job, it's a pleasure."

Today the implosion business makes up about 20 percent of the company's gross revenues and is among the least lucrative of the jobs they do. What with all the television anchors jostling to get their money shot of the next big implosion, the industry is a victim of its own success. "The press has made implosion look like a silver bullet," said Doug. "Solve-all end-all. Where it's probably only applicable to maybe one percent of the projects out there." As Mark's daughter Stacey said, "We didn't intend it, but it's become kind of like the movie *Field of Dreams*—'If you blast it, they will come.' "[67] Paparazzi have decked themselves out in camouflage and camped out in trees perilously close to buildings, angling to snap photos they could sell. One gung-ho spectator stuck his head out of a manhole right in front of a building, with twelve seconds to go. Another time Stacey was on security duty, strolling past a hedge. "Okay you caught me!" a guy suddenly exclaimed, popping up in surrender. The intruder was festooned from head to toe in twigs and leaves, having apparently devoted hours to his elaborate disguise.[68]

For her part, Stacey did all she could to stay away from the madness. "I tried to rebel against the family company in my adolescence; I was the lead singer in three bands over six years but quickly realized that nothing was quite as interesting as this job."[69] She joined the company full-time when she was twenty-two and grew hardened to the realities of the macho wrecking world (which is thought to be 95 percent male). "There is nothing, and I mean nothing, easy about being a woman in this industry," she explained. "When I started 13 years ago, I was young and blond and got a lot of name calling: things like sweetheart, dollface, daddy's little princess. I had a chip on my shoulder about it and worked double time to force people to respect me."[70] And never mind that there aren't a heck of a lot of people who think a woman who travels nonstop and tosses dynamite around for a living is perfect material for marriage. Nonetheless, she's gotten full-gloss coverage in *Cosmopolitan* magazine as a "Blasting Babe"—right alongside other "fun, fearless females" like the Texan bull-riding Miller Lite model Denise Luna[71]—and was once doted on in *People* for wearing a "badge of her femininity": A twenty-four-karat gold pendant that belonged to her grandmother, it's a jeweled bundle of diamond-tipped dynamite sticks, with a ruby on the fuse.

The Loizeauxs have become victims of their own success. For a variety of reasons—the egotism, the accolades, the constantly calling television crews—the company finds itself in an awkward position within the small subindustry of explosive wreckers. Controlled Demolition is "the silhouette on the ridgeline," Mark told me. "Everybody's shooting at us. People are just waiting for us to break a window. If we break a single window, it's an incident. It just goes like wildfire through the industry."

"You're either a hero or a bum," was Doug's take on the business. "If everything goes right, there will be 2,000 people taking credit. If anything goes wrong, the only person standing next to me will be my brother, Mark. Everybody else will be erecting gallows."[72] Frequently in demolition you end up as hero and bum at the same time, a fate the Loizeauxs shared during a mini-imbroglio over the National Tower at Pennsylvania's famed Gettysburg National Military Park. Scorned as "an Eiffel Tower with a pumpkin head,"[73] the 393-foot galvanized steel National Tower opened in 1974, an hourglass-shaped folly with four observation decks marring what Secretary of the Interior Bruce Babbitt called "sacred ground": the place where fifty-one thousand Americans battled one another to the death in a three-day bloodbath in July 1863. The privately operated, $2.5 million structure was also lambasted for looming over the site where Abraham Lincoln later delivered his two-minute Gettysburg Address. As one park official summed up: "It's the mother of modern intrusions on battlefields."[74] The phone soon rang in Phoenix, Maryland.

The National Park Service had commandeered the tower via eminent domain in 2000 as part of its efforts to "rid the battlefield of commercialism" and return the entire six-thousand-acre site to its Civil War–era state. The deal was this: Controlled Demolition donated its services in exchange for the media rights to the collapse and the right to salvage the steel. (The company estimated its costs to be $50,000, throwing in a few "leftover" explosives. The Park Service, on the other hand, valued the donation at $1 million—a figure based on other estimates they had obtained for the job—and called it "the largest corporate contribution toward preservation in the park's 105-year history."[75]) The Loizeauxs were heroes indeed. But a federal judge, in allowing the government to take control of the tower, harangued the Park Service for showing "poor taste" in letting Controlled Demolition use video footage of the blast. Though the plan let taxpayers avoid "significant expenditures of money," the judge said, "it does so by permitting a private contractor to exploit the tower demolition for its own commercial benefit."[76] Still others (namely, the attorney for the tower's owners) objected that the quest for some kind of you-were-there Gettysburg had gone off the deep end. "If we want to be complete," he sputtered, "we could restore the stench of rotting flesh to the battlefield."[77]

Fortunately it didn't come to that when the fateful hour

arrived 137 years to the day after Pickett's Charge, a celebrated battle of the Civil War in which fifty-five hundred of General George Pickett's Confederate troops and thousands of other soldiers made a fifty-minute blitz upon Union forces (billed as "the greatest charge ever seen") and were thoroughly routed. "Even for a town steeped in the tradition of guns, explosions and destruction," noted a reporter, "the demolition was a big event." Oblivious to any controversy, locals were thoroughly keyed up for the July 3, 2000, blast. "Honestly, what brings me here is the whole testosterone thing," one confessed. "If you're going to blow something really big up, I want to be here."[78] As Secretary Babbitt personally gave the order to fire, two vintage cannons manned by Civil War reenactors hurled dummy charges in the direction of the thousand-ton tower, and moments later, cannon smoke still swirling, 15.5 pounds of demolition charges splayed the structure and sent it thudding to the ground. Joy Boden, a battlefield tour guide from the town of Gettysburg, had camped out eleven hours to snag the best view of the destruction. "I've had to look at it for 26 years," she contentedly explained. "I wanted to see every inch of it blown up."[79] In the wake of the blast, battlefield preservation groups who had reviled the tower set about hawking the dead structure's bolts, lightbulbs, and signs as a fund-raiser, a tactic that didn't go over too well with the Baltimore engineer who designed the thing. "It's a hell of a way to go about collecting money," he groused. "It seems like the preservation groups are the last ones who should benefit from the destruction. They're the ones that caused the destruction."[80]

There was certainly a bit of irony to be acknowledged by Richard Moe, president of the National Trust for Historic Preservation, who had backed the tower's implosion. "To a preservationist, 'demolition' is almost always an ugly word," he said in a statement. "But not today. Today it's the right thing to do."[81] The Trust, incidentally, must have enjoyed its destructive adrenaline rush, because Moe and company later gave a thumbs-up to the demolition of the 108-year-old, neoclassical Century Building in St. Louis, a move that had local activists bitterly sounding the alarm: "for the first time anyone involved can remember, the National Trust for Historic Preservation, the country's most powerful preservation group, sided with the wreckers." The Trust had sacrificed the marble-clad structure to ensure the salvation of an even grander building across the street. The Century was razed for a parking garage.[82]

Whatever else you say about Controlled Demolition, the company is almost certainly unique among its peers in having a romance novel based on its high-voltage exploits. Fellow Baltimorean Mary Jo Putney's 2000 work *The Burning Point,* chronicling fictional Maryland implosion firm PDI (Phoenix Demolition International), ably spins the Loizeauxs' raw material into a steamy tale that hits all the firm's high points and more. The story of blasting babe Kate Corsi and her bullheaded father, Sam ("No daughter of mine is ever going to work demolition," he growls[83]), the novel is more or less modeled on the career of Stacey, who is cited in the book's acknowledgments as "clear proof that there is no reason why a woman can't blow things up if she wants to." Wrecking is portrayed as an immensely fulfilling career: Kate wants to rid the world of eyesores "in one beautiful, terrifying instant, and do it with such precision that there would be no need to clear the parking lot next door."[84] But there's also the dumbfoundingly mundane, such as drilling endless holes and fending off wisecracking construction crews. The book covers many other bases, including the rival firm ("Implosions, Inc.") started by a client-stealing cousin and the company's emergency structural response after an earthquake in Mexico City, where Kate "learned that there was a healing sense of catharsis in demolishing structures that had seen great sorrow."[85]

But honestly, by far the most entertaining bits are the romantic one-liners about Kate's star-crossed marriage. You've got the relationship turned sour that mysteriously "ended in an explosion more devastating than dynamite."[86] And there's her partner's psychotically overprotective instincts that were "as volatile and dangerous as nitroglycerin—and now Kate wanted to implode buildings."[87] Fortunately for everyone's sake, a happy ending is in the offing, where love among contractors takes unusual twists. As one demolitionist is surprised to discover: "I'm beginning to find a light dusting of construction debris downright sexy."[88]

| 4 |

HAUSSMANN'S PARIS

AND BEYOND

WHILE ALFRED NOBEL was swishing his sulfuric acids, one of history's most influential *démolisseurs* had just capped seventeen years of ramming boulevards through the teeming center of Paris, clear-cutting entire neighborhoods to make way for what observers called *le percement*—the piercing. In a wrecking jag so stupendous it blew the minds of jaded architectural historians even a century later, urban precincts were wrenched open as if done in by a cataclysm. "A prodigious urban experience, an earthquake in the midst of Paris," a commentator marveled. "Ruins . . . then a new wonder of the world, Paris white and fresh."[1]

Baron Georges-Eugène Haussmann called himself "artist-demolitionist."[2]

Remembered as a "brawny Alsatian, a talker and an epicure, an ogre for work, despotic, insolent, confident, full of initiative and daring, and caring not a straw for legality,"[3] Baron Haussmann reigned as prefect of the Seine from 1853 to 1870. During that time, by one count, 27,500 houses fell to the pickax and the trowel. One of them, a modest home with a front yard and garden, stood not far from the Champs-Élysées. Unflinchingly blotted out for the boulevard that bears his name, it was the house of Haussmann's own birth.

This remorseless urban henchman spawned his own epithet—"Haussmannization"—and as a strapping civil servant, he set the gold standard for creative destruction. The statistics still stagger. Having wrecked tens of thousands of houses, Haussmann built or rebuilt more than 102,000 others. An army of laborers at least fourteen thousand strong laid more than four hundred miles of pavement. Road widths, on average, doubled. He could claim to have laid one in five streets in central Paris. Sewers? He built 80 million francs' worth. Street trees? They numbered nearly one hundred thousand. "The record of his achievement, set down in cold figures, is still without parallel," one scholar wrote. "No one in the entire history of urbanism, neither Pericles nor the Roman emperors nor the Renaissance Popes, ever transformed a city so profoundly during such a short space of time." Haussmann's program of *grands travaux*—his great public works—"was arguably," said another, "the biggest urban renewal project the world has ever seen."[4]

Haussmann owed his preeminence as a demolition artist to Louis-Napoléon Bonaparte (nephew of *the* Napoléon), who served first as president and then as emperor of France during the Second Empire. When Louis-Napoléon returned to the capital city from exile in 1848, he clutched among his possessions a long roll of parchment, upon which was inscribed "a map of Paris, with zebra stripes of red, green, blue, and yellow that ap-

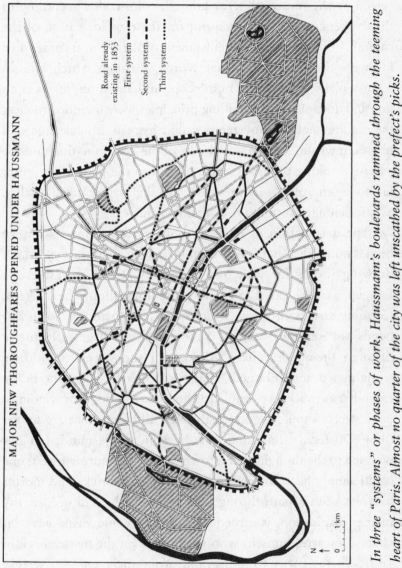

MAJOR NEW THOROUGHFARES OPENED UNDER HAUSSMANN

Road already
existing in 1853
First system
Second system
Third system

N
0   1 km

In three "systems" or phases of work, Haussmann's boulevards rammed through the teeming heart of Paris. Almost no quarter of the city was left unscathed by the prefect's picks.

peared to have been drawn at random."[5] These routes, conceived by the future emperor himself, color-coded according to their urgency, were the blueprint for the transformation of the capital, a "plan for the embellishment of Paris," as it came to be known—the routes, in other words, through which Haussmann's picks would pass. In its scope and ambition, this was an unusual document. "Its guiding principles were intended to meet the requirements of movement, public hygiene, and elegance," a historian wrote. "When one thinks of the determination and the precise thinking that must have gone into the plan, one cannot fail to be amazed by its excessive and slightly deranged quality, as if it belonged more to the dream world."[6]

The destruction of Paris by boulevard-bashing may have been a nutty idea, but it had been kicking around the city's dank drawing rooms for well over a century. The historian Abbé Laugier as early as 1753 was grumbling about the narrow, torquing streets of Paris, which were "so tortuous, so full of bends and senseless angles" that you couldn't get a baguette through them edgewise. "Almost all the streets should be straightened and enlarged," Laugier decided. "They should be extended as much as possible to eliminate too frequent windings. New streets should be driven through all blocks that are longer than 600 feet."[7] Spinning out the plan in his mind, Laugier warmed to the thought that a town was like an unruly forest; one could simply hack through a neighborhood's bricks and mortar like one hews a path through the woods. If he had needed any further inspiration, it turned out, Laugier could easily have invoked Descartes himself, who weighed in on the matter back in 1637. Shying away from a grand pronouncement—"I wreck, therefore I am" was apparently not in the cards—Descartes nonetheless gave demolition a cautious thumbs-up. "It is true that we do not want to tear down all the houses of a city for the sole reason of wanting to rebuild them and thus make the streets more harmonious," he mused. "But it is obvious that some should be torn down and rebuilt and that even at times they must be torn down for reasons of safety lest they collapse of their own accord because their foundations are weak."[8]

If the philosophes had long since declared open season on the "senseless" streets of Paris, it was left to the Bonaparte clan to start smashing up the French windows. For this they had an unnatural appetite. "If heaven had given me just twenty years and a little free time," Napoléon I had wistfully said, "people would have looked in vain for Paris. No trace of it would have been left, and I would have changed the face of France."[9] Napoléon's delusions of creative-destructive grandeur went down the tubes with the rest of his empire in 1815. His nephew, however, was quickly making good on this ruefully lost opportunity. Having settled in as president of the Republic, Louis-Napoléon (roguishly described as "a sawn-off, somewhat comical figure with a pointed beard"[10]) yanked out his parti-colored map and swung into action. "Paris is the heart of France," he announced in 1850. "Let us put all our efforts into embellishing this great city, into improving the lot of those who live in it. Let us open new streets, let us clean up the populous districts that lack air and daylight. Let the beneficial light of the sun everywhere penetrate our walls."[11]

This missionary talk of light could sound corny—"Light before all else" was one of Haussmann's magisterial mottos[12]—but Louis-Napoléon had a point. The city of light needed more light, among other basic amenities, a deficit that only massive demolition could remedy. This was made alarmingly clear when writers pointed up the city's atrocious bill of health in 1834. "Paris is an immense workshop of putrefaction," said Victor Considérant, "where misery, plague and illness work in concert, where air and sun hardly penetrate."[13] At the root of the problem was Paris's population, which exploded from 786,000 in 1831 to more than 1 million in 1846, then nearly doubled by 1870. But in the city's already sardinelike residential quarters, there was simply no place for them to go. Houses were crammed with occupants from garret clear through to cellar. "Everyone is everyone's slave in these dreadful Parisian cages," one account said, "where you are condemned to every sound, every smell, every illness of those with whom you share your chains."[14] Worse, only one house in five had water piped to it. Courtyards doubled as garbage dumps and latrines; alleyways were slicked by the slop bucket. And no one had forgotten the 1832 cholera epidemic, which killed 20,000 of the city's 861,400 inhabitants.

"I wreck, therefore I am" was starting to seem like not such a batty proposition after all. Poor Paris's great blunder, some were saying, was not to have been burnt to cinders like London in 1666 or wrecked beyond all hope like Lisbon in the earthquake of 1757. Those lucky disaster zones could wipe the slate clean, rebuild to modern sanitary standards, spiff up their architecture, kick out the boozers and bums, and turn a pretty penny on the new real estate to boot. Paris, on the other hand, had been forced to proceed catch-as-catch-can—"raising its heights, filling empty spaces, patching up, trimming bits off the street, off gardens, yards, and marshes"[15]—eventually piling up on top of itself like one incurably festering sore. Critics of the day, wrote architectural historian Anthony Vidler, outdid one another in describing the city's ever more baroque pathology. There was "the mud, the awful drains and their noxious exhalations, the rubbish, the dust, the poverty, beggary and crime, the maladies, the epidemics, the political manifestations, the chaotic architecture, the dark and close walls, the smoke, the tragic scenes of death and misery, the comic scenes of picturesque thievery, [and] the mysterious scenes of obscure depravity."[16] The only recourse left for the agonized body of Paris was the total act of surgery: " 'Cutting' and 'piercing' were the adjectives used to describe the operation; where the terrain was particularly obstructed, a 'disembowelling' had to be performed in order that arteries be reconstituted and flows reinstated."[17]

The word *disembowelling* was Haussmann's own, used to describe the triumphant blasting of the Boulevard de Sébastopol through one of the city's intractable working-class districts: "It meant the disembowelling of the old Paris, the *quartier* of uprisings and barricades, by a wide central street piercing through and through this almost impossible maze."[18] Preach all you want about piercing the city's walls with light, but a major fringe benefit for Louis-Napoléon was stamping out those narrow passageways so hospitable to the city's legendary cobblestone barricades, which were mounded up against the authorities in times of insurrection (more than four thousand of them sprouted during the July Revolution of 1830). Also backing the emperor's cause was the archbishop of Paris, Haussmann recalled, who suspected that the topsy-turvy lanes of the day were a big-time impediment to "good housekeeping and personal cleanliness" that hampered the "moral state" of the general population. "In wide and straight streets flooded with light," the archbishop counseled, "people do not behave with the same slovenliness as in dark, narrow, winding streets."[19] Dirty dishes being a direct precursor to guillotining the emperor, it was hardly a stretch of the imagination to say, as architect Le Corbusier once did, that one day Louis-Napoléon simply stood up and screamed: "This can't go on, it's too dangerous. I want all this cleared up, I want this impenetrable warren sliced up into sections, I want straight avenues opened up that my cannons can fire along. Then we shall see if they can still get up these revolutions of theirs."[20]

Demolition contractors descended upon the face of Paris. The streets had to go.

Almost no quarter of the city was passed up by Haussmann's picks. They plundered Paris over the course of three "systems," or phases of ruin and reconstruction. The first system, up to 1858, mainly savaged the central city, hacking north-south and east-west axes through the heart of the "impossible maze." The second system burst outward, making grand diagonal thrusts that did spectacular damage, and the third, launched in 1860, notched around the perimeter to knit suburban communes into the urban network, while polishing off unfinished business in the city's core. The particulars boggled the mind. Smack in the center of town, the Île de la Cité—"the cradle of Paris" and home to twenty thousand people—was sloughed off save for a few sentimental old favorites (the wreckers managed to spare Notre Dame cathedral and the church of Sainte-Chapelle). Running alongside the Louvre, the Rue de Rivoli sliced through a Right Bank slum of noxious quagmires, a spot Balzac had described in 1836 as having "that deeply rooted combination of squalor and splendor which characterizes the queen of capitals."[21] (Haussmann destroyed this zone, as he said, "with great satisfaction."[22]) The ninety-eight-foot-wide Boulevard de Sébastopol reared down from the north, at times threading its way through gardens and courtyards instead of jam-packed blocks, a nicety about which Haussmann chirped: "It is easier to pass through the inside of a pie than to cut into the pastry."[23] The Boulevard du Prince Eugène (today's Boulevard Voltaire) forced its way through the city's pastry-filled eastern flank, inciting minor riots when patrons of the area's popular vaudeville theaters learned that the Théâtre Lyrique, the Théâtre de la Gaîté, and other stages would be stomped out for the public good.[24] The great Boulevard Saint-Germain cleaved the Left Bank. The Boulevard Malesherbes lurched apocalyptically through the northwest. The Boulevard Magenta nipped northeast; the Boulevard Saint-Michel got a running start from the Seine and stampeded to the south. The *grands travaux* seemed never to end. As a song from a revue had it at the time: "Every minute the hammer comes down / On another part of town."[25]

Swinging their hammers day and night under electric light, the hordes of wreckers soon became a fixture on the Parisian skyline, with battalions of horses and carriages queued up below them to cart off the mounting debris. Lording over roofscapes from one end of the horizon to the other, these destructionists traditionally hailed from the countryside region of Limousin, celebrated for its masons and other craftsmen, who poured into Paris during the rebuilding. Some of these "Limousin workers," as they came to be known, were the third generation to come to Paris, and for a time, demand for their services was unquenchable. Forty thousand of them left the region for the building season of 1852, and "none returned for lack of work."[26] (When on the job, they were undoubtedly assisted by Haussmann himself,

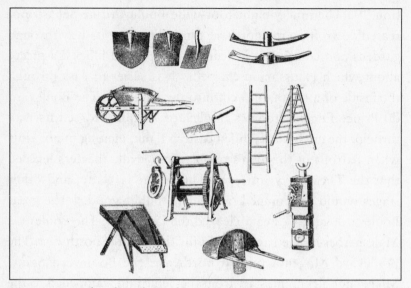

Haussmann's hordes of wreckers revolutionized the physiognomy of Paris with the humblest means imaginable.

who insisted that the demolition wreckage be auctioned off—when he wasn't obsessively tinkering with the details of gas lamps, kiosks, and *vespasiennes,* the city's characteristic street urinals.) That year, 1852, was a doozy for creative destruction in the city of Paris, and the efforts of this wholesome workforce must have duly reassured the emperor. "The people roaming the city were no longer bands of insurgents," recalled a politician of the day, "but squads of masons, carpenters, and the like off to their place of work; if the paving stones were disturbed, it was not to pile them up in barricades but to make water and gas travel beneath the street; the threat to people's houses came not from cannon or fire but from the compulsory purchase order."[27] At the height of Haussmann's work, the wreckers and their constructive counterparts amounted to 20 percent of the Parisian labor force, and the multiplier effect sent cash radiating out into the economy from the city's ruined quarters. As the merry slogan of the time put it: "When building flourishes, everything flourishes in Paris."[28]

Or so the boosters said. A more cynical observer would note a century later: "Construction, destruction, construction: every phase makes money. Only Paris loses."[29] As the wreckers worked their way incorrigibly onward, this latter view proved all too true when Haussmann's demolitions spawned a whole new industry of financial shenanigans known as *expropriations*. The rub was this: As Haussmann's biographer explained it, Paris had historically gone about ripping down citizens' houses under a procedure known as *alignement*—the government's power to set the line of public thoroughfares. This process was meant to protect certain hallowed civic features, in particular the ramrod-straight street line, it being obvious by now that "straight lines are part of France's heritage in aesthetics and regulatory practices."[30] Owners of affected buildings were paid what were called *reduction indemnities* for the blitzing of their homes, but the whole ordeal was subject to public review and could be thwarted at will by property owners. Eager to close this loophole, the city in 1852 authorized large-scale land acquisitions via expropriation, or compulsory purchase. This scheme was vastly more expedient than *alignement* but was based on "a ponderous formal mechanism"[31] that was, in effect, its own undoing. First, in order to be snatched from its owner, a property had to be used for a "public benefit"—for the building of roads or canals, for the erection of public buildings, to bolster sanitary conditions in residential areas, and so on. The bureaucratic machinery then clanked into action. Plans were posted at town halls and opened to public inquiry. Compensation boards convened. Real estate judges were consulted; public benefit was established. Files were sent to the Ministry of Education and Religious Worship, then to the Council of State, and on to the minister of the interior. And finally they landed at the Municipal Council, where the deal was signed and sealed.

Then the money changed hands. By most accounts, Haussmann was more than generous when it came to compensating the newly expropriated, and this sparked off a "thrill of excitement" among landlords when it dawned on them that they'd be hitting the jackpot as soon as their compulsory purchase went through. Petitions started piling up on Haussmann's desk—not pleading to have one's property saved, of course, but begging to be bought out.[32] Now about those shenanigans. Certain barristers, it was said, made a specialty of such cases, and they didn't have many qualms about bamboozling the municipal expropriations committee. This new professional clique "sought out small manufacturers and equipped them with detailed account books, false inventories, and fake merchandise that often was nothing more than logs wrapped in paper," as one account said. "It was a sort of midnight gang that rifled the till of the city government."[33] Thus was born the classic one-liner of creative destruction. When one Parisian *nouveau riche* was asked how he came into such wealth, he replied simply, "I was expropriated."[34]

Still, there were those who couldn't be bought at any price, and they fought Haussmann tooth and nail. "One of the baron's first problems in the western *faubourgs* was that he was obliged, in order to build his new boulevards, to pull down so many fine houses which had been standing for only a handful of years—

and whose owners had influence at court."[35] There was the demolition for the Boulevard Malesherbes, for instance, gashed in a northwesterly tack through one of Paris's infamously squalid precincts—la Petite Pologne, so called after a popular café of the 1830s. The place was famously wicked. "There were no streets, only alleyways; no houses, only shanties; no sidewalks, only a little carpet of mud and trash," wrote the novelist Eugène Sue. "From morning till evening, and especially from evening till morning, there was no end to the shouts of: Help! Guards! Murder! But the guards could not be bothered. The more people were knocked senseless in Petite Pologne, the fewer there were to arrest!"[36] Unfortunately for Haussmann, seventeen town houses had been demolished along with the shanties, and as the new boulevard was inaugurated in 1861, venomous recriminations hit the newsstands. "It was the first time that upper-middle-class residences had been touched by the demolition contractor's pickax, and the event served as a signal for a press campaign of unprecedented violence."[37] Haussmann defended himself by pointing out that the poor had elsewhere endured "the most irksome displacement while showing respect for the duly declared public benefit," while here he only had "to disturb the habits of people blessed by fortune for whom a move of house is no more than a passing nuisance."[38] Haussmann brushed off the abuse in typical fashion. By his own count, he later said that over the course of seventeen long years, he dislodged 350,000 people and their various factories, shops, and taverns, and if it was all said and done without a general revolution, he was counting it an unqualified success. We'll have to take, as a parting shot on the matter, a cartoon by the brilliant illustrator Daumier. Dated December 10, 1852, the scene shows a gentleman standing before an avalanche of crumbling walls and heaps of rubble as a pick blasts away in the background. He remarks to his companion, who is carrying a great pile of possessions strapped to his back: "But here is where I live—and I don't even find my wife."[39]

The municipal coffers thus opened wide, the Limousin workers pounding away, and the boulevards rising from the muck, the transmogrification of the city had begun. "So the entire city dies and is born," wrote one of Haussmann's chroniclers, evoking the panoramic upheaval. "The hard echo of the pick, the rumble of falling plaster, the din of scaffolding sound a refrain to the rhythm of daily life. Everywhere heavy carriages or handcarts trundle furniture, and people expropriated from their lodgings carry bundles of household goods. If a few weeks later you return to visit the tomb of a defunct house, you find that even the ground on which it stood has been taken by a stranger—a boulevard bordered by straight lines of tall buildings, uniformly white, like soldiers on parade."[40]

All that remained was for the city's culturati to boldly take inspiration from the spectacle of ruin, and this was soon to pass. The upending of Paris was fodder for some of the century's greatest creative minds. Artists and illustrators rolled out their easels; poets and novelists stumbled through the rubble, scribbling wayward dispatches about urban life; photographers captured the vanishing city on haunting glass-plate negatives. Never had the poetry of demolition been so richly examined as it was in Second Empire Paris. As the brothers Edmond and Jules de Goncourt fustily lamented in 1860, the demolition of Paris had crumbled a whole world before their very eyes: "My Paris, the Paris in which I was born, the Paris of the manners of 1830 to

In Charles Marville's stunning photograph of demolitions for the Avenue de l'Opéra, pick-wielding wreckers can be glimpsed arrayed across the crumbling rooftops.

1848, is vanishing. . . . I am foreign to that which is to come, to that which is, and a stranger to these new boulevards that go straight on, without meandering, without the adventures of perspective, implacably a straight line, without any of the atmosphere of Balzac's world, making one think of some American Babylon of the future," they famously wrote. "It is stupid to live in a time of growth; the soul is as uncomfortable as a body in a damp new house."[41]

Victor Fournel in 1865 simply called it "the delirium tremens of demolition."[42]

We begin to glimpse the physical enormity of Haussmann's

undertaking in the work of urban photographer Charles Marville, who was dispatched to document the doomed houses and
streetscapes, the brasseries and the arcades, the alleyways and
dramshops and barracks and hostelries. His hundreds of images
are affecting in their own right, as a record of what Victor Hugo
called the city's "inextricable mesh of weirdly ravelled streets"[43]
as they were being summarily ironed flat. But the captions to
Marville's photographs are almost just as haunting. The names
of the tiny, characteristic streets of that lost world are followed
by the word *disparue*—the disappeared. It's an oddly affecting
litany: Rue Saint-Christophe *(disparue)*. Rue des Trois-Canettes
(disparue). Rue des Marmousets *(disparue)*. Disappeared, too,
are the Rue Haute-des-Ursins, Rue de Glatigny, and Rue du
Haut-Moulin. Adieu, Rue du Contrat-Social and Rue Sainte-
Croix and the Impasse des Provençaux and Rues Estienne et
Tirechape. Ditto, Rue Verderet. Bon voyage, Rue du Bon-Puits.
Every last one of them, *disparue*.

Other artists began to take stock of Haussmann's Paris and
its powerful sensations. "There was thus the possibility of a picturesque of demolition," T. J. Clark wrote of the Boulevard
Malesherbes as depicted under construction in an 1861 etching
by A. P. Martial, "surging through the slums of Petit Pologne
like a force of nature, a wave about to burst a flimsy dam, something that could make the city look sublime for a moment if en-
graved with the right degree of detachment; and there are scores
of images from the same decade in which a painter put together
out of broken walls and scaffolding a good semblance of a
ruin."[44] The Italian writer Edmondo de Amicis, having arrived
at the time of the 1878 Exposition, was shocked even then at
"the immense openings" of the Boulevards Haussmann, Ma-

genta, Prince Eugène, and Malesherbes, "into which one glances with a shudder, as into an abyss."[45]

The ruined streets of Paris became a well-trod stomping ground for those souls open to the peculiar majesty of the Baron's labors. The poet Théophile Gautier marched through demolition sites and found a landscape chockablock with "the mystery of intimate distributions." This phrase, presumably, was Gautier's way of saying that wrenched-open buildings betrayed the lives of those who had lived in them, however faintly. "A curious spectacle," he wrote, "these open houses, with their floorboards suspended over the abyss, their colorful flowered wallpaper still showing the shape of the rooms, their staircases leading nowhere now, their cellars open to the sky, their bizarre collapsed interiors and battered ruins."[46] As Gautier knew, there's no accounting for the emotions that well up at the sight of wallpaper aflutter in the open air. "This destruction is not without beauty," he finally confessed; "the play of light and shade across the ruins, over the random blocks of fallen stone and wood, makes for picturesque effects." This was not quite the aesthetic triumph Haussmann had in mind when he declared himself a demolition artist, but it put the prefect at the forefront of fetchingly busted buildings. What is probably the finest compliment ever bestowed upon Haussmann appears in Gautier's 1856 article titled "Mosaic of Ruins." Haussmann, the poet wrote, was Paris's own Piranesi.[47]

For an *artiste* of Haussmann's ambition, this was high praise indeed. No one had nailed the ravishing appeal of rubble quite like the eighteenth-century Italian architect and engraver Giovanni Battista Piranesi, whose etchings of moldering Roman ruins had long dazzled connoisseurs of collapse. Born in Venice,

Piranesi studied as an architect and briefly practiced the trade, but his name would become a touchstone in the realm of demolition—invoked again and again over centuries of tattered structures—thanks instead to his raw talent with copper plates and etching acids. Besotted by the remnants of antiquity, Piranesi rambled around Rome, sketching vine-tangled tombs and toppled basilicas that in his prints were redolent of *terribilità*—an awesome, terrifying power, full of emotional fury. Even his humdrum scenes of monuments and landscapes, which he peddled to tourists to support his wilder work, bristle with fierce energy. Parisians, surveying their hewn and twinging city, might well have found some resemblance to Piranesi's profoundest images: his suite of sixteen etchings known as *The Prisons*. These brooding scenes are a tour de force of light and shadow, depicting imaginary, dungeonlike spaces that recede into whorls of arches, catwalks, and vaults. Every now and then a human figure appears, dwarfed by cavernous stone interiors, gesturing forcefully like explorers in some strange new world. As one scholar put it, these etchings inspire complex feelings of "wonder, a deep sadness and a sense of mystery."[48] This was precisely the impact of Haussmann's Paris.

Gautier was on the right track with his Piranesian musings, but it was not until 1871 that the literature of demolition found what may well be its masterpiece. This was a novel by the great Émile Zola. A journalist before turning to fiction, Zola based his work on meticulous personal observation and sociological research into Second Empire Paris. His father, a civil engineer, was known as a "proto-Haussmann" who toiled over bridges and canals. Sporting these credentials, Zola could not help but brilliantly capture what was called "the intermittence of modern life"[49] during the *grands travaux*—which he did in *The Kill*. "Nowhere," wrote David Harvey, "is the brazen joy of creative destruction better invoked than in this extraordinary novel of Haussmanization in all its crudity."[50]

In his novel *The Kill*, Zola dramatizes Haussmann's demolitions like nothing else before or since. Just listen to Aristide Saccard, the short, ugly real estate finagler whose orations turn wrecking into dazzling imagery: "These big cities are so stupid!" he exclaims, surveying the city from a restaurant window up on the hill of Montmartre. "This one has no idea that one fine day it will be set upon by an army of pickaxes. Some of those mansions on the rue d'Anjou wouldn't gleam quite so brightly in the sunset if they knew that they had only three or four more years to live." Saccard, the epitome of the dastardly double-dealer, eyes the city in a greed-filled frenzy. "Yes, this time, it's all going to burn! Do you see?" he shouts at his wife. "It's as if the neighborhood were being boiled down in some chemist's retort," he went on, arriving at Zola's trademark line on the transubstantiation of real estate. "Yes, yes, as I was saying, more than one neighborhood is about to be melted down, and gold will stick to the fingers of everybody who stokes the furnace and stirs the boiling pot."[51] Chopping up the city with his hand as if with the sharp edge of a cutlass, Saccard sums up Haussmann's operation in its bare essentials: "The buildings that need to be cleared away will collapse in clouds of plaster," he says. "Cuts everywhere. Paris slashed to pieces with a saber, its veins laid open to provide nourishment for a hundred thousand excavators and masons, and in the end you'll have a city crisscrossed by fine strategic highways that will put fortresses right in the heart of the old neighborhoods."[52]

Zola later zooms in for a plaster-cloud close-up. An expedition party trudges out to investigate the indemnities paid to would-be expropriatees and arrives at the gaping hole that had been opened for the future Boulevard du Prince-Eugène. The demolition scene is arresting—the party knee-deep in mud, shattered structures looming up on all sides—as the buildings' revealed innards once again prove uncanny. "Tall buildings had been gutted so that their blanched entrails showed," writes Zola. "Empty stairwells and gaping rooms hung in the air like the smashed drawers of some huge, ugly bureau. No sight could be sadder than the wallpaper in the bedrooms five or six stories up, yellow or blue squares now in tatters marking the places under the roofs where poor, wretched garrets had been—tiny holes that had once housed someone's entire existence."[53] As the party thrusts deeper into this surreal land, the wrecking images come fast and furious. The visitors are mesmerized by the sight of thirty workmen heaving down a still-standing wall. (As it finally toppled, "the five gentlemen of the committee smiled at one another. They were enchanted. A fine powder settled onto their coats, turning their arms and shoulders white."[54]) Elsewhere, demolition workers teeter on the edge of the roof, intently heaving their axes. Someone remarks on their courage: "If their picks had missed their marks, the sheer momentum of their swings would have sent them plunging off the roof."[55] And there's a final vista of a tattered sixth-floor bedroom, where yellow floral wallpaper flaps in the wind as a piece of stovepipe pokes awry. One of the expedition party is suddenly seized by emotion. " 'I spent five years there,' he murmured."[56]

While Zola and the *artistes* before him were contemplating these unsettling new dimensions of demolition, others were still rumi-

The Rue de la Paix, shown here under furious assault, captures the city in Piranesian splendor: rich with wonder, deep sadness, and mystery.

nating—quite eloquently—over the stripping away of the past. "In the new Paris, there will no longer be any residence, any tomb, or even any cemetery," one critic wrote. "Each house will be only a piece of that enormous inn through which everyone has passed and where nobody remembers having seen anyone else." Haussmann's relentless assault on the city had made it one huge revolving door, where without familiar landmarks and moorings, Parisians turned into half-human zombies: "City without a past, filled with memoryless minds, tearless hearts, loveless souls. City of uprooted crowds, a mobile mass of human dust."[57]

Credit for this line of thinking about Paris goes to none other than Victor Hugo, whose despair over the constant wrecking of his beloved city remains unsurpassed. Hugo, besotted with Gothic architecture, declared himself a lifelong foe of the pickax and a determined protector of France's monuments, "as indefatigable in defending our historic buildings as the iconoclasts of our schools and academies are zealous in attacking them."[58] Indignantly roving the streets of Paris, Hugo deplored the mutilation of this chapel or the razing of that palace, all wanton "profanations, demolitions and impieties" perpetrated by those who should know better. "The archbishop's palace has just been demolished, a building in poor taste so the harm is not great," he noted in 1832. "But along with the archbishop's palace they have also demolished the bishop's palace, a rare relic of the fourteenth century that the demolishing architect was unable to tell apart from the rest. He has pulled up the wheat with the tare."[59] *Tempus edax, homo edacior,* intoned Hugo: Time erodes, man erodes more. Or, in his own gladly offered translation: "Time is blind, man is stupid."[60]

Intimately acquainted with the most crafty modes of destruction, Hugo reserved particular scorn for "the necessary decadence of architecture"—in other words, demolition by alteration, especially alterations made by well-meaning but clueless architects to his beloved cathedral of Notre Dame. "Fashions have done more harm than revolutions," he cursed, bewailing the designers of various additions, renovations, and "restorations" who have "stuck their wretched, ephemeral baubles over the wounds in the Gothic architecture, their ribbons of marble, their metal pompoms; and a veritable leprosy of ovolos, scrolls, surrounds, drapery, garlands, fringes, stone flames, bronze clouds, sated Cupids, fat-cheeked cherubims," among other brutalities. "To the centuries and the revolutions, which at least laid waste with impartiality and grandeur, has been added the swarm of architects from the schools, licensed, sworn and attested, defacing with the choice and discernment of bad taste, and replacing Gothic tracery with Louis Quinze chicory to the greater glory of the Parthenon. This is the ass kicking the dying lion."[61]

Beyond the muddling architects, Hugo was convinced that the demolition of architecture was the inevitable result of a single invention: not the pick but the printing press. Architecture—once the universal form of writing, conveying in stone the great ideas of the ages, from the slabs of Celtic dolmens and cromlechs to the sculptured portals of Notre Dame itself—was "the principal register of mankind."[62] But it was no match for the book of paper, which was paradoxically more durable than granite. The book, wrote Hugo, will kill the building: "printing will kill architecture."[63] In fact, he said, the corpse was already starting to rot. "Let there be no mistake, architecture is dead, dead beyond recall, killed by the printed book, killed because it is less enduring, killed because it is more expensive."[64] Hugo finally decided that at the rate Paris was going, it would be built over again every fifty years, and none too nicely, either. "Our fathers had a Paris of stone," he said. "Our sons will have a Paris of plaster."[65]

In his celebrated poem "The Swan," Charles Baudelaire commented on the transformed city under Haussmann. "Old Paris is no more," he wrote. The "form of a city changes more quickly, alas, than the heart of a mortal."[66] But as Haussmann well knew, mortals' hearts change, too. Having wrecked their way through the city of light, neither he nor boss Louis-Napoléon would get much applause for their good deeds, ending up instead as the twin evil geniuses of urban renewal, slum-clearers incarnate. Haussmann may take the rap for wrecking Paris, but blaming the baron isn't entirely fair. Haussmann, some say, was tossed into the midst of a crashing storm of political forces and property values, a weather pattern well known to modernity. "It was, however, a storm he neither created nor tamed, but a deep turbulence in the evolution of French economy, politics, and culture, that in the end threw him as mercilessly to the dogs as he threw medieval Paris to the *démolisseurs*."[67]

Baron Haussmann was shoved out of power in January 1870, a victim of the fading fortunes of Louis-Napoléon, who himself died in exile in 1873. The tumultuous Paris Commune was soon loosed upon the city, as citizens erupted in full-throated revenge against the empire, and Haussmann's former offices, the Hôtel de Ville, went up in flames to cheering crowds: "We have just lighted up the château Haussmann!" went the cry.[68] In the wake of the artist-demolitionist's departure, the urban "embellishments" virtually stopped cold turkey, with condemnations of buildings for public works plummeting from 848 in 1866 to a mere 8 in 1870.[69] Not a single official representing the state or the city of Paris could be bothered to attend the baron's funeral in 1891. "Even the onlookers all along the very streets and boulevards which Haussmann's imagination brought to life, gaze indifferently," one historian said of the funeral march. "Towards the corner of the rue Drouot, a member of the procession cries, with outstretched arm, 'Ingrates!' "[70]

The shocking truth was that after Haussmann's death, it was painfully clear to Parisian urban planners that the destruction of Paris had only just begun. A 1913 report described the city at the time of Haussmann's retirement as "a vast *chantier* of demolitions momentarily abandoned, which it was necessary to continue. There were everywhere dead-end streets to open up, projections of boulevards to prolong, a chaos of obstacles to disperse, and pestilential lanes to demolish. The immense impetus given before 1870 has been continued through the uninterrupted effort of forty years, without, moreover, the end being near to attainment."[71] As late as the 1950s, half the dwellings in certain sections still had no water, 86 percent no toilet, and 98 percent no bath or shower, leading one critic to write in 1957: "That which Paris demands, your task, urbanists, is not little repairs day by day; it is a total reconstruction. It is not a house here and there which it is necessary to demolish, but blocks, I would say even entire quarters."[72]

Haussmann may have been a product of his time, but his legacy stubbornly persists. "Torrential as it was, history flowed in the bed of Haussmann's Paris," wrote Marcel Cornu a century later. "And then, in truth, it isn't Paris alone which remains Haussmannized. Even now in 1972! We ourselves, the Parisians, in our penchants and our aesthetic inclinations, we rest under the dominance of Haussmannism. It conditioned us. We are saturated with it. Paris as remodeled under the Second Empire has been our primary school of urbanism."[73] For better or worse, throughout the twentieth century, Haussmann's particular brand of destruction has exerted a profound pull upon urban visionaries. One enthusiastic disciple was none other than Le Corbusier, the famous French architect who made no secret of his loathing for messy city life: "[I]magine all this junk, which till now has lain spread out over the soil like a dry crust, cleaned off and carted away," Le Corbusier wrote about the thicketed, medieval center of Paris, which he fully intended to destroy in his reviled "Voisin Plan" of 1925.[74] That scheme proposed gutting the entire core of the city and replacing it with a forest of glass-clad skyscrapers towering six hundred feet tall in prairielike parks.

Oh, a few ancient churches could be spared ("They would stand surrounded by verdure; what could be more charming!"[75]) and perhaps a historical doorway or two. Meanwhile, when it came to those straight boulevards (so relentless in Haussmann's day, the joke went, that the Seine itself would need to be straightened, "because its irregular curve is really rather shocking"[76]), Le Corbusier couldn't have agreed more with Haussmann's linear fixation. "The curve is ruinous, difficult and dangerous; it is a paralyzing thing,"[77] he raved, adding that the winding road was "the Pack-Donkey's Way. It is in this way that cities sink to nothing and that ruling classes are overthrown."[78] Le Corbusier, who was so possessed by the baron's spell that he once reproduced a photograph of Haussmann's picks and shovels in his book *Urbanisme,* deemed destruction nothing less than a moral imperative. "We must pull things down," he said. "And throw the corpses onto the garbage heap."[79]

In recent years, less flighty minds have reassessed Haussmann's work and discovered—surprise, surprise—much to admire. One urban scholar pointed out that the baron's tactic of the *percée* called for construction to immediately follow demolition, with highly refined designs for the new streetscapes the world has adored ever since. "American planners, by contrast, cleared broad swaths of land for Corbusian parks; had little control over rebuilding, which was sometimes separated by decades from the demolition phase of a project; and placed even more unreasonable burdens on the poor and the people of color than did the French."[80] The baron's biographer makes a similar case, arguing that Haussmann's indefatigable efforts, for so long scorned as the "mindless butchery" of the beautiful old city, are once more becoming the subject of keen interest among planners and historians, and "sometimes even a model."[81]

Haussmann's work, at the very least, does have a certain forthright elegance when compared to late-twentieth-century clearance operations. Once, the filmmaker Edgar de Bresson had been wandering around Paris, poking his lens into working-class neighborhoods like Belleville and Ménilmontant on the northeast fringes of town. Bresson bumped into a demolition boss in Belleville, where wrecking services included the use of a demonic sort of "Rube Goldberg machine" that terrorized tenants until they surrendered and desperately fled their lodgings. "The machine must have been in great demand around Paris," a reporter joked in 1978, "because a whole new industry in harassment has opened up." The "machine" worked like this: Needy landlords could avail themselves of "experts" who earned commissions based on how quickly they emptied a building, while tactics of the larger developers were not much nicer. One real estate juggernaut, intent on dumping a whole Montparnasse district of eight thousand people out of their homes, "tried to clear a big old building on the Rue de l'Ouest of its last ten tenants by digging an enormous hole in the back yard," the sad story went. "No one left, as it happened, so they kept digging. At forty feet, one of the workmen died in a cave-in, and then the building was declared 'in a state of peril' and the ten tenants who could not be evicted were evacuated for their own safety by the police."[82]

It may be fitting to finish a chapter on Haussmann with the story of Les Halles, the famed central Parisian wholesale food market just a short pig's trot from the Louvre. The name itself "stirs images of exquisite slumming—onion soup and beckoning whores and huge truckers in little blue berets unloading crates of lettuces, and the marvellous gathering rhythms of a marketplace in the morning."[83] Haussmann got Les Halles built during his first days as prefect of the Seine, so perhaps it's just desserts that the market would be wrecked unceremoniously more than a century later, its narrow neighborhood streets, ironically, too clogged with traffic.

Les Halles was lovingly called *le ventre de Paris*—the belly of Paris, its bowels, its soul. Grounded in one of the city's oldest neighborhoods, the glorious, sometimes mucky, always fleshly affair had stood on the site since the twelfth century, boasting the choicest morsels: shad from Bordeaux, flans from Chartres, shallots from Elysium. The place really got cranking in 1851, when architects Victor Baltard and Félix-Emmanuel Callet worked up some iron-and-glass pavilions with peaked vaults and curved arches and filigrees of Gothic tracery, what Louis-Napoléon called *umbrellas of iron*. By 1935, a dozen lacy sheds gleamed amid streetscapes of silhouetted dormers, lined with boisterous, working-class victual vendors, soiled with "the intimate smell of a city."[84] Les Halles, with its butcher boys and she-devils and all manner of aliments, was not the center of Paris, said the historian Louis Chevalier, but the center of other centers—that is, the essential Paris.

Deemed a woeful traffic quagmire and branded a public hygiene menace (never mind that the place was fearsomely scrubbed clean every dawn, the entrails hosed off, and the neighborhood returned to its rumpled bonhomie), the market was expelled to the drab southerly burb of Rungis. Of the traffic-jammed streets around Les Halles, people began to say, "If only the Germans had destroyed Paris," or "Londoners don't know how lucky they are," and one even went so far as to declare, "This is doubtless unfortunate, but we must resign ourselves to it: Paris has not been the victim of an atomic bomb and it is not Brasilia."[85]

Les Halles was bulldozed along with its habitably shabby working-class quarter in 1971 to make way for the Pompidou Center and an underground shopping mall. Editorialists called its demolition "the surgical removal of the secret heart of the city."[86] A few protesters shackled themselves to Baltard's pavilions. Placards came out and were brandished. "To tamper with Les Halles," the slogan went, "was to tamper with Paris."[87] But in the event, the last night of Les Halles played out to only "a few nocturnal creatures, a few nostalgia seekers, a few poets, a few clochards."[88] The beloved market was kaput. In its place stands the subterranean Forum des Halles—"Shopping, culture, leisure: the top brands, the most fashionable shops, the foremost cinema complex in France," blare its advertisements—and the massively popular Pompidou Center, with its exposed, brightly hued ductwork and glass-wrapped escalators, a structure dubbed "an enormous, multicolored, and very venomous insect"[89] and a "building with its tripes outside."[90]

"Where are the powerful odors, the smells by which one recognizes so many cities," Chevalier wrote in his 1977 book *The Assassination of Paris,* ruing what by then was known as the consumer society, a place without the stench of blood from the old Chicago stockyards, without the sweat of labor, without the smell of thighs or the odor of armpits, above all without entrails—"a closed universe, disinfected, deodorized, devoid of the unexpected, without surprises, with nothing shocking, a well-protected universe providing one does not leave one's room and understands that one can always be attacked in the elevator."[91] For Chevalier and others, Les Halles symbolized struggle against "the de-Parisianization of Paris."[92] As Les Halles began to crumble, a hand-lettered sign was soon plastered to a doomed block of buildings. "The center of Paris will be beautiful," it said. "Luxury will be king. The buildings of the Saint Martin block will be of high standing. But we will not be here. The commercial facilities will be spacious and rational. The parking immense. But we won't work here anymore. The streets will be spacious and the pedestrian ways numerous. But we won't walk here anymore. We won't live here anymore. Only the rich will be here."[93]

"Whether or not it was Satan," wrote Chevalier, who died at the age of ninety in 2001, "it must be noted that there was something about the resistance of les Halles, something about the place itself, something mysterious."[94]

Perhaps the mystery was the spirit of Haussmann, lingering over the doomed pavilions, haunting the iron rafters, waiting for the next phase of the unending *grands travaux*. The demolition artist's great creation was, after all, being rubbled in turn. But the baron could rest easy. His oeuvre would last well beyond Les Halles, a feat to be reckoned with for generations. "The city of Paris entered the twentieth century in the form which Haussmann gave it," wrote the German cultural critic Walter Benjamin. "He revolutionized the physiognomy of the city with the humblest means imaginable: spades, pickaxes, crowbars, and the like. What destruction was caused by even these crude tools! And as the big cities grew, the means of razing them developed in tandem. What visions of the future this evokes!"[95]

SACKING PENN STATION

THE SECAUCUS MEADOWLANDS of New Jersey may seem a peculiar place to go trolling for a train station from New York, of 1910 vintage, a little worse for wear, in chunks shaped something like ten-ton Tootsie Rolls. Identifying markings: jackhammer gouges, nice proportions. Color: pinkish, a few soot stains. Style: Roman, very. But Pennsylvania Station was no ordinary terminal, and the Meadowlands, well, stranger things have turned up in these marshy shallows. In 1998, architectural prospectors Alexandros Washburn and Marijke Smit found themselves bushwhacking their way through stands of ragweed, wary of the odd snapping turtle, having grown inured to the damp comfort of hip waders, with a party of ground-penetrating radar operators, some makeshift divining rods, and plenty of blind faith as they hunted down one of the most famed piles of rubble in the history of demolition. For half-submerged among battered bricks and sumacs were, somewhere out there, rose-hued granite drums and velvety neoclassical sculptures, dumped thirty years ago amid cartloads of debris from the wrecker's mother lode. "Tossed into that

This stone maiden from Pennsylvania Station, fixed for all time in Edward Hausner's 1968 photograph, turned the New Jersey Meadowlands into a pretty classy dump.

Secaucus graveyard," wrote *New York Times* architecture critic Ada Louise Huxtable, "were about twenty-five centuries of classical culture and the standards of style, elegance, and grandeur that it gave to the dreams and constructions of western man. That turned the Jersey wasteland into a pretty classy dump."[1]

One of the most stirring transmutations of American civic space unfolded in 1963, when New York City's old Pennsylvania Station succumbed to its inexorable fate as fodder for a flashy new sports complex called Madison Square Garden and a bland, twenty-nine-story skyscraper. As jackhammers gobbled the station's acres of travertine and granite, its eighty-four Doric columns soon to be jettisoned in the Meadowlands, the structure's sorry end would galvanize a generation of civic crusaders and bring architects such as Philip Johnson and Paul Rudolph to the barricades. It would also blow the lid off the wrecker's anonymous toil and help spark a national debate about the dynamic of destruction. "Demolition is a particularly American act," as David Samuels put it more recently, "a concise and visually compelling expression of the belief that history is transient, that a new beginning is always in the cards, that the glories of the past are only a prelude to an even more glorious, everlasting present."[2] Nowhere has the triumph of this "everlasting present" been better staged than in the story of Penn Station, America's archetypal tale of unbuilding.

The headlines gave the blow-by-blow with brilliant economy: GREAT SPACES IN PERIL, rang the alarum in 1961. PENN STATION TO GIVE WAY TO MADISON SQUARE GARDEN.[3] All too soon came the pathetic footnote to the fait accompli: PLAN TO SAVE COLUMNS IS OFFERED.[4] Then, belatedly, CITY ACTS TO SAVE HISTORICAL SITES.[5] And finally, the *New York Times*'s majestic 1963 coda, FAREWELL TO PENN STATION, an obituary that would be remembered as among the finest editorial statements of all time: "We want and deserve tin-can architecture in a tin-horn culture," it read. "And we will probably be judged not by the monuments we build but by those we have destroyed."[6]

The station's denouement in a trackside ditch was "a tearjerker of monumental proportions,"[7] because public opinion had put lines in the mortar beyond which the wrecking ball would not swing. Designed by Charles Follen McKim of the posh firm McKim, Mead and White and completed in 1910, Pennsylvania Station glowed with golden-cream travertine from famed quarries in Tivoli. The main waiting room, modeled after the warm room of the Baths of Caracalla in Rome (with nods to the baths of Titus and Diocletian, plus the Basilica of Constantine for good measure), stood one hundred fifty feet high and two city blocks long, girded by eight massive Corinthian columns and topped by barrel vaults, clerestory windows, and a coffered ceiling. Across its broad walls were Jules Guerin's sprawling murals of the railroad's territory, done up in cerulean blue and ochre. Everywhere were loggia and colonnades and vestibules and fluted pilasters. Behind all this chunky, Roman grandeur was an airily modern concourse, recalling the great train sheds of Paris with its latticed steel-and-glass arches. Cladding the exterior was pink granite from Milford, Massachusetts, with a row of Doric columns standing thirty-five feet high, and a sculptural program by Adolph A. Weinman that included twenty-two stocky eagles (each weighing in at fifty-seven hundred pounds) and maidens representing Day (ringed by sunflowers) and Night (clutching poppies). The station's chief patron, Pennsylvania Railroad president Alexander Cassatt, was the brother of impressionist painter Mary Cassatt. He was a man, it was said, who understood the value of symbols.

On opening day, journalists jabbered as if they'd never laid eyes on a groin vault before. One deemed the $90 million station "a huge structure which covers more territory than any building ever erected by continuous labor in the history of the world."[8] By god, it was "the largest and handsomest in the world," affirmed another. "Any idea of it formed from description and pictures falls short of the impression it makes upon the eye."[9] Sited between Seventh and Eighth avenues, stretching from 31st to 33rd streets, the whole enterprise would engulf some six city blocks—twenty-eight acres of land, including the track yard. More than a little creative destruction was needed to shoehorn the vast terminal into the Manhattan grid, not that the extensive leveling of the cutthroat Tenderloin district elicited a peep from preservationists. "Traditionally, New York had defined itself as the House That Ruthlessness Built, and for more than 300 years the conveniently prevailing assumption had been that whatever got torn down was only making way for something better," a critic noted much later. "No one, after all, had protested in 1903 when 500 buildings had been razed so that Penn Station could go up."[10]

Indeed, it was all glitter and pomp when on February 25, 1903, Pennsylvania Railroad bigwigs posed with house wreckers on the fire escapes at Number 557, a tenement on the north side of 32nd Street. It was the first building to be wrecked for the tunnel that would carry trains under the Hudson River and on into the new station. Fifteen hundred people would eventually be displaced by the project, along with entire blocks of tenements, shops, and factories, although Saint Michael's Church, on a highly coveted piece of land, caught a lucky break and was painstakingly reconstructed—stone by stone, marble altar and all—a few blocks away at an exorbitant expense. By 1907, wrecking crews had hauled off five million bricks and six thousand truckloads of demolition debris, and it gave a man a powerful thirst. In a photograph of the cleared station site in 1904, one lonesome structure sits upright on an otherwise desolate expanse. "The last building standing was a pub," historian Hilary Ballon explained, "no doubt serving demolition crews until the end."[11]

Pennsylvania Station endured for half a century, weathering two World Wars and the Great Depression, but the travertine began to lose its luster with the passage of the Federal Highway Act in 1944, as the whole nation felt a keen upwelling of desire for their Studebakers. And other threats were looming on the horizon. "Business was lousy," complained one proprietor of a cutlery shop in the station's arcade. "People with money aren't riding the railroads—they're riding the airplanes."[12] Meanwhile, what Huxtable called "demolition by commercialization" began long before the station's actual ruin: garish ads popped up; automobiles beckoned from revolving turntables; shacklike shops cluttered the grand space. In the railroad's pièce de résistance, a clamshell-shaped canopy housing swank ticket booths was plopped into the main waiting room in 1958, looking like "a hot dog stand in the Louvre."[13] This ill-advised structure drew no end of irate zingers. A "fluttery fatuous kiosk," went another appraisal, "as appropriate as an installation of juke boxes in Westminster Abbey."[14] The *Times*, meanwhile, harrumphed that the "Age of Elegance bowed to the Age of Plastic when the railroad began to sell tickets on the half shell in the giant plastic clam with which it effectively and tastelessly demolished the building's massive Roman interior."[15] (One can only imagine what Victor Hugo would have said.)

Soon the Pennsy wasn't even keeping up appearances. "Like a once stately mansion that has long been neglected," a reporter wrote as the wreckers descended, "the station now seems to belong more to the past than to the present."[16] Train dispatcher Phil Donnelly recalled that a coat of grime had settled on the exterior's pink granite, adding an ominous note of gloom. "Perhaps this building that now resembled a mausoleum reminded people on some level that the age of railroads was gone," he said, "and it made them nervous to have this relic here, reminding them of something that no longer lived."[17] The whole operation was on the verge of insolvency. In 1955, Pennsylvania Railroad president James Symes hit the panic button and signed an agreement with developer William Zeckendorf to sell the air rights to the station and build a new station underground.[18] "The last wall went not with a bang, or a whimper," Huxtable wrote, "but to the computerized clack of leveraged cash flow computations."[19]

Smashing Pennsylvania Station suddenly became thinkable.

When the dirty deed hit the press in 1961, a drowsy architectural establishment was jolted into action, and soon the wagons were circled with the launch of Action Group for Better Architecture in New York (AGBANY). On August 2, 1962, these grim idealists took out an ad in the *New York Times* proclaiming: "It may be too late to save Penn Station; next month the wreckers will move in for the kill. But it is not yet too late to save New York. We, the undersigned—architects, artists, architectural historians, and citizens of New York—serve notice upon present and future would-be vandals that we will fight them every step of the way."[20] Just after five in the afternoon that day, luminaries such as Philip Johnson, Aline Saarinen, and Lewis Mumford joined two hundred others raising a ruckus in front of the station's Seventh Avenue colonnade, toting placards that said: DON'T DEMOLISH IT! POLISH IT!, DON'T AMPUTATE — RENOVATE, and just plain old SHAME! Came the jaded reply from Irving Felt, chairman of the Madison Square Garden Corporation: "Fifty years from now, when it's time for our Center to be torn down, there will be a new group of architects who will protest."[21] In early 1963, the City Planning Commission approved the railroad's plan unanimously.

At that time, it should be noted, the Planning Commission had no means to preserve buildings even if it had wanted to, and neither did any other group in the city. Aesthetes had been gnashing their teeth over the wrecker's rampages for decades, however, and several years earlier, preservationists got a shock when they went to catalogue the city's must-save structures but found that the final list was a little lean because "almost a third of the buildings they had planned to include had already been torn down."[22] With the perils of Penn Station as a catalyst, on April 21, 1962, Mayor Robert F. Wagner established the city's Landmarks Preservation Commission to tot up an inventory of worthy buildings, which did no good in the station's case, since the commission was powerless to actually pull the plug on demolitions until it finally received such authority in 1965. Preservationists point out, though, that such authority came not a moment too soon in the case of another famed New York rail station. The wrecking ball had been looming over Grand Central

Terminal ever since 1954, when the ailing New York Central Railroad was aching to put a massive office development on the site. The destruction was heartily embraced even by many architects, including Minoru Yamasaki (about whom we shall have more to say later). "Though it is a marvelously beautiful room," said Yamasaki, "Grand Central is in an archaic style [and] does not particularly express the exciting materials or exciting methods of construction we have today."[23] As rage over the proposed razing mounted, however, in 1967 the city declared the exterior of Grand Central a landmark, and following much jockeying among the players (including Jacqueline Kennedy Onassis, who backed the Committee to Save Grand Central Station), the matter landed at the U.S. Supreme Court. In 1978, in the first historic preservation case to reach the high court, justices affirmed the constitutionality of the city's landmarks law. Grand Central was later restored to its full luster, a bittersweet reminder of what might have become of that other marvelously beautiful station had it, too, survived.

Though they couldn't save Penn Station, urban devotees would file away a few lessons for future battle plans. "There's a funny cycle that occurs in the history of a building," explained Kent Barwick, himself once chair of the Landmarks Preservation Commission. "It is very much appreciated when it is put up, then it sort of disappears into the city when other buildings become more noticeable or celebrated. And just a little while before it is rediscovered, it is thought to be absolutely worthless. That's the dangerous moment for a building."[24] But probably the sturdiest advice to the demonstrators marching at the barricades came from the ever pragmatic Philip Johnson. "You can picket all you want, but it's not going to do any good," Johnson counseled the group at one point. "If you want to save Pennsylvania Station, you have to buy it."[25] This pearl of wisdom, as it happened, was echoed by one Morris Lipsett, the demolitionist whose company held the contract to sack the station. "If anybody seriously considered it art, they would have put up some money to save it," he told a reporter in his own defense. "You always have half a dozen societies around trying to preserve everything. In some areas the land is just too valuable to save anything that doesn't fully utilize it."[26]

As demolition day lurched ever closer, many were pointedly quoting James Merrill's 1962 poem "An Urban Convalescence," which opens with the following lines:

> *Out for a walk, after a week in bed,*
> *I find them tearing up part of my block*
> *And, chilled through, dazed and lonely, join the dozen*
> *In meek attitudes, watching a huge crane*
> *Fumble luxuriously in the filth of years.*
> *Her jaws dribble rubble. An old man*
> *Laughs and curses in her brain,*
> *Bringing to mind the close of* The White Goddess.
>
> *As usual in New York, everything is torn down*
> *Before you have had time to care for it.*
> *Head bowed, at the shrine of noise, let me try to recall*
> *What building stood here. Was there a building at all?*[27]

No one among the opinion-makers wanted to revisit Merrill's urban amnesia or dazedly submit to that rubble-dribbling crane. The rhetorical jockeying around Penn Station moved into high gear. The *New York Times* went nuts at the pathetic thought of those "eighty-four disembodied Doric columns banished to Flushing Meadows," referring to one plan that had briefly proposed exporting the columns to Queens. "With what smug, sentimental self-deception we assume that by making some pleasant, picturesque arrangement of left-over bits and pieces, after razing the original, we are accomplishing an act of preservation! Nothing could be further from the truth. Once the total work of architecture is destroyed, it is gone forever," the paper editorialized. "The ultimate tragedy is that such architectural nobility has become economically obsolete, so that we must destroy it for shoddier buildings and lesser values."[28] Indeed, the turgid drawings of the planned new complex—boasting all the grandeur of a potato chip—made it painfully clear that wreckers and real estate rogues were not the only villains in this tale. Architects had eaten their own. "Even the demolition of the first St. Peter's was acceptable when it was replaced by the cathedral of Michelangelo," an urban designer recalled years later. "However, the loss of Penn Station in exchange for the modernist dreck that replaced it was the last straw—the pivotal event after which architects could no longer be trusted to guarantee progress."[29]

Then there was the proposed Battery Park colonnade, a plan to shuttle a few of the columns down to the tip of Lower Manhattan (a public subscription drive was to be taken up to cover the $200,000 tab), where the meager installation would be named for former president Dwight D. Eisenhower. The city's architectural gatekeepers gave the plan their seal of approval, and Eisenhower duly showed up at the site in ruddy good health in 1963, rambling about "the priceless institution of self-government" before taking "half a dozen mild swings with a gilded sledge hammer at a gilded stake marking the site of one of the sixteen pillars of the future Dwight D. Eisenhower Colonnade."[30]

But such piecemeal proposals only seemed to further enrage preservationists, who were beginning to articulate much broader arguments about the phenomenon of demolition. The New York chapter of the American Institute of Architects noted: "Like ancient Rome, New York seems bent on tearing down its finest buildings. In Rome demolition was a piecemeal process which took over 1,000 years; in New York demolition is absolute and complete in a matter of months."[31] Others chided the railroad for cluelessly dumping one of its major brand assets. "That the Pennsylvania Railroad should wish to destroy this monument to itself . . . is incredible," clucked one Harold F. Smith, editor and publisher of the *Mobile Home Citizen,* adding that "the Pennsy will have destroyed a corporate image-symbol of strength, solidity, stability and permanence."[32] (To be fair, there were a few detractors among the crowd of architectural panegyrists. Dissing Penn Station as a "neoclassic behemoth," one sourpuss voted with the wreckers: "It has been said, comparing doctors with architects, that the medicos have the option of burying their mistakes. Let us not pass up this opportunity."[33]) Back at the *Times,* no salvo was left unvolleyed, and the paper brooded the year before the curtain finally went down that Penn Station's fate was that of the whole country. "Of course, there is no happy ending," the editors wrote. "This is really the great American tragedy, being played out in every major city. The growing economic obsolescence of so many of our most distinguished older buildings, the peculiar combination of higher building costs and lower architectural standards of today, a lack of vision—all these factors are making our cities uglier and more ordinary every day."[34]

As ever, Ada Louise Huxtable got in the point-blank parting shot: "What this amounts to is carte blanche for demolition of landmarks," she said. "It's a good way to kill off a city, as well."[35]

The demolition of Pennsylvania Station began on October 28, 1963, at precisely 9:00 A.M. as jackhammers gored the terminal's granite slabs. "Just another job," said John Rezin, the foreman in charge of gutting the station, as its jagged, pink granite innards emerged under a Monday morning's drizzle.[36] Rezin's off-the-cuff remark would forever be attached to the station's demise, his apparent nonchalance confirming for preservationists the whole operation's moral bankruptcy. A few hours later, one of the great stone eagles was ceremonially lowered to the ground, as honchos from the Pennsy and Long Island railroads flanked the bird and photographers snapped away. The images of those proud, fifty-seven-hundred-pound stone eagles being hoisted down by crane, their wings chafing against the strapping, are evocative beyond belief, a moment in demolition history almost more profound than any imploding building. (Two of the poor creatures were eventually set down in front of the new Penn Station, "looking as alien as emperors guarding a poorhouse."[37]) Ton-and-a-half stone slabs were lifted from the facades and hoisted away. The jackhammers munched on forty-foot-wide marble steps, gouged great rifts into the noble columns, and eventually feasted on the shopping arcade, that "miniature boulevard of bookstores, bonbonnières, and haberdashers

Nine acres of travertine and granite were transmuted, in Norman McGrath's shot of the station's rubble-strewn waiting hall, into the bombed-out shell of a great cathedral.

reminiscent of the famous arcades of Milan and Naples."[38] The famous, four-foot-wide Doric columns, it was said, would be dumped on a ninety-acre tract as fill for a swamp intended to be an industrial park. "An ignoble, if practical, end will eventually be served by the tons of granite."[39]

Less than a year later, the grand main waiting room "looked like the bombed-out shell of a great cathedral," a historian wrote. "Coils and wires hung like entrails from its cracked and open walls. The men with jackhammers filled the air with noise and dust. The noise violated memory; the dust smelled of death."[40] Photographs show cranes wedged into the cramped construction spaces and the new Madison Square Garden complex rising amid the destruction of the old, as all the while, trains continued to disgorge bewildered, grimly perspiring passengers into a maze of dust and debris. That dazed-and-confused feeling would turn out to be a permanent feature of the new Pennsylvania Station, a cramped warren compared to the monument it replaced, the vast main waiting room swapped for charmless, low-ceilinged corridors. "Through it one entered the city like a god," Vincent Scully famously wrote of the old station. "Perhaps it was really too much. One scuttles in now like a rat."[41]

Days after demolition began, the racket reverberated around the city with the publication of the *New York Times*'s scathing farewell to Penn Station. "Until the first blow fell no one was convinced that Penn Station really would be demolished or that New York would permit this monumental act of vandalism against one of the largest and finest landmarks of its age of Roman elegance," the paper said in its editorial Wednesday, October 30, 1963. "It's not easy to knock down nine acres of travertine and granite," the editors went on, "84 Doric columns, a vaulted concourse of extravagant, weighty grandeur, classical splendor modeled after royal Roman baths, rich detail in solid stone, architectural quality in precious materials that set the stamp of excellence on a city. But it can be done. It can be done if the motivation is great enough, and it has been demonstrated that the profit motivation in this instance was great enough." In its acid concluding lines, words that would be hurled in the path of the wrecking ball for the next forty years, the paper flung down the gauntlet before a culture of destruction. Even when we had Penn Station, the paper said, we couldn't be bothered to keep it clean. "The final indictment is of the values of our society. Any city gets what it admires, will pay for, and, ultimately, deserves."[42]

Morris Lipsett, the man whose company wrecked Pennsylvania Station, was "a tall, portly, and congenial man of humble beginnings" who boasted an often imaginative approach to demolition. He had no college degree and no formal engineering training, but his native prowess with an adding machine and a wrecking ball turned him into "a multimillionaire and something of a personality in a field given more to anonymity than celebrity."[43] The secret to successful demolition, Morris confided as Penn Station crumbled, is "rhythm . . . our boys have got rhythm."[44] When they weren't swinging their hips, though, Morris's minions cased their quarry with a cold eye to salvageable steel, appraising original architectural drawings and checking them against a structure from cornice to sump pump before making a bid. Pennsylvania Station, said Morris, yielded up only about fifteen thousand tons of scrap metal—a yawn compared to your typical sixty-thousand-ton steel mill, which the company was also taking down at the time. It might have comforted the raving editorialists to know that in 1963, the year Morris began mauling Penn Station, Lipsett's parent company, Luria Division, lost money for the first time in its seventy-six-year history. Cratering scrap metal prices had wiped out its artfully calculated profits.

Morris Lipsett began his illustrious career as a junk dealer in Jamestown, New York, "with $20 and a tired Hupmobile roadster" that launched the estimable concern known as "Lipsett's Auto Wreckers—Home of a Thousand Parts."[45] His brother

Julius, having tired of running a circulation route on a Rochester newspaper, joined up in 1930, and the siblings' first building demolition was an aging hotel in Bemus Point, New York. An auction of the furnishings fetched a handsome $3,000, but any notion of profits evaporated in their ruinous attempt to take down the structure and sell its parts for salvage. Morris was unfazed. "In fact," the story went, "such was his faith in the future of wrecking buildings he announced to his wife that, from that time forward, he would no longer eviscerate automobiles. Mrs. Lipsett reminded her husband of the substantial loss they had just taken on the resort hotel." Morris replied philosophically, "You should always look for money where you lost it."[46]

The hunt began in earnest, and the sign on Morris's auto wrecking yard was promptly repainted with the phrase "industrial dismantling." Having borrowed $10,000 to wreck an oil refinery in Charleston, South Carolina, the Lipsetts found that one refinery led to another (wonderful thing about destruction), and in 1940 they landed their headquarters in the heart of burgeoning wrecking opportunity, New York City. Wartime demand for scrap steel was a massive boon to the young company and helped them turn a profit on one of their first high-profile gigs— a bid to scrap the fire-ravaged ship *Normandie* in 1946. The Lipsetts paid $161,680 for the massive vessel, which was built for $60 million and served as a French luxury liner before it burst into flame and capsized in its Hudson River berth in 1942 while the U.S. Navy was converting it into a troopship. Julius called the purchase "strictly a gamble," but the price of scrap nearly tripled over the first eight months of the job.[47] After the *Normandie* came the aircraft carrier *Enterprise* and a few battleships to boot. "Indeed," commented *Architectural Forum,* "in their efficient, businesslike way, the Lipsetts have done almost as much damage to the U.S. Navy as the Japanese did to it at Pearl Harbor."[48]

Wrecking ships was all well and good, but soon the brothers' sights were set back on terra firma, namely the defunct elevated train structure of New York City's Second Avenue line. This, too, was a rousing success. They paid the city $40,000 for the job, and seven weeks later had a $25,000 profit in hand. Emboldened by this coup, Lipsett Brothers went on to stun the industry when it bid on the job to vanquish the Third Avenue elevated transit line in 1955. The city had been prepared to plunk down $750,000 to get the eyesore out of the way, and other contractors had swaggeringly demanded $1.7 million for the job. So newspapers were aflutter with the announcement that the Lipsetts had calmly offered to pay the city $331,000 for the privilege. Some suspected the brothers were high on hits of acetylene, but of course they were just mildly delirious from pumped-up prices of scrap metal, of which the rail line would generate forty thousand tons. (In fact, a week before bids were due, the sum they offered was $230,000. But the city delayed its decision due to rising scrap steel prices—in that time they went up about $3 a ton—and snared itself another $100,000.) At the going rate of $40 a ton, Lipsett could pay the city its due and still gross over $1.2 million—even with their contract's proviso that stated "no steel from the Third Avenue structure may go to any foreign power whose interests are inimical to those of the United States."[49]

In marked contrast to the Pennsylvania Station job, razing the Third Avenue line turned the demolitionists into overnight civic saviors. Just before its demise, a throng of twenty-five thousand Third Avenue residents turned out to kiss the blighted seventy-seven-year-old line good-bye. "In a rousing, polyglot wake for the quaint elevated structure," said a report, "merchants and tenement dwellers who came from many lands to settle alongside the rattly railroad sang and drank sidewalk toasts to future, sundrenched days."[50] City officials led a raucous "four-hour street pageant" in a 1909 Mercedes from Chinatown to Harlem, passing an incredible confluence of celebrating citizens along the way: Greeks at 77th Street, Hungarians at 79th, Irish at 84th, and Germans at 86th. There were Puerto Ricans at 106th Street and Italians at 116th, happily serving Mayor Wagner "pizza, spaghetti and clams and Chianti, while a band played the 'Tarantella Napolitana.' "[51]

When the party was all over and the wrecking began, the steady clip of positive press reports barely ebbed. Swiveling cranes and torch-wielding workers enchanted the city with their dramatic destructive sallies. "The burners use delicate blue oxyacetylene flames to hiss and glow through girders at 6,300 degrees Fahrenheit," residents were informed. "The lifters swing the cut steel away on ninety-foot booms as easily as if they were maneuvering sugar tongs."[52] The ins and outs of wrecking were further elaborated for the crowd of sidewalk superintendents. A strict order of precedence, said Morris, governed even demolition jobs. "You don't just turn any gang loose to work where it will," he lectured about his craft. Only housewreckers could remove station woodwork and most anything else not requiring outside power. The steel burners waited until the wood men were done, and then miles of copper cable, called *spinach*, were socked away, while twenty-five-ton chunks of rusted steel were loaded up on barges and shipped to U.S. Steel. Meanwhile, citizens were so exultant about the reviled structure's demise that they were clamoring to cart home bits and pieces for their own collections. NBC executives put in an order for three hundred fifty track spikes, which were to be chromed and inscribed as paper weights. "A rich squire's wife in Pennsylvania," on the other hand, "tried to get the Lipsetts to take a whole station apart for reassembly on her estate, for sentimental reasons, but they had to turn her down. It would hold up the job too long." A Long Island gentleman just wanted a load of crossties. "Best fireplace logs a man can get," he wrote. "A small lot of old oil-soaked Long Island Railroad cross-ties kept me all one winter."[53] It was noted, however, that the Lipsetts themselves never toted home so much as a turnstile for their own abodes. A demolition superintendent, it was said, develops a philosophy that shuns sentiment. (Morris was once queried about how the era's wondrous new engineering feats were changing the wrecking business. "These new curtain wall buildings," he simply deadpanned, "will be much easier to wreck than the old ones."[54])

Lipsett Brothers was lauded as "the world's biggest wreckers" by *Architectural Forum,* but by the time Morris died of cancer in 1985 (and Julius passed on in 1990) it was clear that nonstop destruction left even the wrecker feeling a little empty. "Just tearing things down didn't make Morris Lipsett happy," a reporter had written as early as 1955. "Some years ago he went into construction, as a sort of balance." Morris was enjoying laying a transmission line across South Dakota, blasting a tunnel through a mountain in Pennsylvania, and toiling on a new subway in Philadelphia. "Makes a man feel better," he said.[55]

On July 13, 1966, Morris Lipsett's tin-hatted demolition crews lowered the last of Adolph Weinman's four sets of art nouveau maidens to the ground as fifty men with jackhammers still pelted the stone columns around Pennsylvania Station's grand entrance. Crane operator John Tarallo, wiping sweat from his eyes, pulled a lever in the cab of his sixty-foot-tall machine and plucked the top half of a maiden into the air. The final phase of demolition had begun. Ralph Stephenson, a counterman at the station's famous Savarin restaurant, had earlier provided his own bon mot for the epic occasion. "This city's got the right name—New York," he said. "Nothing ever gets old around here."[56]

Pennsylvania Station's three-year-long disappearing act became an engrossing affair in its own right, drawing a whole cadre of photographers to the unusual spectacle unfolding before them. The architect Percival Goodman's comment wryly captured the spirit of the time, invoking the glorious ruins in the etchings of Piranesi. "I have a good idea," he said. "If we can get the wreckers to leave the old room at the right moment stripped of its plaster decoration, etc., we might have a Piranesi right in the heart of New York—a real tourist attraction."[57]

People like Marijke Smit, later foraging for the station's ruins, testified to the awesome power of the wreck-in-progress. "I dream about Penn Station," she said. "Claustrophobic dreams, of a place I never saw. It's probably the photos of the building's last days, which are heartbreaking."[58] The architectural photographer Norman McGrath, who happened to be working part-time right across the street, roamed around the site and captured the rubble-strewn scene. Expanses of ripped-out marble; vistas of jagged steel fretwork; light streaming in through lunette windows and falling upon scaffolding and the station's scarred remains: It was a staggering sight. Many of the most stirring images were made by photographer Peter Moore, better known for his shots of the Fluxus avant-garde performance group, a free-form collective of experimental artists and musicians whose "happenings" were legendary. It turned out that Moore was the right man for the job. His images capture a sublime territory coming into being in the heart of the metropolis. A typically arresting frame shows one of the towering Corinthian columns, stripped of its marble fluting to expose a sharp-edged steel skeleton—the actual support of the column—poking out nakedly under the genteel marble facade. A description of this shot sums it up: "The grand illusion of a classical past has been stripped away and discarded."[59]

Pennsylvania Station's Piranesian rapture was mirrored in the work of Chicago architectural photographer and wrecking site habitué Richard Nickel. Though he didn't loom large in talk of Penn Station, Nickel's documents of Chicago spanned nearly the same moment in the history of unbuilding, and his frank gusto for guttered structures helps us understand the brute magnetism of the destruction of New York. "Marvelous being in a work of art under rape," Nickel wrote to a friend in 1972. "Tonight, more specifically late afternoon, I was telling the wrecker what the demolition involvement meant to me. How often do you experience the bones, veins, skin of a work of art, even if it be in dissection?"[60] Like the ruins on Seventh Avenue, buildings looked best to Nickel during demolition. But it wasn't simply the frisson of dereliction; he found an edifying quality in his half-wrecked structures. "A building under siege allowed Nickel to explore fully," a commentator wrote. "As a building gave way to the relentless hammering, Nickel could see things that had remained hidden for decades. Exposed beams and girders disclosed how buildings were put together. Muddy foundation pilings clarified how weight was supported. Trusses and

This photograph by Peter Moore shows Penn Station's great Corinthian columns stripped away to sharp-edged steel skeletons: sublime territory in the heart of New York.

cantilevers hinted at the engineering gymnastics covered up in the finished product. Watching the wrecker's 'clam shell' punch out floors, the headache ball close in on walls, and sledgehammers rip a building naked heightened the experience."[61] Nickel, a one-time paratrooper who hired cemetery workers to hoist half-ton corbels from their moorings—and no stranger to salvaging terra-cotta ornaments from dumping grounds on the shore of Lake Calumet—did admit a bit of a fetish for the wrecking scene. "Honestly," he said, "I'm more at home in a wrecker's environment: dirty clothes, using rope and pinch bar, moving weights out in the air and wind. Very exhilarating, especially when you get a choice piece of a building up high and then take it home and look at it in various kinds of light."[62]

Before Penn Station hit the press in June 1960, Nickel had been instrumental in attempting to save Chicago's doomed Garrick Theater, designed by the firm of beloved architect Louis Sullivan. As protestors hit the streets to decry the destruction, the reaction in the local press says a great deal about how much Penn Station's saga would later change the game. "As unlikely a crew of agitators as ever assembled are whooping it up (sedately, of course) in front of the Garrick Theater these days," wrote Mervin Block in a *Chicago American* story entitled "Picket Garrick Razing: Eggheads Plead for Culture." He wrote: "Doctors of philosophy, Phi Beta Kappas, professors, architects, and others of that intellectual ilk were picketing, passing out handbills, circulating petitions, and declaiming yesterday."[63] (Philip Johnson had even joined in, practicing for the upcoming New York picket line.) Unfortunately, at that early date, the eggheads couldn't raise enough interest among certain key interest groups. "Not enough people really care," Nickel said, "especially the architects."[64] As many preservationists also knew well, it was a big challenge to interest the average citizen in the fate of buildings unless, paradoxically, demolition had begun. Richard Cahan, Nickel's biographer, pointed out that Chicago's passersby "were bored by the subtlety of great architecture; only a wrecking ball made them pay attention."[65]

Nickel died in an accident while salvaging ornaments from Louis Sullivan's Chicago Stock Exchange building in 1972. It was, in its way, a fitting end. Sullivan himself couldn't be bothered by the destruction of his own masterworks. A half century earlier, when the great architect lay on his deathbed in a tiny hotel room, the story goes that someone rushed in and exclaimed: "Mr. Sullivan, your Troescher Building is being torn down." Sullivan raised himself up and retorted, "If you live long enough, you'll see all your buildings destroyed. After all, it's only the idea that counts."[66]

Sullivan died destitute in a Chicago hotel room in 1924. Another of his pithy maxims was: "Out of oblivion into oblivion, so goes the drama of creative things."[67]

As Penn Station turned into an extended Fluxusesque photo shoot and the Meadowlands began mounting with their strangely sought-after debris, no one—even thirty years later—could get those luscious, twelve-foot-tall maidens off their minds.

Alexandros Washburn was scouring a trucking company lot on Secaucus Road, poking around eight-foot-tall swamp grasses and dodging snarling German shepherds. It was all in a day's work for the president of the Pennsylvania Station Redevelopment Corporation. He had been on the hunt for relics from the old terminal that might be brought back to life in a planned reincarnation of the great rail gateway, spearheaded by Washburn's onetime boss, the late Senator Daniel Patrick Moynihan. Washburn's mother is Greek; his aunts lived across the street from the Temple of Olympian Zeus in Athens, with its Corinthian capitals and fallen column drums splayed out in the sun. Washburn knows about the drama of creative things. "If you just saw a single column capital, you could often reconstruct a whole building, if not an emblem of what society believed," he told me. "I always thought there was true power in fragments. If any of these pieces survived, they would bring a dividend of authenticity to the project, and a real tactile remembrance of things past. In the 1960s we were in this era where architecturally you didn't want to compete with history, so you erased history. I do think that what was committed there was a crime of sorts."

So in 1998, he roamed around the Meadowlands with associate Marijke Smit and other aficionados of the station's demise, gamely convinced that they could stumble upon what Huxtable had called "a setting of macabre surrealist vérité"[68]—the cache of pink granite columns and half-busted maidens littered upon the Jersey marsh. Many before them had made the same desperate search, often goaded into action by a magnificent 1968 photograph taken by Eddie Hausner of the *New York Times*. Called "probably the most evocative single image of the demolition of Pennsylvania Station," it shows an upturned maiden (the allegorical depiction of Day) garlanded by sunflowers and an arc of bayberry wreath. Heaps of granite columns are jumbled in the background. A train crosses gravely on the horizon. "It grabbed you," Moynihan said, remembering the shocking scene. "You thought: 'What have we done? Has the city been sacked?' "[69]

As Washburn soon discovered, the picture had grabbed

many people. In 1968, a New Jersey conservation commissioner named Robert A. Roe saw the photograph, nabbed a number of remnants, and socked them away at a state park. One "Day," meanwhile, turned up at a salvage yard in the Bronx, leading to gallows humor that this "winged victory" otherwise "could have been someone's patio."[70] (Fortunately, the concrete recycling facility had put it aside, their lawyer said, when workers noticed its "appealing and attractive" statuary qualities.) When word spread that Washburn's hunt was on again for pieces of Penn Station, closet archaeologists clambered out of the woodwork. One newspaperman, it turned out, had loaded his Ford with dumped artifacts. A full thirty-five-foot Doric column had been reassembled by crane in Woodbridge, New York. Numerous stone eagles were scattered from Maine to Virginia. A pair of statues adorned a fountain in Kansas City. "We've found threads from the fabric of Penn Station stretching across the country," Washburn said. "Few buildings can inspire that continuum. It makes you want to reweave those threads."[71]

Another explorer slightly beating Washburn to the punch was author Robert Sullivan. Researching his book *The Meadowlands,* Sullivan had rapturously discovered some of the station's granite columns on a trucking lot in 1996. Hugging the cold stone and pumping his fist into the air—"relishing the fact," as he wrote, "that I had laid hands on a piece of re-ruined Rome"—Sullivan chipped off a chunk or two to take home as a souvenir, but not before stopping off to have photographs of his cache notarized for the public record.[72] He may not have been first, but Washburn's own Meadowlands adventures also yielded ersatz antiquity, turning up a half-buried pile of fragments in that trucking company lot. (The initially apprehensive lot owners "were amused by the idea as soon as they saw we weren't there to steal the TVs," he recalled.) Despite high-tech toys like ground-penetrating radar, otherwise deployed to hunt for dead bodies, the eureka moment came the old-fashioned way: "The way we actually found the thing was by going 'boom' and stubbing our toe on it." One pair of maidens remains unaccounted for, but for Washburn, the reassembled collection—should the new Pennsylvania Station ever get built—would be impressive enough. "These statues are an irreplaceable physical tie to the late, great Pennsylvania Station," he declared at the time. "Finally, the mute stones speak."[73]

Ground-radar buffs still trolling for those wayward maidens could be looking for a long time. The end of Pennsylvania Station coincided with a burst of cash-transaction activity around wrecking sites, the product of a booming market for freshly liberated antiques. Just a few years before the great terminal went down, home-decor dabblers were alerted that razing a building—yes—raises decorators' spirits, too. "The plunder (and, at the prices charged, it amounts to that) gathered by professionals and amateurs since the end of the war, a boom era for demolition, is probably second only to the pillaging of Rome," *Times* readers were advised in 1958, adding that intrepid connoisseurs needn't even bother to change into comfortable shoes. "Wreckers are, by and large, a cordial group and quite accustomed to leading women in spike heels over partly ripped-out floors."[74] Soon the great rush was on, with homemakers prowling around every mud-spattered demolition site and peppering city hall with queries about areas slated for rebuilding. "Antique shops aren't alone in providing a happy hunting ground for families seeking individuality and a change-of-pace in the decoration of their homes," as *Better Homes and Gardens*, clearly jumping on a good story, reported in 1961. "Wrecking companies are another source."[75] Yes, "today's slum buildings, now being torn down, were yesterday's mansions," the magazine noted, citing acres of leaded and stained glass, fine marble, and ornamental ironwork practically yours for the taking. Hot tip: "Well-known mansions often rate feature stories before being torn down. Advance news of wreckings can also be found in the classified section."

Salvage, incidentally, is now a major business (though not wildly profitable: "Once I sold an entire lawn for a dollar," one fanatic noted), with treasure hounds staking out doomed Silicon Valley mansions, including one formerly of the du Pont family, stripping away white-oak kitchen cabinets and grand staircases moments before the wrecking ball's blitzkrieg. The market is booming for high-class scavengers such as Wyatt B. Childs, the Georgia entrepreneur who makes monthly expeditions to Normandy to plunder falling-down French châteaus for their walnut doors and farmhouse mantles, which he then piles into containers and ships back to the United States to unload at hefty profits to aspiring Long Island sophisticates. "What I'm after is age and history," Childs once explained. "What I sell is romance."[76] Certainly there's romance for the taking in a slightly down-market end of the business—places like Detroit, that is, where looters make do with the city's stock of abandoned buildings and help themselves to terra-cotta facing, cast-iron sinks, and stone pillars "that look gorgeous in gardens, fueling a thriving trade in antique artifacts," one report said. Some building owners even plunder their own prize possessions, such as those that had control of Detroit's much-abused Book-Cadillac Hotel, "just long enough to sell some of the ornate copper roof panels to a sal-vager and pay the tax bill."[77]

Back in the Lipsett Brothers' day it was all called "gargoyle snatching," and it was news around the country's decaying urban districts even then. "But nowhere has gargoyle snatching reached such staggering proportions as in Manhattan," said *Time* magazine as Penn Station crumbled. "There a dogged band of New Yorkers, who call themselves the Anonymous Arts Re-covery Society, has managed to cart off for posterity more than 100 tons of chips off notable old blocks." Founded by the thirty-eight-year-old pop art dealer Ivan Karp, the society laid claim to a hundred dues-paying rubble aficionados who "rally wherever the wrecker's ball threatens," even roving side streets on patrol for any furtive wrecking ball activity. ("Anonymous" referred not to the society's members but to the ornaments they saved, which carried no pedigree from a classical school or period, hav-ing been carved by unknown stonemasons, typically European immigrants.) When called for, the group would stage midnight raids on demolition sites with their small pickup truck, scooping up a cast-iron fox from near the Brooklyn Bridge; ornamental capitals from a Louis Sullivan building; and a small bestiary of griffins, sibyls, cherubs, angry lions, and grotesque brownstone heads, replete with tongues lolling out of grimaced mouths. Lug-ging all this loot around had taken a toll on Karp and company, however, with the damage standing at four hernias, three wrecked cars, and wallets emptied into the upturned hard hats of countless demolition bosses. Karp would foist a wad of cash upon the wreckers, but in the "desperately competitive" demoli-tion business, costs were spiraling alarmingly, and items once going for around $25 had been commanding three times as much. "We've got to negotiate with them," said an exasperated Karp. "They're a rather cynical race, and the whole building would be destroyed if we didn't bargain with them."[78]

The society, which became known around town as "a kind of respectable architectural ambulance-chasing organization,"[79] also helped finagle a fourteen-ton figure of "Night" from Pennsylvania Station, which was stashed along with other cherished relics in a safe house of sorts at the Brooklyn Museum. "Night" can still be found languidly ensconced at the museum's Frieda Schiff Warburg Memorial Sculpture Garden, gripping a couple of poppies and looking every bit the beauty she was in her original incarnation. "Her sister, Day, is still in Secaucus, on the mud flats," said Ian White, the museum's assistant director, in 1966. "I wanted to save Day, but she was split in half, and I couldn't find her lower quarters. She was a handsome girl, made of dense pink granite, with sunflowers on her shoulders."[80] It was a tragic end to a tragic tale. "Secaucus reminds one of Persepolis," a museum curator added. "Truncated columns lying as far as the eye can see. It's quite a visual experience. A monument to American architecture in ruins."[81]

[6]

WRECKER FOREVER

IN 1975, OVER THE course of a cocktail-drenched convention at Caesar's Palace, more was swinging than just the hips of the bleary-eyed delegates. These were swingers of a higher power, a motley confederacy of wreckers, razers, and topplers hell-bent on hoisting not the disco ball but the wrecking ball. "We will no longer be willing to accept a stepchild status," Sheldon J. "Red" Mandell told the fledgling National Association of Demolition Contractors, huddled in Las Vegas for its second annual meeting. "We want respect," he said. "We, the lowly wreckers, are here to stay."[1]

And stay they would. Because the wrecking ball had become more than a job. It was more like a gestalt. And it was the American way. "A lot of people would like to preserve every damn building where Millard Fillmore ever used the public convenience," spat George F. McDonnell, an industry consultant. "There's a lot of sentimental drivel about all that," he added, calling it a blemish on the national heritage to go blubbering on about buildings and institutions and laws that had grown bowlegged with age. "When they don't work anymore, they should be dismantled and the parts recycled," he railed. "Let the wrecking ball swing!"[2]

America's unbuilders had lashed themselves together as a permanent front in 1972, but their Vegas visitation three years later was a watershed moment for the world of wrecking. Shrugging off decades of niggling regulatory scrutiny, cackling editorialists, and put-downs from famous poets—poets, even!—the wreckers would finally have their beef-and-beer-fueled day. The scene abounded with sweaty camaraderie. As a postconference rundown gushed: "Las Vegas (cocktail parties), Caesar's Palace (cocktail parties), interesting exhibits (cocktail parties), informative business meetings (cocktail parties), great shows (cocktail parties), headaches, upset stomachs—it was all there!"[3] Between slugs of Pepto-Bismol, though, were diatribes over prevailing wage laws and refreshers on the "ferrous scrap cycle." Wreckers boned up on cooperative buying plans and heard how to transmute "just plain garbage" into profit-rich "prepared refuse." There were recession-era wisecracks ("I was told to be brief and funny here tonight," drawled the emcee. "It's easy to be brief and to be funny—I'll read you a list of the contracts I got last month"[4]). There was nervous, cryptic talk of International Harvester's hydraulic hose situation. A magician roved the floor. There were banquets and more cocktail parties and dismantling dignitaries from the United Kingdom. And piping hot under the collar was George F. McDonnell, who hollered on about the "millions upon millions of government bureaucrats" he said were hog-tying that giant called "American enterprise." After this four-day-long frenzy of fetes, shoptalk, and bootstrapping raillery, one thing was clear: The lowly wreckers weren't just here to stay. They were about to bash their way to the big time.

"We are entering a great new era of demolition," Harry Avirom had presciently announced as Pennsylvania Station was torched into oblivion. "All of the little garbage has been torn down, so now we are sinking our teeth in the big stuff."[5] They haven't stopped gnawing since. Ripping and tearing with the blunt tools of the trade—medicine balls, jackhammers, excavators, and grapplers—that ragtag band of renegades would grow into a precision-rigged wrecking machine, a federation nine hundred firms strong chomping through more than $3 billion worth of contracts every year, while exporting their savvy to sites of destruction on nearly every continent.

The big garbage waited to be bagged. But first wreckers would have to bludgeon away at something closer to home. That was the industry's own forty-ton inferiority complex.

It took two civil engineers in Edinburgh, Scotland, to deliver the dread truth about demolition. Having surveyed the tiny body of literature on the topic of modern, large-scale wrecking—the sum total of which could probably still fit in the cab of your average miniexcavator—these chaps were gobsmacked by the state of the art. Even though many specialist wreckers such as the Loizeauxs were doing pioneering work at the time, relatively few contractors in the wider world of demolition had paid much mind to the ruin of tall buildings. First off, "it is imperative," the engineers wrote with palpable alarm in 1974, "that the demolition of tall buildings should be viewed as an urgent research topic."[6] Bigger and bigger buildings were being sketched up, built, declared goners, and destroyed; no one, least of all architects and planners, seemed to care about what happened when these structures were to be snuffed. The Scots thus implored their worldwide colleagues to ponder the ever-more pressing problem of "planned obsolescence," adding that "it is essential to be aware of the many problems which can arise when a site or area is due for demolition and redevelopment."[7] Wrecking methods of the day were "often crude and wasteful," while the neglect of land-clearance operations often resulted in collapses, accidents, and other unmitigated horrors.[8] (Their suggested remedy: Design engineers would be badgered into submitting a credible demolition scheme for any planned building, well in advance of its construction.) Obviously, "the safest and most sensible" way to wreck a tall building "is simply to reverse the construction process in every detail."[9] But that was a laughable prospect. Remember the "Upside-Down" Volk brothers and their desperate attempts to ride out the whirlwind of creative destruction? A good deal of brow-furrowing, therefore, needed to be devoted to brilliant methods of wrecking new structures, along with an "urgent reappraisal of current wastage of materials from demolished buildings," since fine old masonry was smashed and dumped, reusable timber torched, and valuable reinforcing steel deep-sixed, still embedded in its concrete.[10]

Industry pundits were well-nigh unanimous on this point. Whether wreckers liked it or not, their profession was truly a stepchild of the construction and scrap trades—and they had growing pains galore. "The demolition of buildings on site has so often been virtually an afterthought," lamented a British wreckers' manual in 1977, "and carried out as quickly and cheaply as possible."[11] One big beef was the lack of skilled labor for what was demanding and dangerous work. Much of the destructive labor force was "peripatetic," as it was tactfully termed, roving bands of casual workers with next to no specialized training. "Reputable contractors do not like to rely on this sort of labour," one demolition historian remarked, "but, in many areas, they are forced to employ it."[12] This state of affairs did nothing to salve the industry's interminable "splinters, cuts, burns, eye injuries, nail punctures, strains, bruises and fractures," to name a few.[13] And it led to casualties of other persuasions as well. "The damage that is sustained in many cases by mature trees which the Architect may have wished to retain as part of the new scheme," said the manual, "is one of the most common causes of bad feeling between the Demolition Contractor and the Architect." Indeed, there seems to have been little love lost between said warring parties, what with wreckers constantly botching up the flora. "Damage is most commonly caused either through the trees being scorched by fires lit on the site (indeed for some reason demolition operatives are strongly attracted to the practice of heaping bonfires up against trees), or through their being hit by lorries or machines."[14]

There were other quarrels to be had with the industry's reigning practices, but one of the more serious was the wreckers' penchant for pulling over structures by means of a wire rope, which, despite "having a number of disadvantages," was probably the method "most widely used for masonry and brick structures, which form the bulk of present-day demolition projects."[15] You don't need an advanced degree in physics to suggest the potential dangers involved in lassoing a building and trying to yank it to the ground, but the success rate was sufficient—and the speed of the technique self-evident—to make it a perennially attractive option. This was duly confirmed, many years later, by an American demolition contractor reminiscing about his early days in the trenches. "When we first broke into the business," he recalled, "we had a Cat 977 loader and if the job included, say, a small building demolition, we put a cable around the structure, pulled it down, set the debris on fire and called it a day."[16]

Many a quick buck was made in the bad old days of the wrecking business, and even the Americans began to recognize that they had a problem on their hands. In 1975, for example, the titans of the industry opened fire on their own fringe elements ("boot-leggers," "fly-by-night" firms, and "weekend wreckers") who undercut legitimate contractors with a gamut of shady tactics. Most pointedly, contractors complained of being "plagued by an apparently significant number of unscrupulous operators who cut corners by burying combustible debris in basements or in holes."[17] This demolition no-no was a major nuisance in wrecking wonderlands like Chicago, where large city contracts to raze abandoned urban properties were being low-balled by the fly-by-nighters. The rules required wreckers to cart off a structure and leave a graded empty lot. Moreover, below-grade cavities like basements had to be filled with clean soil or some other inorganic material, because organic material—namely wood—causes sinkage, is a fire hazard, and provides a fun habitat for rodents. But weekend wreckers would simply dump the crunched-up debris in the basement, chuck a thin layer of dirt on top to fool city inspectors, and pocket their profits. Wrecking a two-story house legitimately, it was estimated, would cost you $1,700. But cut out the trucks, drivers' salaries, and dumping fees, and you could slash your bid by up to 25 percent. Reputable wreckers were getting a raw deal.

All this would drive any self-respecting destructionist to dyspeptic fits of howling; you could even begin to glimpse where berserkers like George F. McDonnell, the excitable consultant at Caesar's Palace, were coming from. But there was one further matter to bedevil the lowly wrecker. The industry's hand-me-down status meant that it had no founding father, no mad chemist like Alfred Nobel or strapping adventurer like Charles Lindbergh, whose reputation could be burnished and forever gazed upon as the guiding light of wreckerdom. Instead, well, you got some kind of Neanderthal. Yes, the first wreckers in history, according to industry lore, were burly, unidentified, Fred Flintstone–like cave dwellers. In pursuit of that Paleolithic duplex penthouse, it is supposed, these hulking protocontractors hefted a granite boulder and hurled it at a primeval partition wall. Badda-bing, badda-boom. With a world-jarring whomp of stone upon stone and a shower of pebbly silt in the air, a goofy exaltation must have crept over the brow of *homo deconstructus*. Man vs. edifice: An industry was born. No Stone Age demolition permits have turned up on the limestone walls at Lascaux, of course—not even a jeer from loincloth-clad picketers, clamoring for historical cave districts—but so goes demolition's origin myth. Unfortunately, the image of the Cro-Magnon wrecker would prove all too enduring. For all the public cared, the preliterate troglodyte would be the trade's unofficial mascot for the next hundred thousand years.

So as a nascent sense of collective pride began to dawn, you could hardly fault wreckers for dredging up some of the industry's more illustrious cameo roles. Fast-forward a few millennia, for instance, and hang a left at the walls of Jericho (some people call it "demolition by faith") where in the Old Testament book of Joshua, the Israelites, dead-set on conquering the snugly fortified city, march around its ramparts for seven days blowing seven trumpets of ram's horns, and then give a great shout-out. The walls come tumbling down, as everyone knows, and the city is sacked. (Purists are wont to point out that, actually, the King James text says that "the wall fell down flat."[18] The tumble-down version, made popular in the spiritual tune and immortal-ized by Elvis, certainly has more curb appeal.) Joshua is probably the closest anyone will come to being the grand pooh-bah of demolition. The official title is still up for grabs, however, since among certain wreckers, no Biblical unbuilder is more revered than Samson, who, in what's treasured as one of the ear-liest recorded examples of a deliberate collapse, was hauled as a captive into the temple of the Philistines.[19] As the story goes, Samson grasped two middle pillars holding up the structure, budged the columns outward, and brought the house down, crushing to death a crowd of his enemies—and himself in the process. Samson "was a good Structural Engineer," one demo-historian joked. "He knew exactly how the building would be-have. Mind you, the Health and Safety Executive wasn't too happy for he killed over 3,000 people."[20]

As the wrecking ball barreled ever more righteously through the 1970s, firms launched a variety of outreach efforts to give their funereal work a perky twist for the general public. "Some companies even add a touch of humor to the rather depressing business," a writer noted. The wrecker T. M. Burgin, while raz-ing a local movie theater, wasted no time in slapping his banner up on the marquee: NEXT ATTRACTION: T. M. BURGIN—DOING HIS THING.[21] Along these lines, the slogan for the Billy L. Nabors Wrecking & Excavating Company in Dallas jovially boasted: "We could wreck the world."[22] That was impressive, but it was probably beat by the merry ambitions of Chicago's

Three Oaks Wrecking: "We wreck anything in the Universe," their business cards said. "Not yet equipped for Outer Space."[23] Spurred on by these modest ego-boosters, the demolition home office was soon mounting an all-out effort to demonstrate that not only were wreckers apple-pie-munching Americans like the rest of us, but they were properly the envy of all humankind. "While a lot of people might think they're too civilized to have such base instincts, the fact is that there is something soul-satisfying connected with the physical act of destruction," the demolition association's magazine said in a remarkable article headlined BLAST YOUR TROUBLES AWAY. "Is there anyone who is so dishonest with himself he won't confess he gets just a little bit of a kick out of knocking out a window light?" they pointedly wondered. No, siree. And so, "envy the demolition worker," the advance guard of a new race of professionals "who can vent their destructive instincts, avoid going to the pokey and get paid for it to boot." As if copying pages straight out of Freud's *Civilization and Its Discontents,* the editors worked themselves into a lather over the wrecker's virtuously unshackled id. "The point is," they went on, "the demolition contractor doesn't have to smother any of his compulsions. He can shatter, smash, maul and haul to his heart's content and it's all nice and legal."[24] Demolition contractors, in sum, had gallantly assumed responsibility for "stabilizing the mental health of the American people by letting them get their thrills 'by proxy.' "[25]

Now that your average wrecker was something like Joshua, Clark Kent, and King Kong all rolled into one, it was time to settle the score with that nagging enemy camp, the historical preservationists. "As those in demolition know, historical societies and the ladies of the DAR have long been thorns in the demolition contractor's side, making him out the heavy when plans for a landmark tear-down project are announced."[26] Elsewhere lambasted as "Hysterical Societies," preservation groups, especially in the years after Pennsylvania Station, had stepped up their vigilance over wily developers. It was not uncommon, for instance, to roll out the bulldozers in the wee hours of a Saturday morning, making short work of a structure before the alarm could be sounded. Such deviousness prompted calls for "a code of ethics" to govern demolition projects, but wreckers weren't exactly raring to cooperate. Besides, as they said, they weren't judge or jury, just the executioner. That argument didn't sit so well in places like Ocean Springs, Mississippi, which once imposed a sixty-day demolition moratorium while officials pondered their wrecking policies. The town was shocked to find that an 1893 bakery building had been bulldozed by a local church on an expansion binge. "As it stands," said one baffled resident, "you are required to go through more processes to have a small magnolia tree removed than you are to remove a building."[27] Destructionists, for their part, just let the id hang out. "The demolition contractor has the satisfaction of walking away with history," as an industry veteran put it. "You tear down a building, it's yours."[28]

Even in post–Penn Station New York, if you played your cards right, you could own that chunk of history with hardly a scowl from prowling preservationists. In 1967, for instance, wrecking began on what was billed as the tallest building ever to be demolished: the Singer Building at Broadway and Liberty Street in Manhattan. "Passers-by below paused to gaze up at the structure, which many—especially the younger among them— had ignored until the demolition men began attacking it."[29] It was little loved then, but at its completion sixty years earlier, the ornate, forty-seven-story structure was the world's tallest building, and among its Beaux Arts splendors were slabs of silver-gray marble; a cacophony of consoles, rosettes, pediments, and cartouches; a vast mansard roof; and an observation balcony known as Suicide Pinnacle. Still heavy on the minds of New Yorkers, apparently, was good old Italian engraver Piranesi, ever a touchstone for sublime destruction. "Piranesi, anyone?" asked Ada Louise Huxtable as the Singer Building's domed vaults devolved into rubble. "The master never produced a more impressive ruin than the Singer Building under demolition." Those curious enough to risk being beaned on the head by a chunk of Pavonazzo marble, she said, "will find a scene of rich, surrealist desolation."[30]

No picketers were noted amongst the luxurious destruction, perhaps because the Lipsett demolition company's superintendent on the job, Mr. Harry Glick, was by then a familiar face to journalists on the Piranesi beat—and he had a rueful way with words. It was said that the Singer's architect, Ernest Flagg, had loftily pronounced his creation "as solid and lasting as the Pyramids,"[31] but the pyramids didn't have profit margins to meet, and Flagg's triumph was being torn down to make way for a modern, fifty-story office building. Glick, who greeted his visitors "by pushing back his helmet and giving a short sigh,"[32] was a soft-spoken, circumspect man who had been in demolition for forty years. His father, he explained, was also a demolition man. He took down an old riding academy to make room for the Savoy-Plaza, which his son had just wrecked to make room for the General Motors building. "History moves fast," Glick said.[33]

History was soon bumping along at a fearsomely rapid clip,

and by the end of their power decade, wreckers were proudly copping to an appetite for destruction. "It was a love affair," one New Jersey wrecker said in 1978, owning up to his hankering for dangerous things. "Wrecking and I were made for each other." The possibilities, at that time, were unlimited. "It's always been my dream to tear down the Empire State Building," he said. "It would be a challenge. I wouldn't mind tearing the Trade Center down either."[34] That same year, an official of the Cleveland Wrecking Company claimed that his firm had "demolished more buildings than all the earthquakes of our time." (They counted an impressive eighty-eight thousand structures, bridges included.)[35] The bravado built to a crescendo as the industry trade publication slugged an article entitled: YES . . . YOU CAN RAZE AN OCCUPIED BUILDING. (It turned out that a tenant in a commercial structure remained in the first floor while the wrecking ball chewed its way around the site, gingerly avoiding the tenant in question).[36] But the tenor of that era was most winningly summed up by one of wrecking's leading lights, Richard J. Burns of Pearland, Texas, who was given to signing off his communiqués with a two-word flourish that radiated more native pride than any boast uttered by a phalanx of boozy conventioneers: "Wrecker Forever."

History got a budge in the right direction around that time from an unlikely wrecking industry ally—the IRS. Contractors might not have had the United States tax code lying around on their nightstands, but beginning in the 1950s, they could have told you something was afoot just by looking at the shoddy buildings they were bulldozing. It all circled around how the Internal Revenue Service handled depreciation, or tax deductions taken to account for an aging structure. As scholars John Jakle and David Wilson have shown, prior to World War II, most buildings were granted a forty-year useful life. An owner could depreciate them on a tax return at 2.5 percent each year, allowed as a "set-aside charge in anticipation of ultimate replacement." But pushed by aggressive building industry lobbyists, in the 1950s, the IRS let owners of new commercial buildings ramp up depreciation and grab hefty tax deductions early in a project's life. If a new project was financed 90 percent by loans, for example, an investor in the 70 percent tax bracket who plunked down $100,000 could make back $77,000—before a backhoe even touched the ground.[37] "Buildings that are intended to be written off quickly need not be durable," the authors dryly noted. "They need only function efficiently for the short run before capital gains are taken, and the cycle of tax incentives repeated elsewhere. Tax laws and related accounting procedures have not engendered permanency in the American landscape."[38] Yes, folks, it's creative destruction at its finest, and a boon to those who ride the wrecking ball.

Sometimes, of course, the cycle gets a little too amped up for even wreckers to keep under control. What with so many flimsy facades to crunch up, one starts blurring into another, and soon enough the Associated Press gets ahold of a juicy story like this: "A couple was at their dinner table when a bulldozer rumbled into their home and tore their ceiling down. The bulldozer operator had the wrong address, officials said."[39] Yesenia Reyes and Carlos Suarez had just settled down for a cozy supper in the kitchen of their rented home in Hollywood, Florida, when at 5:30 P.M. a dozer that had been munching on other neighborhood houses as part of an urban renewal project abruptly veered off course and rumbled toward the couple's three-bedroom home. "Just then Suarez, 26, grabbed his wife by the shirt and pulled her out the front door to safety, and they watched the bulldozer knock a huge hole in their roof, sending pieces of it onto the television and table." BULLDOZER PLOWS INTO WRONG HOME, trumpeted the *Miami Herald,* noting that a harassed, seventy-four-year-old demolition contractor could be seen hobbling on a cane behind the bulldozer, frantically bellowing, "Not there! Not there!"[40]

It's enough to bring back those horror-show days of the marauding troglodytes, but in an industry with notoriously low entry barriers and cutthroat competition—all fanned by frenetic bouts of rebuilding—well, these things do happen. An even more embarrassing case of the wayward bulldozer was reported in the late 1980s, when one Bob Harvell of Las Vegas hired a dozer to crunch down a fence and level some soil around the $80,000 house he had rented to a tenant. Having dashed out to get some groceries, his tenant returned to find the fridge in a heap—along with the rest of the house. Harvell confronted the man at the controls, but "the smell of liquor on his breath almost knocked me down." The dazed and confused dozer operator managed to reply, "All right, there is no problem. I'll get my business partner and insurance papers and I'll be back in 15 minutes." Harvell never saw him again.[41]

Piranesi was all peachy pastels compared to the bizarre tales that sometimes attend the subject of demolition—nightmarish, Gothic images tossed off in the maelstrom of creative destruction. Once, there was a lone house standing on a large city block that had otherwise been leveled for an urban renewal scheme. The owner was holding out. Much to his unpleasant surprise, however, his house had been commandeered by the entire block's cohort of rats—two tons of them in all, done in by exterminators and shoveled from the basement. One witness, describing the teeming scene just before the rats were gassed, wrote that she "will never forget the extraordinary hum of the vermin that came from the house even though all windows and doors were sealed. Nowadays there is a rule that all buildings must be 'ratted' before demolition begins."[42]

If that vision keeps you awake at night, blame the IRS.

As George F. McDonnell made bruisingly clear back in 1975, wreckers and the government didn't always get along. The National Association of Demolition Contractors was born shortly after the dawn of two federal regulatory giants that would take a bitingly skeptical look at the destructionists' whirling world: the Occupational Safety and Health Administration and the Environmental Protection Agency. The timing of the wreckers' confederation was no coincidence, since their brotherly bond with the EPA was pretty much soured from the get-go. In 1978, the contractors scored national headlines (the biggest blitz of publicity the insurgent wreckers had ever seen) when the group emerged victoriously from a legal battle against the EPA that stretched from an asbestos-laden Detroit wrecking site all the way to the United States Supreme Court. It would prove a defining moment for the righteous wreckers in more ways than one.

The basic facts of the case were clear enough. The Adamo Wrecking Company of Detroit had been indicted in 1975 for destroying a building without wetting and removing the asbestos insulation and fireproofing on its boilers, a procedure called for in a two-year-old EPA regulation under the Clean Air Act. Asbestos, of course, was a substance Congress had deemed an "intolerably dangerous pollutant" that could cause cancer twenty or thirty years after even low-level exposure. The legal wrangling began over the nature of the federal requirements and quickly degraded into a semantic battle that even the court's majority opinion discussed with some sarcasm: "The basic question in this case may be phrased: 'When is an emission standard not an emission standard?' "[43] In an effort to limit the EPA's impact on the wrecking business, lawyers for Adamo had argued that such requirements were "procedures" rather than "standards," and therefore could not be challenged in court. In a 5-to-4 decision handed down on January 10, 1978—a date hailed by the wreckers as "V-EPA Day"—the Supreme Court agreed.

By some accounts, the substance of this case, *Adamo Wrecking Company v. United States,* looked like the age-old gripe of Gulliver against the meddling bureaucrats: The wreckers wouldn't stand for the government telling them how to do their job. But as critics pointed out, the wreckers were just dodging the inevitable bullet—comprehensive asbestos compliance—and the case's minority opinion affirmed as much when it worried that "the Court's holding today has effectively made the asbestos regulation, and any other work-practice rule as well, unenforceable." By letting the wreckers off the hook, the justices decided, "the Court today has allowed the camel's nose into the tent, and I fear that the rest of the camel is almost certain to follow." As it happened, the camel was sent packing in short order. The EPA soon tightened its asbestos regulations, mooting the wreckers' victory. The case had nearly bankrupted the association. Scrounging around for a silver lining, the wreckers noted that publicity from all that Supreme Court coverage attracted a gaggle of new members.

The contractors' Pyrrhic legal victory made one thing

painfully clear: Wreckers could bluster about Gulliver all they wanted, but the bureaucratic terrain was fast shifting under their own steel-toed boots. When they first huddled together in 1972, safety practices were barely regulated, asbestos was "one of the miracle products of the age," and there were landfills as far as you could drive a dump truck. "There was a time not so long ago," an industry report said, "when a structure's owner would call in a couple of local wreckers to look at his job, take some bids and the building would simply disappear a few days later. Soon after, a bill for the demolition, often on a single sheet of paper, would appear."[44] Now the lowly wrecker was up to his hard hat in billowing piles of paperwork, crammed to the margins with everything from hazardous material regs to groundwater contamination protocols. The group's long-time executive director, Michael R. Taylor, wrote that the business of demolition had "faced an explosion of legislative initiatives and government regulations that have changed that lovable 'simple wrecker' into a lawyer, an environmental scientist, an industrial hygienist, a hydrogeologist, a safety engineer, and human resources expert."[45] The wrecker's vaunted id, in other words, was getting forcibly restrained. And the public would need to be notified.

So with great fanfare in 1988, at the industry's fifteenth annual convention (held in, you guessed it, Las Vegas), the image-conscious theme "Demolition for Progress" went out over the wire. This "Orwellian-sounding" motif (as one pundit put it) was later unpacked in rambling verse and broadcast throughout the industry. "Like cleaning a closet of forgotten joys, space is cleared for storing new toys," went the poem. "Demolition, destruction and disturbing noise, equipment, torches and hard working boys, / This we contribute toward progress for all."[46] This disarming little number was soon worked into a more polished promotional overture, which hinted once more at the industry's perpetual efforts to strut its stuff in the face of a wary and often hostile new world. "Demolition is a silent partner in progress. It, too, is often an unnoticed trade, but it is demolition that sets the stage and gets the ball rolling, the wrecking ball!" The copy writers continued grandly, "We are coming of age, 'The Demolition Age.' "[47]

Despite decades of earnest press releases, revamped logos, and constantly rejiggered mottos—from "Demolition for Progress" to "Reinventing the World" to the newest couplet, "Preserving the Past, Preparing the Future"—fifteen years later, demolition still couldn't get no respect. "The role of the demolition contractor," the industry flat-out admitted not long ago, "is not clearly understood by most Americans."[48] After yet more soul-searching, in 2004, the National Association of Demolition Contractors rebranded itself as the National Demolition Association, the group's most drastic push ever at "revolutionizing people's perceptions of who we are and what we do," replete with "one of the most aggressive public relations programs in the Association's history" to get everyone hip to "what being a demolition contractor really means."[49]

Rampaging bulldozers? Porcelain-crushing cowboys? The last great bastion of rugged individualism? It was time to finally set the record straight. To the ever-blasé public, who hadn't necessarily been keeping abreast of lead-based-paint regulations, demolition meant flipping on CNN any Sunday morning to find another stupendous implosion splashed across the tube, or,

The hydraulic excavator, gnawing here on a pile of reinforced concrete columns, is a very exotic hunk of history-munching machinery.

failing that, a wrecking ball slamming into another flimsy, tax-depreciated pile. But when the "Loizeaux Channel" came calling for another quote about the God-given gift of gravity, industry honchos would push back their demolition helmets, heave a sigh, and point out that implosions account for less than 1 percent of all demolition work, "and most contractors would be hard pressed to lay their hands on a wrecking ball."[50]

It was time for a full-frontal public relations assault upon the American people. And the first order of business—CNN producers be damned—was a doggedly mundane history of the modern demolitionist. It runs something like this: The modern demolitionist is an investment banker who trades in very exotic

hunks of history-munching machinery. Long gone are those halcyon days when all you needed was a front-end loader, a reliable
brute on Caterpillar tracks, and a large, wide bucket on the end.
You could shove a two-story house over in one fell swoop, then
load it up to be trucked off to oblivion. No fuss, no muss. But
just as jackhammers replaced sledgehammers, so hydraulic excavators stormed the scene in 1980, transforming the industry
overnight. These versatile, limber beasts look something like a
backhoe on steroids: a compact, rectangular cab and body with
a large, rotating arm protruding from the machine's front end.
At the top of this arm, which in some models reaches over one
hundred sixty feet high, are placed all manner of computer-
controlled attachments (grapples for plucking, huge shears for
snipping steel, and breakers and crushers and such) that can delicately sort metal from wood, munch concrete on the fly, and
wax your truck in their spare time. In the hands of the right operator, you could wreck away like some turbocharged Ginsu
knife. "An equipment operator has to be like a rabbit, very alert,
always with an eye on everything because things happen so
quickly," one wrecker explained.[51] You munch on your building,
observe its reaction, and munch again, and there is no end to
variations on the theme—witness the "sag-and-chew" method,
where you knock a support out from under one corner of a
structure; as it sags, an excavator can reach up and nibble away.

A contractor's bank account doesn't go unchewed, either.
These supermachines cost anywhere from $250,000 to over $1
million, and commercial creditors have come calling. "Demolition is a capital-intensive trade with high-dollar equipment demands and substantial working capital requirements," one
analyst happily reported. "Lines of credit can be quite profitable

due to the considerable cash required to fund some contracts, but a bank's most profitable loans to demolition contractors tend to be for equipment financing because of the enormous price tags attached to specialized heavy machinery."[52] Even while forking over money for the machines, the contractor has had to spend extra on skilled labor to run the beasts, jacking up costs even though the number of people on the payroll has dropped. Some old hands find this creative destruction of the labor force rather too depressing. "You used to have people who had to sit up on a wall and take it down by hand," one wrecker lamented. "Many of those people were small in stature, but highly skilled. Today, you have people skilled in maneuvering so-phisticated equipment, but you train people for that. I think the older skills were inborn traits."[53]

Sorry to say for the sentimentalists among them, all that so-phisticated machinery has largely consigned the wrecking ball it-self to the dustbin, even though crusty contractor types still call the "skull cracker" the most efficient and profitable way to wreck. Already, demolitionists throughout the United Kingdom are ditching the venerable ball—insurance companies have fi-nally had enough—and America's wreckers are beginning to openly wonder: "Does this mean the end of the wrecking ball in the UK? What are the implications of this policy for the North American market? Are the days of the wrecking ball num-bered?"[54] As a beloved icon of the lowly wrecker, though, the cast-iron clobberer may never die. To the relief of old-school de-structionists, the wrecking ball found a place for itself on the in-dustry association's shiny new logo.

Having vastly accelerated the means for munching away the past, the modern demolitionist has a new problem: There's nowhere to dump it all. The demolition of buildings in the

United States produces nearly 125 million tons of debris each year, according to the Deconstruction Institute—apparently enough to erect a wall thirty feet high and thirty feet thick around the entire coast of the continental United States. With skyrocketing disposal costs and ever scarcer opportunities to dump (many European nations already ban demolition debris in landfills, a trend fast catching on in the United States), add to the wrecker's new job description: recycling evangelist. "The biggest trend in the industry is the continuing move toward recycling. I like to call it 'green demolition,'" one contractor explained. "In order to secure work, you have to be able to recycle. And it's cost-effective."[55]

This healthy attitude toward waste management stands in marked contrast to the live-and-let-dump olden days. In 1966, for example, New York City banned the burning of waste lumber and ordered the material cut into three-foot lengths if it was to be picked up by the city's sanitation department. The wreckers moaned in agony. "This is the death knell of our industry," declared a lawyer for the city's Wrecking Contractors Association. Truckloads of wood littered wrecking sites around Gotham, and a whole shady subindustry had sprung up of "gypsy" carters who were "dumping it in the country."[56] Fast-forward to 2004 (there are some upsides, thank Shiva, to creative destruction) when recycling and salvage can kick in as much as 50 percent of some companies' revenues, and the industry recycles, on average, 40 percent of the total materials generated on its project sites.[57]

As in the days of the Lipsett brothers—when rising steel prices drastically altered bids for wrecking metal-dense structures like the Third Avenue elevated rail line—the volatile scrap steel market can still wreak havoc on the demolition business.

Lately, of course, the havoc has been caused by buyers showing up at wrecking sites and flashing wads of cash. In 2004, scrap steel prices soared to more than $300 per ton, up from $77 a few years earlier, driven among other factors by China's warp-speed building boom. (In 2003, China became the first country ever to import more than $1 billion of American scrap.[58]) That's swell news to scrap metal purveyors such as Chinese-born David Pan, whose Los Angeles–based firm sometimes ships five hundred containers a month to China, "filled with battered pipes, fine metal shavings, doorknobs, jumbles of wire, crumpled cars and all other manner of flotsam. He is even negotiating to buy the remains of a steel factory in Utah; he would ship it, as scrap, to his native country."[59] On the downside, note wreckers, metal is one of the few recyclable building materials with an actual market value. Concrete and some types of wood can also turn a profit, but markets for used brick, drywall, glass, and carpet will apparently have to wait until China finds some desperate need for them.

Burgeoning interest in recycling, in any case, has sparked off jostling between wreckers and a rival "deconstruction" industry. This nascent business has been promoted as the systematic disassembly of buildings, often by hand, with the aim of extending the "embodied energy" of all the materials encountered during the course of a "de-building" project—the solar energy, say, that goes into a tree used for lumber. Reuse the lumber, and you extend the life of those sunbeams. The same goes for the nuts and bolts of a building that typically end up in the dump: insulation, siding, switch-cover plates, you name it. One California deconstruction firm summed it all up in the title of its newsletter: *The Velvet Crowbar*. Fueled by a spate of positive media reports ("The press loves deconstruction," said a decon partisan. "They think it's really sexy"), the field at first looked like it could turn into serious competition for the old-school wreckers. At the Rebuilding Center in Portland, Oregon, a clearinghouse for deconstruction, the place was initially so swamped with business that "its 13 workers cannot keep up with the demand for building removals."[60] The wreckers weren't about to take this lying down and launched a preemptive strike against the budding decon craze. "Deconstruction is nothing new to the demolition industry," they haughtily declared in 1999. "Deconstruction, or hand demolition, is the stage from which the professional demolition industry evolved decades ago."[61]

Indeed, many contractors were ahead of the curve. Dan Costello of Costello Dismantling in Middleboro, Massachusetts, for example, hated the thought of using a wrecking ball as his company's logo, since he rarely had cause to deploy the old monster. "What we did was not symbolized by the wrecking ball," he explained. "We consider ourselves dismantlers." Having cast around for a catchy image, Costello hit upon the praying mantis, which he learned dissects its prey before eating it. "So now the image of the stick-figure-like insect adorns everything," a reporter said, "including the company letterhead and promotional brochure, the outside of the office building and the weathervane on top of Costello's house."[62] With so much convergence, the wreckers and the deconstructors appear to have negotiated an uneasy truce—working hand in velvet glove, as it were—and squabbling with the "crunch-and-dump guys" has died down.

It was only a matter of time before the experts on all manner of dereliction and debris would bust open another hefty realm of wrecking expertise: brownfields. Aiming to cash in on what the industry called a $1.2 billion brownfields "windfall" (that's billion with a capital *B,* colleagues were reminded), wreckers geared up for six demolition-intensive years that would flow from the passage of the 2001 brownfields law, which kicked off the cleanup of all manner of long-abandoned and wretchedly polluted industrial sites around the nation. Still blocking and tackling their industry turf, the destructionists announced that they were not necessarily going to let all those billions flow into the coffers of environmental engineering firms. "The industry has been doing tank pulls since God invented tanks and clearing contaminated soil for our industrial clients back since the reign of Charles II of England," said industry representative Michael Taylor. "We know how to do this work quickly, safely and profitably."[63] Indeed, contractors were fast ramping up their skill sets to encompass vast new arenas, including hazardous materials management, soil decontamination, mold remediation, and groundwater cleanup. Adding these fields to their long-standing brio with asbestos, lead abatement, and PCBs, demolition contractors were ready to hit the brownfields as lean, mean, remediating machines.

Though brownfields provided a major opportunity for wreckers to strut their stuff, in terms of revving up the excavators, they weren't the only chunks of federal legislation in town. First came the Intermodal Surface Transportation Efficiency Act of 1991, which was hailed as nothing less than "the unleashing of an estimated $151 billion dollar economic bonanza for the American construction industry."[64] This act jump-started demolition projects across the board by green-lighting bridges, highways, and transit-system improvements, and it helped put wreckers in the middle of another impending growth industry. A decade later, that is, cities began ripping up their urban freeways with a destructive frenzy unseen since the days of urban renewal. "In downtowns across the country, where developers find it increasingly difficult to assemble full-block sites," the trade magazine *Planning* reported, "freeing up 15 or more contiguous acres is a real estate dream."[65] Freeway wrecking was going whole hog or was under serious study in Milwaukee, San Francisco, Toronto, and Portland, Oregon—the blacktop was getting blitzed thanks to the federal TEA-21 program, which doled out funds for transportation-related projects. Mayors everywhere were only too delighted to discover that they could forget about refurbishing their dilapidated highways and instead flatten them for a fraction of the cost—while selling off the land for condos. "The relative cost of replacement versus demolition, combined with new sources of money from TEA-21," experts said, "is likely to make highway demolition more common in cities across the country."[66]

When not brushing up on sick-building syndrome or bidding on an earthquake-damaged section of the San Francisco freeway, wreckers could look forward to one other big bonanza looming on the horizon: nuclear energy sites. The U.S. Department of Energy estimated that $1 trillion will be spent over the next sixty years to decommission obsolete nuclear facilities worldwide. And the spigots are already flowing. Even in 2003, one of every three dollars in the Department of Energy's $21 billion annual budget was spent for nuclear site cleanup projects.[67] As more and more complex, contaminated, and top-secret structures are being blasted away around the globe, the lowly wrecker, dare we say it, has become the go-to professional to get the job done. These former stepchildren of the construction and scrap trades might even suggest that they've got an exciting, fast-paced, immediately available opportunity on their hands. A few years ago, notably short on hot prospects with high school diplomas, the wreckers got cracking on the college job-fair circuit. "Young people aren't coming into our industry like they used to and we want to change that trend," an official explained. "We want to encourage them to think about demolition as a great career choice."[68]

It might be a tough sell. Today's contractors rove through an ever-changing landscape of environmental hazards, structural failures, and sundry perils that has made wrecking sites subject to an overwhelming array of federal safety regulations—the capstone to the modern demolitionist's advanced wrecking degree. There's no getting around it: Demolition is a rough trade. Though it is not considered among the most dangerous jobs in America (that honor goes to the likes of timber cutters and fishing workers), wrecking is not far behind. The construction sector as a whole has the fourth-highest fatality rate of all industries, and the demolition business logs an average of twenty worker deaths per year, according to the U.S. Department of Labor. In Britain, things are not much better. "We are all familiar with the accident data, and we are all aware that the industry has one of the poorest accident records in the UK," researchers railed in an unvarnished 1992 report. Of ninety-five industry deaths over a five-year period, they said, sixty-seven were avoidable.[69] And a British engineer scolded the industry for its "appalling" safety record, "with a demolition worker being seven times more likely to die than his construction counterpart."[70]

Any demolition contractor will tell you that safety is paramount, and for the majority of wreckers, there's no doubting that it is. Industry leaders have campaigned feverishly on the issue, and, with a little prodding from the Occupational Safety and Health Administration's inspectors, the business is a far cry from Albert Volk's dangerous days. Indeed, the relative concern for today's wreckers is what makes reports like the following so startling. In a 1992 study of two Bronx demolition jobs, researchers found that workers were not provided with hard hats, safety shoes, or gloves (they had to bring their own, and many didn't bother). Wreckers yanked down whole walls "in an uncontrolled fashion," sending debris showering onto the protective sidewalk bridge and then bouncing into the street. Fall protection? Nonexistent. Fire protection? Nope. Respiratory protection? Bring your own. Among the "extremely hazardous" work practices logged, wreckers "often stood on top of a brick wall while breaking the bricks out beneath them." As for toilets, they used the first floor of the building as a latrine.[71]

It sounds like horrid fly-by-nighter stuff, another flashback from the bad old days. But even in 2003, government regulators could cite one particularly egregious Rhode Island contractor for "employees working without fall protection at the edge of seventh and eighth floors of the partially demolished structure," while other wreckers at the dangerous site were exposed to falling debris "while working directly beneath floors as they were being ripped out by a crane." Protective equipment was in short supply, and to add insult to injury, "a wrecking ball was not correctly attached to its rigging." Safety officials slapped the company with more than $250,000 in proposed fines. As they declared: "This worksite could easily have become a graveyard."[72]

Accidents involving explosive demolitions are rare, but

when they do happen, they're heartbreaking. On July 13, 1997, two hospital buildings were being blasted on a lake-flanked peninsula in Canberra, Australia, when a "deadly rain" of shrapnel shot into a crowd of forty thousand people gathered on the other side of Lake Burley Griffin. As the branches of nearby trees got sheared off by platter-sized debris—later found as far as a kilometer from the blast—twelve-year-old Katie Bender was nailed in the head and killed, and several others were injured. Katie's family had dropped by to watch the blast on the spur of the moment, after attending Mass at nearby St. Patrick's Church. "We just went over to have a five-minute stop," her sister said. Demolition workers blamed the "unexpected brittleness" of the fifty-year-old steel girders.[73] Reaction from the industry was swift. "We have editorialized before against turning implosions into entertainment for the masses," fumed *Engineering News-Record*. "But promoters of hotels, movies, charities and such have continued to create these events as spectacularly effective, cheap advertising."[74]

"One irresponsible contractor," as Jack Loizeaux had worried in the 1970s, "could wreck the future of explosives demolition for all."[75] The Loizeauxs' own safety record has come under particular scrutiny from their detractors. In 1996, a Controlled Demolition crew blasting electrical transmission towers near Memphis had finished its work for the day and was returning explosives to a storage magazine on the site. When they arrived at the magazine, according to the accident investigation, keys were nowhere to be found, so a supervisor grabbed a propane torch, and a thirty-nine-year-old worker began cutting two locks away. One lock came off without incident, but as he was cutting off the second lock, a ferocious blast blew the worker to his death, while two others barely escaped a flying steel panel. In another heartbreaking incident in 2000, a chunk of an Illinois coal storage silo broke off as twenty-two-year-old Kevin Auchter of Glen Arm, Maryland, and a worker from another company drilled holes for the placement of dynamite sticks. The wall collapsed and killed the two men. Auchter, described as "a former chef who found his dream job in blowing up buildings," had been working for Controlled Demolition for just three months. "I can't remember when I saw such a bright person that young approach us for work," Mark Loizeaux recalled. "Every single task that was put in front of him, he mastered at a frightening pace." Auchter's mother told a reporter that her son would be buried with a pair of drumsticks, a symbol of his passion for drumming in a rock band called the Negatives. "He died doing what he wanted to do," his mother said. "He truly had found his niche." The headline on his obituary read: KEVIN CAMPBELL AUCHTER, 22, DEMOLITION WORKER, DRUMMER.[76]

"Sometimes the mistakes," Mark once said to me, "are more poignant than the successes."

THERE GOES THE GHETTO

MODERN ARCHITECTURE DIED in St. Louis, Missouri, on July 15, 1972 at 3:32 P.M. (or thereabouts)," wrote the architectural critic Charles Jencks, "when the infamous Pruitt-Igoe scheme, or rather several of its slab blocks, were given the final coup de grâce by dynamite."[1] In a series of blasts during the spring of 1972 that ricocheted across television sets around the globe, Pruitt-Igoe, the notorious thirty-three-building public housing complex, became the poster child for American public policy gone bad. Lauded in *Architectural Forum* in 1951 as a triumph of slum surgery that would save "not only people, but money" from the squalor of "rat-ridden old houses,"[2] this fifty-seven-acre expanse of buff-colored brick and concrete (once home to ten thousand residents) became within a decade a brand-name bombshell, "a household term," in the words of sociologist Lee Rainwater, "for the worst in ghetto living."[3]

Pruitt-Igoe would hit the history books as "one of the most disastrous public housing projects ever built,"[4] and its commensurately colossal destruction, first with dynamite, later with the old "headache ball," would give wreckers a redemptive new role: expiation for the government's sins. Over the next three decades, repenting public housing officials and shell-shocked former residents would punch down ceremonial plungers across the ghastliest ghettos of St. Louis and Chicago, Baltimore and Kansas City, even Paris and Belfast and beyond. Blotted out of the landscape was a parade of downtrodden dwellings, among them Robert Taylor Homes (Chicago), Jeffries Homes (Detroit), Carver Homes (Atlanta), Stella Wright Homes (Newark), Scudder Homes (ditto), Christopher Columbus Homes (ditto again), and Hayes Homes (where else?). Six towers here, five towers there, ten towers toppled in one Newark project alone; atonement came fast and furious, and the bulldozers rolled in to mop up. But public enemy number one was Pruitt-Igoe, the original two-hundred-ton gorilla of the urban jungle. "Other big buildings have been demolished in the same way without great fanfare," a 1973 report said. "Pruitt-Igoe was different. Here was the King Kong of public housing being brought to its knees by 90 pounds of dynamite."[5] Indeed, those thirty-three stark brick buildings proved so seductively distressed that even years before their demise, they had made the quantum leap into the realm of myth. "Pruitt-Igoe also is a state of mind," *Architectural Forum* lamented in 1965. "Its notoriety, even among those who live there, has long since outstripped the facts."[6]

The Captain W. O. Pruitt Homes and the William L. Igoe Apartments were plopped down on a fifty-seven-acre tract in the St. Louis neighborhood of Carr Square, just blocks northwest of the city's downtown core. The shanty-strewn stretch was once colorfully known as "Kerry Patch"—after the Irish immigrants who settled there from County Kerry—but the Irish long ago moved on, and newer waves of African American settlers had landed. Soon enough, "St. Louis was getting ready to cut two big sections out of the collar of slums which is threatening to strangle its downtown business section." Spearheaded by Mayor Joe Darst—a real estate man himself—and created under the United States Housing Act of 1949, Pruitt-Igoe was part of Darst's multipronged assault on five square miles of the city that were corroded by "slums among the worst in the world." With whites skedaddling for the suburbs and "St. Louis Big Money" in a tizzy, it was high time for serious slum surgery. "We must rebuild, open up and clean up the hearts of our cities," said Darst. "The fact that slums were created with all of their intrinsic evils was everybody's fault. Now it is everybody's responsibility to repair the damage."[7]

Heading up the emergency cardiopulmonary team was architect Minoru Yamasaki of the firm Hellmuth, Yamasaki & Leinweber. The architects first sketched up a remedy of high-rise, mid-rise, and walk-up buildings, but surgery quickly went awry. Cost-cutting housing officials took their own scalpels to the plans: Apartment size was put on a diet; children's play areas were scrapped; landscaping had to go. As density spiraled upward from thirty to fifty families per acre, Yamasaki griped that he fought the good fight, but was stymied as the "Public Housing Authority was working to save every nickel they could."[8] Soon little was left but the thirty-three cookie-cutter slabs in their dirt-filled patch of St. Louis. But even still, architectural journals of the day gushed over the drawings. Nothing was more praised than the ingenious elevator system, which opened on every third floor so that no resident had to walk more than one flight of stairs to his or her apartment. On the elevator floors were eighty-five-foot-long, glass-enclosed galleries that doubled as sunny corrals for toddlers. "A mother can do her laundry with her child playing in sight and still be near enough to her apartment to keep an eye on the stove," *Architectural Record* said in 1956. "Many a high-rent city apartment dweller would envy the storage area just off the elevator, instead of in the basement." The whole point of the skip-stop elevator plan and its connecting galleries, the magazine added, was "the economical creation of individual 'neighborhoods' within the buildings."[9] The whole arrangement tickled the architects so much they rushed out to patent it.

When it opened in 1954 and 1955, the $36 million project was hailed as a beautiful solution that could cram 2,870 families together and still vastly outclass the horror it had replaced—a hodge-podge of junkyards and four hundred hovels languishing in "an atmosphere of debris and despair."[10] And to some tenants, at least, Pruitt-Igoe was a dream come true. At first it was "perfect, the nicest place I'd ever had," one resident remembered. "I'd never had any place—never seen any place—as nice as Pruitt."[11] The complex was widely described as "award-winning," though oddly, one historian concluded, the project "never won any kind of architectural prize."[12] It was a telling oversight, because the dream soon unraveled into the nightmare on O'Fallon Street. Costs were arbitrarily slashed during construction, leading to a litany of mechanical woes: Locks and doorknobs busted the first time they were used; windowpanes popped out; one elevator broke down on opening day. Some critics were even bluntly categorical. "On the day they were completed," one summed up, "the buildings in Pruitt and Igoe were little more than steel and concrete rabbit warrens, poorly designed, badly equipped, inadequate in size, badly located, un-ventilated, and virtually impossible to maintain"—despite having construction costs said to be 60 percent above the national average.[13] And that, it turned out, was just the tip of the iceberg.

Initially, Pruitt-Igoe had been planned as a segregated project. Wendell Oliver Pruitt was a black Tuskegee airman from St. Louis who distinguished himself in World War II; William Igoe was one of the city's white Democratic leaders. Pruitt's twenty buildings were thus for blacks and Igoe's thirteen were for whites, until a court order forced the project's desegregation. At that point, most whites scrammed, making Pruitt-Igoe "an exclusively black project virtually from inception."[14] By 1965, the complex was 99 percent black, with a large number of tenants who were female heads of households and dependent on public assistance. More than two-thirds of residents were minors, 70 percent of them under twelve. The project became the de facto "dumping grounds" for slum clearance in St. Louis when, in that same year, housing officials jettisoned their strict screening procedures and allowed problem families onto the site. The root cause of the carnage, said one scholar, "was that very poor welfare families, with large numbers of children, with a deep fatalism about the power to influence their environment, could not cope with this kind of building, nor it with them."[15] There was much chuckling, indeed, about families just off the farm who found themselves shooed into a high-rise when they hadn't even been in an elevator before. "We had people in Pruitt-Igoe," said Thomas Costello, executive director of the St. Louis housing authority, "who actually thought the way to defrost their ice-boxes was to light fires in them."[16]

What some called the "systematic decimation" of Pruitt-Igoe had begun. Soon the place was a disaster area: Rubble and debris littered the streets; abandoned cars piled up in the parking lots; bare wires dangled from light sockets. There were broken windows galore, mud-caked walks, mice, roaches, vermin, you name it. And about those "patent-pending" elevators: "Unquestionably the greatest source of bitterness and frustration is the elevator system," workers reported after an exhaustive, door-to-door survey in 1966. "No problem was more frequently cited."[17] For starters, the elevators were constantly out of service, and though weekly inspections were required, no tenant in the development ever recalled witnessing such an event. (The elevator contract was held by a private firm; only one mechanic was employed to service forty-three cars.) Visitors who actually set foot in the lifts were floored by what they found. "The infamous skip-stop elevator is a revelation even for those considering themselves prepared for anything," said one vivid account. "Paint has peeled from the elevator walls. The stench of urine is overwhelming; ventilation in the elevators is nonexistent. . . . When the visitor emerges from the dark, stench-filled elevator on to one of the building's gallery floors, he enters a grey concrete caricature of an insane asylum."[18]

One could go on and on. "Manager talks to you like a dog," said one resident. "Need more guards, some that will work and not flirt," said another.[19] Then there were boiler tanks rarely cleaned; insecticide sprayed once per year; and two security workers assigned for the thirty-block development in any twenty-four-hour period. It was an open invitation for mayhem: "Derelicts from all parts of the city come to this concrete ghetto, knowing they can perpetrate crimes easily, with little fear of detection."[20] As for those happy homemakers, only two asphalt play areas—netless basketball hoops and all—were provided for five thousand children, while the site's two rubbish-crammed wading pools were plowed under for a new street. Matters went from bad to worse in 1969, when Senator Edward Brooke of Massachusetts got the housing laws amended so that no tenant would pay more than 25 percent of his or her income for rent. With plummeting proceeds and no money to cover the gap, Pruitt-Igoe was in a death spiral. "It was like building a battle-ship that would not float," said the housing authority director in 1970. "The damn thing sank."[21] By 1972, twenty-seven build-ings were unoccupied. Residents simply dubbed it "the Monster."

In hindsight, the verdict was plain enough to see: "Pruitt-Igoe condenses into one 57-acre tract all of the problems and difficul-ties that arise from race and poverty," sociologists reported shortly before the development's annihilation, "and all of the impotence, indifference, and hostility with which our society has so far dealt with these problems."[22] Architectural design was neither the culprit nor the cure at doomed Pruitt-Igoe. Rather, "economic crisis and racial discrimination played the largest role in the project's demise."[23] That didn't keep poor Yamasaki, alas, from lying awake at night. Despite mountains of evidence that he had honorably discharged his duty, the shock of seeing his own structure put out of its misery was apparently hard to shake. "It was one of the sorriest mistakes I ever made in this business," he once warbled. "Social ills can't be cured by nice buildings."[24]

But social ills could be cured by destroying those "nice buildings." In March 1972, desperately seeking strategies to cut

Pruitt-Igoe's theoretical population density, King Kong's keepers called in Jack Loizeaux and sons to try their hand at what was called a "carefully controlled cost analysis that may lead to the radical rehabilitation of the development."[25] A whole smorgasbord of demolition techniques was laid on the table for the public's delectation. One building might be blasted in toto. A second would have its upper six stories blown away, while the unblemished lower floors would be renovated as walk-up apartments. (This slightly zany idea was ultimately dropped after "a long discussion with local officials.") A third building was to be revamped using old-school jackhammers and torches. And every step of the $200,000 wrecking experiment would be chronicled for cost efficiency by the Chicago office of architects Skidmore, Owings & Merrill and various other bean-counter types. Pruitt-Igoe would get penny-pinched to the bitter end.

Despite the exploratory nature of this first phase of destruction, the arrival of dynamite on the premises marked a definite juncture in urban American history. "For the first time since the inception of public housing, the Federal Government is giving up," said an epitaph. "There is an immediacy about the desolation, as if the holocaust had occurred the night before."[26] The first salvo—the beginning of the end of Pruitt-Igoe—was readied on March 16, 1972, as the western half of 2207 O'Fallon Street stood wired for the blast. Choppers scurried overhead, packed with news cameras from national television networks peering down on the scene, and anxious dignitaries trooped into a nearby building to take in the unprecedented ordeal. The anxiety mounted. The 1:30 P.M. blast hour ticked by and nothing happened. A rescheduled time of 2:15 came and went. Pruitt-Igoe apparently wasn't going to go down without at least making the wreckers look bad. Finally word arrived that the Loizeaux's blasting machine had mistakenly been whisked off to the airport, where someone had gone to pick up Arthur Dore, the main contractor for the job. At length, the blasting machine materialized and was hastily rigged up. Forget about the countdown. Spectators watched as the plunger was given a shove and dust shot out from the lower floors of the tower. The blast rippled upward, and the building seemed to kick itself free from the adjacent structure, its top half hanging canted in midair, before heaping to the ground. "It was a good shot," Jack told the press. "I'm delighted with it. But when we say we're going to do something at a certain time we like to do it at a certain time. We take pride in being punctual, and I'm embarrassed. Somebody took our blasting machine."[27]

Fortunately for Jack's sake, another chance at the history books was waiting, and photographers from *Life* magazine were standing at the ready. The most famous shot of Pruitt-Igoe in extremis was taken on a cloudy Friday afternoon in St. Louis as a hush settled over Dickson Street. It was April 21, 1972, and one of Pruitt-Igoe's anonymous eleven-story slabs stood prepped for its date with posterity. Building C-15 was a long, straight hunk of brick-faced concrete with squared-off sections at either end. It had once housed two hundred families, who trudged up urine-soaked stairwells and lived among gauntletlike spaces, often at the mercy of muggers and thugs. Still tinged with menace and impregnable as ever, Building C-15 was no slouch of a foe. Its executioners—the flying Wallendas from Maryland—steeled themselves for battle with characteristic nonchalance. "St. Louis is no different from many other cities," twenty-four-year-old Mark Loizeaux explained before blasting one part of the complex earlier that year. "All of them have old buildings that need to come down, and the sooner the better, for more efficient use of the land," said the young guillotiner, ticking off the milliseconds needed to nix old Pruitt.[28] Having sussed out their quarry, dodging the occasional gunshot from antsy local residents, wreckers drilled sixteen-inch-deep holes in concrete pillars on the ground and first floors and in two small basements. Delayed percussion caps and dynamite were fitted in place amid the tower's ravaged remains. Someone asked the prime contractor, Peter Taylor of Dore Wrecking Co., how much salvage he had netted from the vacant structure. "That seems to have been taken care of before we entered the building," he replied, alluding to the junkies and looters who had long since picked Pruitt-Igoe to the bone. A few scrubby trees teetered out front; the lowering skies turned gray; downtown St. Louis brooded on the horizon. King Kong was ready to rumble.

"Six, five, four, three . . ." Mark intoned over a bullhorn moments before 2:00 P.M. The countdown hit zero and the high-tension hush—"like that of a football crowd awaiting the outcome of a crucial place kick in the last seconds of a bowl game"—abruptly came to an end as 152 charges sequentially fired, and a spontaneous holler welled up from the crowd. Photographers, crouched on the ninth floor of an adjacent building, snapped away as the scene unfolded. The building bulged at its center, and then those three-hundred-sixty-foot-long walls were wrenched downward at a raking angle like some capsizing ship. Dust billowed from the ground floor, and the brick facade fractured, window hangings still flapping from their open frames. The building's midriff lingered for a moment and then lunged to the earth as the end walls folded in. When the dust cloud lifted, all that remained was a thirty-foot-high pile of acrid brick and memories, and "a general outpouring of crowds cheering at the success."[29] For the adrenaline-dizzy wreckers, it was time to mount a Kong-sized trophy brick up over the hearth. "It's all worth it," Mark would soon comment, "because when that thing's down you look up there and you say, oh, man, we did that. It's like winning the Grand Prix or bagging your elephant."[30]

There were other stalking sessions in the wilds of Pruitt-Igoe, but that ten-second implosion of Building C-15 was the ultimate money shot. Splashed across the pages of *Life* a few weeks later (with St. Louis' famous Gateway Arch looping poetically across the background), this "instant demolition in a St. Louis slum" would endure as one of the most potent images in wrecking history.[31] The death of Pruitt-Igoe served up a ready-made icon for a whole social system on the brink of collapse. That day, a scholar wrote, the implosion became "an instant symbol of all that was perceived as wrong with urban renewal, not merely in the United States but in the world at large."[32]

After the big moment, Pruitt-Igoe proceeded to wither with touches of the absurd. "The last optimistic effort to rejuvenate the dying project had elements of the comic, and the pathetic," the *New York Times* reported in 1973. After the vacant buildings had been dynamited, the rubble was to be sodded over and gently graded into sloping "green oases" for the remaining residents. But after a bout of squabbling over this plan, the rubble was quietly carted off. Then housing officials noisily ordered a halt to the experimental demolition program as last-ditch remodeling plans were bruited about. This, too, turned out to be more Grand Guignol theater, and officials finally ordered the razing of the rest of the project. At that time, $32 million in construction debt was still owed on the property. The buildings were imploded, and

The colossal implosion of Building C-15 at Pruitt-Igoe, on April 21, 1972, would become one of the most potent images in wrecking history.

they were not even paid for, and the Department of Housing and Urban Development (HUD) "faced the hard fact that it would be paying back bondholders until 1995."[33] Meanwhile, the absurdities kept getting richer. One proposal suggested that the remaining buildings would serve admirably as "a medium-security state prison," but that plan understandably died on arrival.[34] Residents, for their part, got used to the gallows humor. One tenant affairs board member suggested half-jokingly that the project be kept open as a tourist trap like the old Nazi concentration camps in Germany and Poland. "We should put a fence around it and charge admission," she said. "You go to places like Kansas City and the people say the big thing they want to see in St. Louis is Pruitt-Igoe."[35]

For other former residents, the complex's destruction was no

less surreal. "It was in 1972 when I had the out-of-body experience of going with a group of architecture students to Pruitt-Igoe
to see it be demolished," recalled Michael Willis, who was five
years old when his family moved into Pruitt-Igoe in 1956, the
apartment freshly painted, the grounds newly scrubbed and
open for business. "It was kind of like a party to watch that
headache ball smashing into those buildings." Willis, an architect who would go on to design award-winning public housing
projects of his own, remembered the man they called Mr. Orange, the maintenance man, who would troll Pruitt-Igoe's
grounds scooping up litter with a nail-tipped stick, prompting
the local children to rig up their own sticks and nails, picking up
trash in a vignette that is bitterly poignant. The building-repair
budget soon tanked, of course, and the familiar "comedy of er-
rors" commenced. Cranks that opened the casement windows
fell off, nary a replacement to be found. Wind would snare the
open window like a sail, torque it around, and slam it into the
tower's brick facade. The glass would fall out, and you'd put in
the plywood, since the glazing crew replaced eight panes of glass
each day, but more than twenty panes daily were wrecked.

As Pruitt-Igoe ran its disastrous course, Willis's family soon
moved to LaClede Town, a low-rise public housing village in St.
Louis heralded as, yes, a paragon of diversity and urban living (it
was the nation's first public housing complex with a swimming
pool), a place that was "cool, hip, cheap and populated by people committed to making integration work"—"our own little
United Nations,"[36] residents said. Providentially for Willis, it
was déjà vu all over again. Bulldozers blitzed LaClede Town in
1995, and two years later not one of the fourteen hundred apartments or town houses was left standing. The place Willis fondly

remembers as being packed with "poets, madmen, writers, and university swimmers," where "the colors and the vibes mixed freely," was now dust. "For the second time in my life I saw a newly planned community where I used to live razed to the ground," Willis told me. The vision still deeply resonates. "In a way I think it was proper for a bunch of architects in their formative years to stand and watch something that once held great promise come down into a heap. The lesson may be subtle, and may take a lifetime to learn—what makes our projects succeed may not have anything to do with the architecture whatsoever, but with the kinds of community we are able to engender."

The lessons were poignant indeed. But as the buildings crumbled, any deeper truths lingering in their galleries got scrunched into that one world-jarring photo op of Building C-15. As an aide to the St. Louis mayor testified, the implosions drew surpassingly strong ratings: "It got more coverage than anything we've ever done in this city—good or bad."[37] It was the ultimate architectural mea culpa, and it spawned a whole new motif—"the architect as whipping boy," as another commentator argued. "Here we get the photo in *Life* magazine and elsewhere, dynamiting all that brick and glass, 11 stories worth. The high-rise ghetto as bombsite becomes a potent media image, less personal in its outlines than the shot of the mourning witness of Kent State, but a measure of human tragedy for all that."[38] Then the cameras were packed up and the blasting machine was carted off again, and $45,000 worth of chain-link fence went up around the site. Though dynamite was spectacular, the headache ball was trundled in to do most of the damage. The slab construction, wreckers had discovered, was "much tougher than expected," with concrete made from river-bottom crushed stone that was harder than nails and highly abrasive. Cleaning up the dynamited rubble "proved not to be economically feasible," according to one wrecker. "The buildings came down a mess."[39] And so the slow, methodical, TV-averse wrecking ball would batter Pruitt-Igoe to the ground, concrete falling first and steel piling on top, making for one efficiency, at least, in the project's short history—the swift separation of its recyclable materials.

By 1976, just after the twentieth anniversary of its opening, Pruitt-Igoe was gone. The site was going to be a horse-racing track. Single-family houses. A golf course. A fishing lake for inner-city folk. Part of the land was eventually cordoned off for an "educational park," but most of it remained a grubby waste. In 1977, Charles Jencks had half-waggishly proposed saving the Pruitt-Igoe rubble as a kind of garden folly, "a great architectural symbol" to be "preserved as a warning. . . . Without doubt," he said, "the ruins should be kept, the remains should have a preservation order slapped on them, so that we keep a live memory of this failure in planning and architecture."[40] Almost thirty years later, Jencks would effectively get his wish. "Today, tall, brown, white-tipped weeds cover the grounds like sickly wheat," one ghetto-naturalist wrote in 2005. "What was once home to 10,000 people is now 34 acres of fenced-off weeds, ghostly trees, broken glass, construction waste and feral dogs."[41] Trees on the grounds seem to have soared nearly as tall as the eleven-story slabs.

The architect Philip Johnson once called public housing towers "monstrous brick prisons rising from the streets like untidy asparagus."[42] And Pruitt-Igoe was just one stalk in the forest.

Throughout the 1980s and 1990s, housing towers crumbled with numbing regularity, and nowhere more numbingly, of course, than in Newark, New Jersey. Take the Edward W. Scudder Homes, the direst public housing project in the state when the first of its sixteen hundred apartments were razed in 1987. The project's four stalwart towers loomed over a bombed-out Newark ghetto. Urban ethnographer Camilo José Vergara, who had walked through the emptied buildings prior to their demise, found the telltale detritus that somehow never made it into the evening news clips: stars often painted on apartment ceilings; portraits of Malcolm X taped to the walls; a Valentine's box of chocolates from 1963; discarded missives from the Welfare Department; a grade sheet with two Fs, two Ds, and a C. The only diploma to be found congratulated the candidate on a six-month training program to be a church usher. On May 27, 1987, PR flaks threw a lunch reception and handed out press packages, which probably didn't note that in New Jersey's high-rise projects in 1984, a family of four had a 75 percent chance of a member's becoming the victim of a serious crime over the course of a year.

As at Pruitt-Igoe, Scudder's so-called "demolition ceremony" was not lacking in mordantly unscripted theater. An elderly former resident hit the detonation button, and pushed again with the aid of two helpers, and the first tower began to topple. "The sides folded inward and the huge structure collapsed," Vergara recalled. "Then came the acrid smell of explosives and a mortar and plaster cloud rose, covering everything with a pale dust." Approaching the scene, a local resident took in the great winding-sheet of dust and deadpanned, "They finally made a white neighborhood out of it."[43] The Scudder

Homes were twenty-four years old—quite ancient by the grim standards of the day—and people like Vergara were pointing out the woefully obvious. "Here were well-dressed city and Federal officials," he wrote, "whose role is to provide decent housing for poor people, blowing up unpopular but solid buildings—200 apartments in all. The press, out in force, focused not on policy, but on the spectacular implosion."[44] No one listened, naturally, and the rhetoric only got cranked up further when Newark's Christopher Columbus Homes bit the dust a decade later. Mayor Sharpe James, by far the most demolition-minded mayor in the nation, grandly told the press: "This is the end of an American dream that failed." The detonation of four 13-story towers was "one of the largest in the history of American public housing," and the end of the project took on the customary "oddly festive air," with dozens of officials turned out to "express their joy and relief that the towers were finally being turned into gnarled rubble."[45]

These towers may have once been home, but short of a revolutionary shift in American housing policy, no one was particularly pining to go back. To be sure, many ghetto denizens reveled in the destruction. A high-rise project the Loizeauxs toppled in Kansas City, Missouri, in 1987 (five towers at the Wayne Miner Court complex) was a wrenching case in point. At the time, it was the largest building implosion in U.S. history, with 666 apartments in the towers, built for $12 million in 1960. Twenty-five-year-old Rick Duncan explained that his sister was shot and killed at the project by drug-addled thieves. "I was with her that night," he told the press. "They shot her over some stereo and TV. I want [Building No.] 2011 to go down. I want to see that one go down. I wish those fiends were in there."[46] It was the same brutal story over in Atlanta, where even Techwood

The Christopher Columbus Homes in Newark, New Jersey, were razed in 1994: expiation for the government's sins, with help from 3,800 pounds of dynamite.

Homes, called "the nation's first federally subsidized public housing development," was toasted in 1995. Despite being on the National Register of Historic Places, celebrated for its "unusually high-quality engineering" and deemed "nearly indestructible physically, and economically rehabilitative,"[47] the situation was deemed terminal. "By 1989," one report said, "drugs and violence were so prevalent that Atlanta public housing residents begged the governor to send in the National Guard."[48]

The wreckers were sent in instead, compliments of the $5.5 billion the U.S. government has issued in so-called HOPE VI grants that have underwritten the demolition of more than ninety-seven thousand units of public housing—and many of the boffo implosions that fire up federal housing officials. HOPE VI, deemed "one of the most ambitious urban redevelopment efforts in the nation's history,"[49] was launched in 1992 with the mandate to knock down "Soviet-style subsidized apartment blocks"[50] and replace them with mixed-income housing (in addition to other remedies, including the Section 8 housing vouchers allowing low-income residents to afford privately owned housing in less poverty-wracked areas). HOPE VI (Homeownership and Opportunity for People Everywhere) grew out of the National Commission on Severely Distressed Public Housing, established by Congress in 1989. Having scoured ghettos from coast to coast, the commission found that eighty-six thousand, or 6 percent, of the nation's public housing units were in such dire shape they needed to be put definitively out of their misery. The commission begged Congress to spend $7.5 billion and turn these units into dust by the year 2000. Within months, Congress had doled out its first $300 million, and HOPE VI was off and running.

Wreckers swung immediately into action, but the percussion caps didn't get truly popping until one glitch in the program was fixed. A long-standing HUD policy—made explicit in the 1987 Housing and Community Development Act—required housing officials to replace every housing unit they demolished. For already dirt-poor housing authorities, this requirement pretty much nixed the prospect of demolition. But when President Clinton signed the Congressional Rescissions Bill into law in 1995, local authorities were free to dump the one-for-one replacement requirement. The floodgates had opened. "That was a real big stepping stone," Doug Loizeaux once told me, sitting behind his desk in Maryland. "Because, man, right after that they all started coming down at once. Baltimore was rockin' and rollin' for five years, and other cities were too. I mean some years we would take 50 buildings down, just take 'em down six at a clip, five at a clip. As fast as you could prepare 'em." Pointing to a photograph on the wall of housing blocks crumbling, Doug explained a couple of nuances to the government's infatuation with implosions. "Right here are six that we did in Baltimore at the same time," he said. "Why did we do those jobs? Number one, it's highly visible. It showed that the HUD money was being used." Furthermore, he went on, one of the major goals of the HOPE VI program was to funnel money back into the community, preferably to minority contractors who could benefit from the destruction. The problem was this: Few minority companies had the resources and bonding capacity to wreck the nation's mammoth towers. But if HUD brought in the roving executioners and blasted the towers to bits, a complex demolition project became a mundane material-handling job—in other words, one easily conquered by local contractors with a couple of trucks and excavators. "By doing this we were getting 46 percent minority participation," Doug said. "It might have cost more, but we were in a position where we could put it right on the ground. The money was going where it should go."

Some 446 grants (of up to $50 million a pop) and 166 cities later, the HOPE VI blitz has finally begun to peter out—much to the dismay of wreckers and implosion junkies everywhere. In 2003, with conservatives urging the federal government to ditch its affordable housing program, Congress slashed HOPE VI funding from $570 million to $149 million per year, and the slate-clearing cash cow now "faces almost certain death" as the administration of George W. Bush turns to other housing tactics.[51] Heady as it was, however, HOPE VI was just a sort of midnight snack compared to the federal government's previous demolition binge. A whole lot of wanton destruction went into building all those high-rise hovels. Let us pause to appreciate the singular wrecking achievement known as *urban renewal*.

Whether you call it "slum surgery" or just demolition as a de facto planning tool, urban renewal took a breathtaking bite out of the American landscape. Between 1949 and 1973, when President Richard Nixon unilaterally quashed the program, the federal government shelled out $12.7 billion to bulldoze 2,500 neighborhoods in 992 American cities.[52] One million people were said to be dispossessed by the nation's vigorous quest to give every American family "decent, safe, and sanitary housing." Yes, this was the era of "the Busy Bulldozers," as news stories blithely dubbed it, and it actually began in 1933 with the creation of the Public Works Administration. This juggernaut's housing division doled out some of the first cash for slum clearance projects, flattening tracts of unimaginable despair in over thirty cities. The dozers started growling in 1937, however, when Congress passed the Wagner-Steagall Low-Rent Housing Bill, creating the United States Housing Authority. This unleashed more than $800 million in loans and subsidies,[53] and eventually four hundred thousand slum units had been chomped away. Unfortunately, this was a pittance compared to the 5.6 million substandard units that would soon be discovered needing urgent destruction in metropolitan areas everywhere. Daring new attitudes toward wrecking were required, and the government readily obliged.

Many a wrecker went into business with the Housing Act of 1949—doing a joyful dance of Shiva in thanks for the law's Title I provision in particular, which dangled federal funds in front of developers to help banish blight from diseased urban patches like the one plowed under for Pruitt-Igoe. Armed with the power of eminent domain to condemn vast stretches of slums, and offering subsidies to underwrite the acquisition of rickety, run-down tenements (and the soon-to-be filthily valuable land underneath them), the act sparked off a rampage of rubble-making as bulldozers fanned out across the land. As Herbert Gans pointed out, in addition to swapping slum dwellers' rat holes for that "decent, safe, and sanitary" housing, the program's fringe benefits helped boost "large-scale private rebuilding, add new tax revenues to the dwindling coffers of the cities, revitalize their downtown areas, and halt the exodus of middle-class whites to the suburbs."[54] What was good for wrecking was good for America.

By that time, demolition for progress was fully engaged, but a big turbo boost was applied in 1953, when a presidential committee composed largely of businessmen irritably complained that the wreckers were woefully understaffed for the work at hand. "If we continue only at the present rate of clearance and rely on demolition alone to eliminate slums," they said, "it will take us something over two hundred years to do the job."[55] What cities needed was a whole new concept called "urban renewal." And so with the Housing Act of 1954, all the pieces were in place, including, in that year, broad new powers of eminent domain allowing the seizure of any property whatsoever if a state legislature declared a public purpose for the land. The hardest part of a wrecking job, it was said in that rip-roaring decade, was getting residents out of their freshly condemned buildings.

Indeed, the busy bulldozers and all their trappings were a rude shock to pundits who followed the craze, even though the basic metaphors had been around since the days of that original disemboweller, Baron Haussmann. "The concept is a little like that of a dentist: drill out the infected cavity and fill it with nice new wholesome cement," smirked Harrison Salisbury, a newspaperman better known for his dispatches from Siberia. "It may hurt a little at first but the end justifies the pain." However, Salisbury went on, the slum-clearer does not have the finesse of a dentist, and his wayward drill uproots solid enamel as well as decay. The wrecker rips down churches, local business, neighborhood lawyers' offices, and synagogues. "Bulldozers do not understand that a community is more than broken-down buildings and dirty storefronts," he stammered. "It is a tight skein of human relations. It has a life all its own. The wreckers tear this human fabric to ribbons."[56]

Urban renewal was officially finito by 1975, but that didn't mean decrepit housing and wreckers parted ways. In that year, a whole new epidemic reared up in fast-rotting cities across the country—the abandoned, fire-ravaged, and otherwise broken homes of the ghetto that would keep the bulldozers chomping well into the twenty-first century. "By 1975," researchers said, "there were an estimated 199,000 abandoned housing units in New York City, 64,500 in Chicago, 62,000 in Detroit, 33,000 in Philadelphia, and 30,000 in St. Louis. Between 1973 and 1977, more than 1.1 million home-owned and 1.5 million rental units were removed from the national market." The bulldozers would be working overtime, it turns out. Nearly one in twenty-five U.S. residences in 1973 had been wrecked, with more than 520,000 units lost every year to abandonment between 1974 and 1980. In New York City alone, almost 294,000 dwelling units were lost over a fourteen-year stretch beginning in 1970—that's more than 190,000 units demolished, 98,000 burned out or boarded up, and 3,000 condemned.[57]

The ever-ravaged New York, as we have seen, was no stranger to all manner of housing destruction, particularly not since the days of that "Commissioner Plenipotentiary and Rubblemaker General,"[58] Robert Moses. To build his monumental expressways in New York, Moses evicted 250,000 people from their homes and, in just one notorious binge on the Cross-Bronx Expressway, "demolished a solid mile of six- and seven-story apartment houses—fifty-four of them—thereby destroying the homes of several thousand families."[59] That episode was so lurid that one resident would never forget the scene: "While people were still living in it, they were tearing it down around their heads!" Meanwhile, such massive demolition had other familiar consequences, said the astonished witness: "The rats were running like cats and dogs in the street."[60] Moses, of course, was a ruthless follower of the Haussmannian ways. "You can draw any kind of picture you like on a clean slate and indulge your every whim in the wilderness in laying out a New Delhi, Canberra or Brasília," he archly explained, "but when you operate in an overbuilt metropolis, you have to hack your way with a meat ax."[61]

All that hacking, many have since pointed out, took the soul out of the South Bronx and helped inaugurate a vicious cycle of neighborhood clear-cutting and disinvestment that has been called "contagious housing destruction."[62] The poxed face of the urban beast was brought to national attention on October 5, 1977, when President Jimmy Carter made his dramatic visit to the South Bronx, hiking around in what was described as "the middle of a block on which all buildings on both sides had been demolished and the bricks had been bulldozed into heaps that in some places were eight feet high."[63] It was a shocking realization to many who had been comfortably ensconced in the suburbs to learn that large chunks of some of America's largest cities were vast demolition-cum-war zones. "The Presidential motorcade passed block after block of burned-out and abandoned buildings, rubble-strewn lots and open fire hydrants, and people shouting 'Give us money!' and 'We want jobs!' "[64] This apocalyptic scene duly impressed reporters, who immediately assigned the visit world-shaking proportions. "The Bronx that President Carter saw yesterday," said one typical account, "has become a national symbol of what is wrong with urban America."[65]

Yes, it was total chaos in that "social sinkhole in which civilization has all but vanished," according to one report on the poor South Bronx, noting that even the wreckers had trouble operating under such rampant disorganization. "On several occasions, rehabilitation teams and demolition crews working under separate city programs have appeared at the same building on the same day."[66] In truth, the destruction of houses in New York had been quietly proceeding apace for well over a decade, with the South Bronx finding 250,000 apartments destroyed between 1960 and 1975, "despite concerted public efforts to ameliorate housing conditions there."[67] Arson, for example, famously grew into a "a new industry" driven by corrupt property owners, mortgage bankers, and insurance adjusters. "We're losing 300 to 400 buildings a month by fire and the majority are arson," reported a coordinator of New York City's new two-hundred-fifty-member arson task force in 1977, what with owners of rotting tenements torching them away and collecting the insurance cash to recoup their losses. The business arrangements of this demolition-by-arson craze could be squirrelly indeed. "A New York police investigator," said *Newsweek,* "recently traced $1,000 paid by a businessman to burn out a rival; before the match was struck, the job was subcontracted six times—and the ultimate torch was a 14-year-old who said he was paid little more than a six-pack of beer."[68]

There goes the ghetto. As sensationally ruined as St. Louis or Newark or New York have been, another site looms large on rubblemakers' radars: a 139-square-mile city with its very own "site-specific engines of demolition," and plenty of them, too— implosions, racism, freeways, fires, politicians, and good old Henry Ford. These ever-revving engines, one critic noted, are "where the real history of the city is being written: by the vernacular forgetting machines that render the past natively unrememberable."[69]

Hold on to your frontal lobe. Welcome to demolition central, Detroit, Michigan, United States of America.

DISAPPEARED DETROIT

THE ODOMETER ROLLED over on another modern era with typical to-the-minute precision: "For Detroit, the 20th century ended at 5:47 P.M. Oct. 24, 1998." True to form in the Motor City—mythic land of the annual new model—Detroiters got a head start on the coming century as the rubble met the road. "With a deafening roar that will echo in the hearts of Detroiters for decades," said the local press, the long-barren J. L. Hudson Company department store careened its way into the dustbin. "Explosions raced across the building, shearing off pillars as they moved northwest: men's suits on two; junior dresses on five; the community auditorium on 12," until even the cork-lined fur vaults on the seventeenth floor (capacity: eighty-three thousand furs) blew apart, and "the mammoth structure wobbled like a drunk, hesitated, then collapsed into a 60-foot-high pile of rubble."[1] The sprawling, twenty-eight-story downtown emporium had been branded "the symbol of one of the most notorious episodes of urban decay in America's history."[2] The store hit its peak sales year in 1953, and it was all downhill from there. Its bronze doors slammed shut for good in

1983, entombing memories of Santa Land, elevator ladies, and Maurice salads within its brooding shell—a "decrepit behemoth's carcass," detractors said, blighting the city. The Downtown Development Authority wanted it blitzed. The Loizeauxs were happy to oblige.

Standing 439 feet tall and sprawling 2.2 million square feet (the second-largest department store in the nation, after Macy's in New York), Hudson's was billed as "both the tallest and largest single building ever imploded."[3] (Taller stacks had been downed, but this was the tallest once-inhabited structure. It remains a matter of industry bickering over who takes the cake for the largest single building blasted, with Hudson's and the Sears center in Philadelphia, razed in 1994, vying for the title.) The formidable building, constructed over twelve stages between 1911 and 1946, had 76 elevators, 705 fitting rooms, and a woman's restroom boasting 85 stalls. It took twenty-one workers nearly three months to scout the structure, plus four people to work up the implosion, which was fired by 2,728 pounds of explosives. "It's the most we've ever used for one building anywhere, anytime, anyhow," Mark Loizeaux said.[4]

When the big day finally came, television anchors were rushing to complete their own hectic preparations as they juggled the once-in-a-lifetime implosion with the all-important Wisconsin-Iowa football game (one news director vowed to run both ratings-grabbers live, using a picture-within-a-picture insert). But you didn't need a wide-angle lens to catch the broad smile on the face of then Mayor Dennis Archer. Radiating bliss at the downtown redevelopment prospects opened by the $12 million blast, Archer grabbed Doug Loizeaux in a hug as they watched atop a nearby building, pumping his fist when Hudson's tumbled into a 330,000-ton pile of history. Visions of the office-retail complex that was slated for the site (ironically called Campus Martius or "field of Mars," named after the Roman god of war) must have danced amid the detonating charges as Archer punched the ceremonial ignition switch. "Today, we say good-bye to years of frustration," he declared. "Let the future begin."[5]

As the blast commenced and the "symphony of failure" reached its crescendo, spectators duly took note. "It sounded musical," sighed one rooftop partyer, munching on shrimp and pastries. "It was so graceful."[6] As it happened, there was an added tinkling effect when the 27.7-second blast shattered 132 windows in surrounding vacant buildings. The Loizeauxs said that 92 windows were already cracked, and they expected the breakage, which they thought would cost about $10,000 to fix (seven separate glass companies were already on high alert for the occasion). The sheet music took a more consequential detour, however, when six columns went akimbo during the implosion and landed on a nearby concrete box girder, knocking out service on a three-hundred-fifty-foot chunk of Detroit's elevated People Mover railway, only a dozen feet away. ("The People Mover won't be moving any people for a while," was the press's mordant take.[7]) After an initial glance, a manager downplayed the damage as "cosmetic," but it ultimately took a year to fix the line and restore the system to full capacity, irking Detroit bigwigs who claimed the incident cost $1 million in lost People Mover revenue, stymied thousands of riders, and just plain looked bad. After various lawsuits, quarreling engineers, and sparring insurance companies had all been accounted for, the total bill came to more than $4 million.

You might call it the curse of Martius—and he wasn't fin-

Men's suits on two; junior dresses on five: It's one mammoth closeout sale for the beloved J. L. Hudson Company department store in downtown Detroit.

ished with Detroit yet. Moments after the blast, carousing crowds were abruptly confronted with a ten-story-tall dust tsunami emanating from the building, which "hurtled swiftly toward spectators to the south and east," a witness recounted. "[Mayor] Archer ducked into a stairwell while nearby construction workers stood their ground, toasting with Budweisers as gray soot enveloped them."[8] Other spectators, too, seemed to take the deluge with impressive savoir faire. One seasoned blast junkie came armed with mask, goggles, hard hat, and buttoned-up overcoat, so amply fortified she was dubbed "Miss Implosion" by envious friends. Meanwhile, sixty-seven-year-old Joyce

Hurthibise bore the billowing cloud with stoic good cheer. "To see that building come down and then that cloud come at you, was just the most amazing thing I've ever seen," she said. "When the dust started coming, we just turned our backs to it."[9] There was even a silver lining for restaurateurs at nearby Greektown eateries, who were swamped by an early-dinner mob: Folks diving for cover ended up lounging around for drinks and a meal. "It helped us because it happened during a time that is usually slow for us," said the manager at Trappers Bar and Grill.[10]

Not everyone was so blasé about it, though; what some called the "attack of the killer dust" darkened the skies, sending a few spectators fleeing in fear and driving others into coughing fits. "The 50,000 guests followed the mayor's lead to come downtown and party," one resident later complained. "Surely, they had no expectation of the black cloud of dirt. It is these kinds of surprises that give rise to panic."[11] Though the blasters warned that dust would blanket the area and advised those with respiratory concerns to shun the spectacle ("This is not a publicity stunt," they said a week before the blast[12]), that didn't stop television stations from helpfully rushing dust samples to waiting labs and reporting lead levels of more than five hundred parts per million, enough to "cause serious damage" if ingested, according to one environmental expert.[13] While dust samples did turn up lead and asbestos, further analysis concluded it was "not enough to be a health hazard for those who watched the downtown Detroit implosion."[14] City, county, and federal environmental officials all agreed, claiming that peeling lead paint in an old home would pose a much greater danger than the Hudson's dust, not to mention the months-long exposure to dust that a wrecking-ball-style razing would entail. Nonetheless, a law-

suit was promptly lodged against the demolitionists by a spectator alleging "unspecified injuries as a result of contaminated
dust particles 'being heavily emitted into the air of the general
public.' "[15]

That suit didn't get very far, but the fallout over fallout went
on for days, with some judging the dust episode a media-brewed
tempest in a teapot. "Detroit makes a perfect laboratory for
studying mass hysteria," one Michigan attorney commented,
"thanks to some irresponsible TV news coverage of the aftermath of the imploded J. L. Hudson Building." Amid breathless
accounts of toxic dust loosed upon the city from the sinister-
looking cloud, the Hudson's terror could be a case of "hysteria-
induced illness," the attorney wrote, owing mainly to a
dour-looking doctor who popped up on Channel 4—clad in an
authoritative white coat—discoursing gravely about stomach
pains, headache, and fatigue. Asbestos is a serious health issue,
no doubt, but depending on the financial rewards, "the syndrome may spread to people who were nowhere near any dust
cloud," she wrote. "And soon there are class-action lawsuits."[16]

Martius finally relented, it seemed, and the media soon
blipped off to other pressing matters (BOY SPRAYS WD40 IN
TEACHER'S SPORTS DRINK, the headline read one day later). The
Hudson's smoldering remains, meanwhile, yielded up some
crowd-pleasing artifacts, which Homrich Wrecking, the Detroit
company overseeing the demolition, offered to local charities.
More than twenty-six hundred bricks from the site were sold off
at an area Goodwill store in two days at $5 a pop. "The newest
fad?" You guessed it: "A hunk of rubble from the Hudson's
building."[17] As the loss of the beloved structure soaked in around
the nation, however, the high fives gave way to melancholic

afterthoughts. "A piece of me died when I saw on national television the implosion of the venerable Hudson's department
store," a former Detroiter wrote in from Austin. "I certainly
hope that somebody was astute enough to rescue the ornate
brass drinking fountains scattered through the store. They were
lovely."[18] The copper and brass fixtures, it was said, had long
since been stripped out by vandals.

The demise of Hudson's (more a drama-drenched opera, as it
turned out, than a symphony) may have blasted Detroit out of
the twentieth century, but the implosion was well in keeping
with an august city tradition. When in 1979 the J. L. Hudson
Corporation tried to take a wrecking ball to its opulent but failing department store, an architect, Lewis Dickens, campaigned
to save the venerable redbrick pile. He began riffing on the shifting syllables of the city's name. "When the French were here,
Detroit was pronounced 'De-twah,' " he told a preservation
council. "Then it was 'Detroit,' and then it was 'Dee-troit.' Let's
not now make it 'Destroyed.' "[19]
    Fifteen years later, Detroit had become synonymous with de-
struction. Architect Dan Hoffman, ruminating on the disappearing city, put it most poignantly. "Unbuilding," he said, "has
surpassed building as the city's major architectural activity."[20]
Between 1970 and 2000, more than 161,000 dwellings were demolished in Detroit, amounting to almost one-third of the city's
occupied housing stock—that's more than the total number of
occupied dwellings today in the entire city of Cincinnati.[21] Between 1978 and 1998, only 9,000 building permits were issued
for new homes in Detroit, while the city doled out over 108,000
demolition permits.[22] "Demolition is so much a part of the city's

culture," an investigative report concluded not long ago, "that in 2001, when he was running for mayor, Kwame Kilpatrick pledged to knock down 5,000 abandoned and dangerous buildings in his first year in office. After he was elected, he found there wasn't enough money in the budget to fuel such a ravenous demolition machine."[23]

Detroit is disappearing because Detroiters themselves have disappeared. The city has shed 48 percent of its population—almost nine hundred thousand residents—since its population peak in 1950. And they didn't all move back to France. Like many a metropolis of the era, against a background of shifting economic fortunes and stark racial divides, Detroit was walloped by "a five-decade exodus of middle-class families to the suburbs."[24] Its 139 square miles of turf, once upon a time the province of elegant Queen Anne duplexes and gabled Flemish houses and stout Georgian piles with Palladian windows, went into terminal shock. Bungalows went belly-up; cottages crumbled. The diagnosis: demolition by neglect. Fleeing owners sometimes ditched their houses altogether; others bailed out after defaulting on mortgages; still others sold to scurvy real estate types who wrung some income out of the properties and then bolted. The cycle was wearily familiar to the city's swamped demolition-permit department: "An owner would default; the property would fall into the hands of the federal Department of Housing and Urban Development; HUD would give it to the state, which would then give it to the city; and the city would demolish what by then had become a dangerous vacant building."[25] By that time, of course, scavengers had ripped even the bricks out of the walls and sold them to builders, who paid $200 for a thousand-piece lot. Whatever rubble remained was dumped into the basement, and the whole mess topped off with dirt, a cheap demolition trick, as we have seen, that drove up redevelopment costs because a builder would have to haul out the debris. The tainted properties languished, and the owner next door would start packing up. As one analyst summed up the city's predicament: "It does gravitate to a graveyard spiral."[26]

Adding fuel to Detroit's great bonfire of unbuilding was, well, fire. In an annual rite on October 30, the night before Halloween, thousands of torch-bearing arsonists and riled-up spectators would take to the streets in a frenzy known as "Devil's Night." On October 30, 1984, the city's worst night, 810 fires burned over the three-day Halloween period in a ghastly bacchanalia that seemed to clinch the city's slide off the deep end. Some torched their own properties for profit; others just got kicks from watching abandoned houses go up in flames. Suburbanites would even drive downtown to enjoy the fray. "Some people like the Fourth of July," a resident of suburban Warren explained as he videotaped a blaze. "I like Devil's Night."[27] Over the years, the city struggled mightily to stamp out the menace—a chief tactic being yet more demolition, a sort of preemptive strike that would deprive the arsonists of their quarry. As part of its "Angels' Night" campaign in 2001, for example, during a three-day period, officials wrecked 716 vacant structures (and towed 2,060 abandoned vehicles for good measure).[28] Critics pointed out the rather ironic fix in which the city then found itself. On the one hand, officials deplored the wanton torching of their urban assets, while on the other they "privately corroborated" the arsonists' illegal activities "by developing, funding, and implementing one of the largest and most sweeping demolition programs in the history of American urbanism." The upshot was painfully clear: "Vast portions of Detroit were erased through this combination of unsanctioned burning and subsequently legitimized demolition."[29]

Many houses that did get torched would simply be left to rot, much to their neighbors' consternation. This proved a source of further unintended ironies in Detroit. What with an endless backlog of buildings to demolish—and often no budget for the bulldozers—the city was not known for rushing wreckers to the scene after a call came in from a burned-out citizen. Dan Pitera, who directs the Detroit Collaborative Design Center at the University of Detroit Mercy, sensed a creative-destructive opportunity at hand. "If you look at a burned house," he once told me, "they actually can be quite beautiful, if you don't have the

Detroit gravitated to a graveyard spiral. This collapsed house was found on the city's East Side in 1998.

negativity of what it means for them to burn." So Pitera and colleagues launched the "Fire-Break" project, a series of installations in and around picturesquely charred houses on Detroit's east side. Working with community members, they created sites such as the "Sound House" (where musicians from the neighborhood played Cajun tunes, while brightly colored fabric hung from its openings) and the "Hay House," covered with five thousand tiny bundles of hay in a nod to urban farming. (In the city's fallow building lots, alfalfa is a popular crop, as it helps detoxify contaminated soil. It's hard to believe, but numerous residents have also turned derelict "crack houses" into "hay houses," used to store bundles of hay.) "We do all this without permission," Pitera explained. "They're intended to be mercenary acts." They hit their mark. In some cases, neighbors had been clamoring for years to get these particular houses destroyed, and a little art worked wonders. The design group's installations attracted the eye of city authorities, who sacked the structures within weeks. "Every house we've done so far has been demolished," Pitera said proudly. "When you consider there are 8,000 houses and we've gotten five torn down, it's pretty daunting."

Whether via neglect, fire, or the odd Cajun musician, block after block of Detroit succumbed to the bulldozer over the decades, but it wasn't until Monday, April 26, 1993, during a budget presentation to Detroit's City Council, that the city's unbuilding binge rocketed to national attention. On that day, Marie Farrell-Donaldson, Detroit's ombudsman, proposed that blighted sectors of the city be put out to pasture. Detroit would literally be downsized at "20, 25 blocks or so at a whack."[30] The plan called for residents to be ferried from moribund districts to those where a spark of life could still be found. Derelict houses would be demolished, empty stretches fenced off, and the whole mess turned over to "nature." Farrell-Donaldson, a former city auditor who was Michigan's first black female certified public accountant, titled her report "Management by Common Sense." She explained in terms familiar to the Motor City's hard-pressed automobile executives: "What we would be trying to do, in reality, is to downsize the community. We're talking about rightsizing the city to correlate with our budget."[31] It was an oddly intriguing idea—in some quarters, anyway—and proponents pointed out that "mothballing" was a common practice for bombed-out neighborhoods in European cities after World War II. If it's good enough for Dresden, it's good enough for Detroit. Demolition costs for the project were put at up to $4,000 per house, but since the city was spending $4 million each year to maintain its sixty-six thousand vacant lots, this was a modest sum indeed. Plus, wrecking one-third of the city would make vast parcels of land attractive to developers.[32] Having got hold of the story, the *Economist* mustered a stiff upper lip, concluding that "wholesale abandonment of parts of the city begins to make grim sense."[33]

Official reaction around town was frosty (city budget director Ed Rago rebuffed the plan as a "bizarre notion"), and editorialists blasted the proposal as a wrong-headed "clearance sale for Detroit."[34] But the scheme kicked up unexpected enthusiasm among the bombed-out sectors under discussion. "The mayor thinks it's ridiculous," one reporter wrote, "but some residents are asking, 'When's moving day?' "[35] So bitter had Detroiters become over pothole-pocked roads and weed-choked lots that the destruction of their own houses made perverse sense, especially if the city bought them out at a premium. "I've suggested to the city that they tear down more houses because there are too many blighted areas now," said one supportive homeowner. "Maybe some of the people who live next to these [fenced-out areas] can throw some grass seed in there."[36] That attitude showed outstanding pluck, but others were more noncommittal. So much demolition had already taken place, some said, that it had made the old neighborhood downright homey. "Now everyone has moved out and everything has burnt down," allowed seventy-three-year-old Bessie Graves. "It's a bit like living in the suburbs now. You could say it's almost a better neighborhood." In 1993, Graves's house, the one "with peeling yellow paint and a roof that sags almost comically at both ends," was the only one left standing on the block.[37] It was the same story for Delores Reese, her home flanked by the hulks of houses destroyed by arson. "When people come to visit, I tell them to look for *Little House on the Prairie,*" she said with amazing good humor. "It's like living in the country."[38] She wasn't exaggerating. At that time there were sixty-five thousand vacant lots in Detroit, and the whole city was reverting to what it must have looked like when the French were wandering around the place and calling it "De-twah." "Covered by huge fields of brush 6 feet tall, many Detroit neighborhoods resemble prairies," one observer said. "Houses squat like pioneer outposts amid sprawling expanses of white Queen Anne's lace, blue cornflowers and other wildflowers."[39]

The notion of full-scale urban clear-cutting may have shocked Detroit's polite society, but the concept wasn't exactly new, even for Detroit. Three years earlier, the City Planning Commission had prepared a report—apparently quickly buried—that has become known as the *Detroit Vacant Land Survey*. This remarkable document for the first time assembled maps of the city showing its vacant parcels, which were blacked out with marker in ominous expanses. The report is full of disarming bureaucratese—". . . Master Plan proposes concentrating spot demolition of vacant structures along with a vacant lot cleanup campaign . . . the few remaining families should be encouraged and assisted in moving into better housing . . . over 70% of the parcels in the area are vacant . . . simply vast areas of open space . . . future of the remaining residential area remains unsure . . ."[40]—that nonetheless proposed a revolutionary program of urban nonrenewal. Observers later admired the document's "unsentimental and surprisingly clear-sighted acknowledgment" of the postindustrial maelstrom that had bled the city of its building stock, to say nothing of other basic resources. For once, planners had boldly come to grips with the "urban erasure" that had already taken the city by storm.[41]

Prior to Detroit's woes, no city knew urban erasure like New York, and Farrell-Donaldson could easily have gone to Gotham for backup in the matter of demolition-minded urban remedies. In 1976, for instance, New York City began "thinking the unthinkable" when its top housing official, Roger Starr, urged all sensible Americans to get hip to the thought of "planned shrinkage." The city already had pockets of dwindling population—namely the South Bronx and Brooklyn's Brownsville neighborhood—and if you can't beat 'em, join 'em. Public policy would accelerate that shrinkage so that blighted areas could be scratched off the list of neighborhoods needing expensive city services.[42] No doubt about it, Starr said. "The stretches of empty blocks may then be knocked down, services can be stopped, subway stations closed, and the land left to lie fallow until a change in economic and demographic assumptions makes the land useful once again."[43] It was strong medicine for an American dream obsessed with building up and growing ever bigger, as Starr himself acknowledged. "I surely cannot underestimate the fears engendered by this notion of growing smaller," he said, "in a social milieu in which growing bigger has been the hope of those who have not had a fair share."[44]

This romantic vision of destroying the city in order to save it continues to tantalize urban thinkers. The scholar Witold Rybczynski was still working out the finer points of the concept just a few years after Detroit's dustup over downsizing. The de facto abandonment of America's corroding cities was to be encouraged, he said, echoing Starr's bold thesis. "Housing alternatives should be offered in other parts of the city, partly occupied public housing vacated and demolished, and private landowners offered land swaps," Rybczynski wrote in 1995. "Finally, zoning for depopulated neighborhoods should be changed to a new category—zero-occupancy—and all municipal services cut off." Thus was born the dream of the "comprehensive downsizing of cities," an urban slash-and-burn operation that made Detroit's demolition binge look like kid's stuff.[45] Meanwhile, captivated by this apocalyptic panorama of "de-densified" cities wrecked beyond all hope, still other scholars have tried to get a grip on the broader phenomenon of "shrinking cities." Pointing out that shrinkage is a growing, worldwide affliction (the United States, Britain, and Germany are faring the worst, but places as disparate as Phnom Penh and Johannesburg have shed more than a third of their population), this camp reports that for every two cities that are growing, three are shrinking. And that's a recipe for destruction. "Traditionally, urban planners advise bulldozing eroded neighborhoods and starting from scratch," said Philipp Oswalt, project director for the $3 million research project earnestly studying the newly diagnosed "shrinking city syndrome."[46] As in so many things, it seems, Detroit was ahead of its time.

In an extraordinary series of reports in July 1989, the *Detroit Free Press* counted 15,215 empty buildings in the city, a cancer the paper called "an infection more pervasive than ever documented" and testimony to the exodus of middle-class families "that is both a cause and a result of the economic decay that has crippled many Detroit neighborhoods."[47] The saga of Detroit's struggle to demolish this staggering inventory makes for one of the oddest episodes in modern urban history. It's a *Pilgrim's Progress* of vigilante wreckers and emergency demolition orders, a perilous journey through the eye-opening wilds of what one writer called Detroit's "spontaneous evolution of aggressive dismantling."[48] The city had plunged into the slough of wrecking despond at least as early as 1958, when a survey estimated that it would cost $1.2 billion to raze all of Detroit's blighted buildings—that's $60 million a year for twenty years. By the time of the *Free Press* survey, however, officials had gotten a little behind in their demolition payments. At that time, Detroit had razed an average of two thousand buildings a year since 1982— at $9 million per year, or $4,500 per home, a figure that had shot up more than 50 percent in five years. That was serious wreckage, the paper reported, but it wasn't even holding the line. Every year in Detroit, an estimated twenty-four hundred structures became newly vacant and in dire need of destruction.

There was smashing to be done, and Detroit rolled out the wreckers. In April 1989, Department of Public Works director Conley Abrams was appointed the city's demolition czar, and he drew up separate demolition contracts for the city's four quadrants. The deal was this: Each of the four contractors had to wreck at least ten houses every week; within each quadrant, smaller wrecking firms were contracted to raze three buildings per week. As part of the new blitz, crews were free to crunch up multiple houses in the same area simultaneously, which was a boon to wrecking productivity: One crew ripped down five "dangerously abandoned" houses on one block in just four hours. The city was justifiably purring over this lightning-speed action, but given the gargantuan task before them, it was no surprise that expectations might run a tad high. Just months after the bulldozers were unleashed, Curlee Shorter, a twelve-year veteran of northeast Detroit, could be found in his front yard sounding off about a half-story-high pile of rubble mounded up next door. What with the slam-bam wrecking pace, a vacant house had been demolished by mistake; no one even bothered to haul away the debris, which was perfectly framed by Shorter's dining-room window. "You're sitting here eating and you've got to look at that," he said. "And the rats. We even killed some possums."[49]

But at least that house got wrecked, even if it was the wrong one. Other Detroiters weren't so lucky, and they were taking blunt tools into their own hands. Disgusted by waiting for the city to demolish houses that had been on the to-be-wrecked list for over a year, by early July, two posses of self-appointed

"house busters" had descended upon three long-vacant structures, one of them a crack haven and the others fire-damaged rat
warrens. Jubilantly bashing away with sledgehammers, crowbars, baseball bats, and their own vans, they toppled the hated
houses and hauled the debris into the middle of the street,
smugly forcing the city to cart it off. The scene was one of law-
less frenzy, crossed with some sort of neighborhood demolition-
industry recruitment drive. "I saw them working and there was
nothing else to do so I came to help," nine-year-old Roscoe
Childs explained when reporters caught up with him. Others
were simply aglow with that primal wrecking euphoria. "I'm ecstatic," twenty-four-year-old Karen Reeve said. "I'm on top of
the world right now."[50]

The high was contagious, and soon, roving thirty-person-
strong gangs of what the media were calling "residents-turned-
amateur-demolishers" were stalking the city with chainsaws.
The "do-it-yourself demolition bug" was particularly catching
among teenage boys. "We always bust up this place," explained
thirteen-year-old Devin Laird, who boasted that he had started
the whole craze by throwing rocks at one of the neighborhood
eyesores. "Now everybody's doing it."[51] One civilized group of
residents circulated a petition to get a consensus of twenty-two
signatures on their block before dragging an offending house
down, and the sudden blush of high-spirited cooperation
seemed to put a spring in the whole city's step. Police cruised by
amateur wrecking sites without stopping, and neighbors didn't
even care when a wayward plank smashed out a window or
two of their own basements. Meanwhile, demolition supporters
pledged to post bail for comrades who might get arrested.
"They're sticking their necks way out, and they're brave to do

it," affirmed a seventy-three-year-old. "They're helping the city out. It's not illegal."[52]

Professional wreckers were slightly less gung-ho about this upswelling of sledgehammer-swinging competition. Larry Lewis, then director of the Inner City Black Wreckers Association, urged the demolition vigilantes to cool it for their own safety. "It's a risky business. Once you start to tear down a house, it could fall to the right or left," he said. "It's not predictable. It can fall on a fence, another house, or a person."[53] There was also fretting about live electrical wires, gas main explosions, and burst sewer lines. But no one could seem to get too worked up about the lurking hazards, least of all city officials. City councilman Jack Kelley, having made the rounds of the wrecking sites, wistfully remarked that if there was a vacant house next door to his own home, he'd be first in line. "I'd get five gallons of gas, call the fire or police and I'd take it down very quietly," he said. "I know that's wrong, but you can't blame them."[54]

As the days went on and media coverage mounted, public opinion swung decidedly behind the wreckers. One newspaper survey found that a resounding 91 percent of readers approved of their "free-lance rubble-rousers." ("Not only do I agree with their action, I think they should be reimbursed for their time," averred one reader.[55]) The whole scene was getting out of control, and at length the city was forced to move. Five men were hauled off in handcuffs for wrecking without a permit and slapped with $100 fines, with Mayor Coleman Young denouncing them as "reckless vigilantes." Lest he look bad, Young hastened to add that the budget for the city's new fiscal year included $15 million to fund "the largest demolition program in our history," which he thought would take down three thousand structures.[56] As it happened, the brief jail time didn't have much of a deterrent effect on the opposition. "I'm so angry I could start tearing other houses down," seventeen-year-old Arthur Wirgau seethed. "And I'm going to."[57]

Demolition had touched a nerve in Detroit. No one remembered this spontaneous outpouring of commonweal and chainsaw oil better than the city's next great wrecking impresario, Mayor Dennis Archer, who gleefully cheered on the imploding Hudson's building. It was 1997, and Archer had been on a rampage, vowing to bulldoze every abandoned building in the city deemed too far gone for rehabilitation—as many as 8,922 of them—preferably in a single summer (the one before the mayor's November reelection vote, that is).[58] In a stroke of brilliance, Archer asked the federal Housing and Urban Development office to pony up the cash. Amid grumbling about ballot-count boosting, days before Archer's reelection, HUD officials swept into town with some timely good news. "Secretary Andrew Cuomo granted Archer a campaign wish: a $60 million loan guarantee, slated to finance the demolition of nearly every abandoned residential building in Detroit." Housing honchos boasted that it would be the "largest such bulldozing ever undertaken by a U.S. city."[59] At the time, Detroit officials couldn't say how many structures would be razed, other than to hint that there would be plenty going down, in every voter precinct, for sure—as many as ten thousand. For his part, Archer was on such an adrenaline high he could hardly see straight. "When you start talking about stadiums or even the $900 million for the Chrysler plant, it doesn't touch or concern every citizen," he said after the HUD announcement, nearly shaking with emotion.

"When you say you're going to tear down abandoned houses," he went on, "to be able to say you're going to start on it and tear them all down, I think creates an enormous pride in the entire city."[60] Archer's bulldozer hosannas struck some observers as pure pandering. "There's a 'Tear it down and they will come' mentality," one preservation officer complained. But as it turned out, the mayor had thornier problems to worry about than carping preservationists. "For more mundane reasons, Mayor Archer may miss his demolition deadline," a reporter wrote. "The city, which by law must award half of all its contracts to Detroit-based businesses, is expected to have trouble finding enough construction companies to do the job."[61]

Despite decades of streamlining, wheel-greasing, and general head-butting, Detroit's demolition machinery was a shambles. Crowbar-toting citizens could wreak more havoc than the city could on a good day. Only months after Archer was returned to office, a comprehensive study called for "a complete overhaul of the city's demolition process," noting that the mayor's dream of razing ten thousand dangerous structures was pie in the sky given Detroit's "seriously fragmented" bureaucracy and "ineffective inter-department communication." You would sooner see bunny rabbits hopping around in demolition helmets than the city wrecking so many buildings at its dysfunctional pace. One citizen had been trying to get a vacant house torn down on her street near Eight Mile Road for a decade. In 1988, the city's building and safety engineering director acknowledged her request and confirmed that, yep, the structure was as wretchedly deserving of destruction as she had described it. Then it was officially green-lighted for demolition—in 1996. Two years later, the house was still standing. The report finally recommended the drastic step of rolling the entire demolition process into one mega-agency to get rid of bureaucratic bobbling. Renewing his ardent appeal to the public, Mayor Archer was vowing to raze 3,655 houses in one year, but by late 1998 the city had yet to pay out any of the $60 million HUD had given it for demolition, with editorialists concluding that "demolition isn't likely to outpace the rate of property abandonment in Detroit for years—if at all."[62]

Fully three years later, the city's wrecking woes were still a code-red crisis. Vacant structures were decried as festering havens for rapists, crack dealers, arsonists, and marauding packs of feral dogs, prompting one reporter to describe the distinguishing architectural style of Detroit as that of the "gigantic, fecal-stained doghouse." The hand-wringing and violin-playing grew so absurd it made *Waiting for Godot* look like a model of lucid good government. "Understandably, the city has difficulty keeping up with its demolition needs," the *Detroit News* lectured in an editorial. "Since the 1960s, the rate of abandonment in the city has outpaced the city's ability to take vacant and dangerous structures down."[63] Even though Detroit at the time razed five buildings per day, costs by then had gone up to $7,100 each, the number of vacant structures had stayed steady for years at about twelve thousand, and the fitful bouts of wrecking had "done little to shrink the city's swollen inventory of empty buildings near schools," a source of particular outrage after a spate of ten schoolgirl rapes in late 1999, three of which were linked to derelict buildings.[64]

As bulldozers munched picturesquely on a junked building in the background, Mayor Archer, never one to miss a photo op where a toppling edifice might be squeezed into the frame, rolled out yet another plan in late 2000. With Shiva as my witness, he said, Detroit would raze eleven hundred vacant buildings in five months and bugger the city's never-ending backlog of bombed-out properties. At the time, the Detroit City Council, which under city ordinance had to approve all building condemnations, reviewed at most ninety-six structures per week, a figure Detroit's Buildings & Safety Engineering Department was begging to have jacked up to 252 to help bring the problem under control. As Deputy Mayor Freman Hendrix groused, the Department of Public Works, which was feeding demolition orders to sixteen contractors, didn't have enough orders from the council to keep the companies hopping.[65] The city administration suggested that the council hold hearings only on properties where a demolition was being challenged; the council refused but eventually began whipping through an average of a hundred fifty cases in its Monday sessions and cranked out as many as two fifty in a single day.[66] (Later, the city would even roll out "blight court," a streamlined administrative tribunal giving officers power to remedy building code violations by such tactics as attaching wages and bank accounts, staffed by three full-time hearing officers.[67]) By that time, Archer informed the electorate that $43 million of the $60 million HUD loan had wrecked 6,211 buildings since 1998, and he vowed to use the balance for more demolitions until October 2001.[68] All across the city, the blitz was under way, with the most dangerous abandoned buildings now tagged with a big yellow *D* for demolition. But there were still other snafus. Those *D*-marked buildings, as it happened, were not on a list to be boarded up by city workers. Why? "If they were boarded up, they wouldn't qualify as dangerous, and couldn't be demolished," said the city's interim public works director. "So for years the buildings sit open, where squatters and drug addicts take over."[69] And the violins played on. "The more they tear down, the more become abandoned," said one Detroit school principal. "Are we making any headway here?"[70]

The Perils of Detroit, Scene III, Act 1,652: exeunt Dennis Archer and bulldozer entourage; enter Mayor Kwame Kilpatrick. In early 2002, Kilpatrick's administration hit the ground running with yet another "emergency citywide cleanup program" and yet more press releases vowing to take down five thousand of Detroit's vacant buildings by that fall. In that budget year alone, Detroit earmarked $13.2 million for demolitions.[71] But just as the curtain went up—foiled again! By March, the city had run out of cash for its wrecking program and was scrounging around for private contributions for the effort, with the city's demolition firms flat out of luck. "The bottom line was, 'Ain't no more money; you'll have to wait,' " said Deb Taitt of Smash Wrecking Inc. as the city was pondering slashing its demolition contractor base from twenty firms to ten. One bright spot finally appeared on the dismal horizon in the form of seventy-year-old asphalt-magnate-turned-urban-booster Robert Thompson, who in 2003 gave the city $10 million to get the wrecking back on track. The cash, doled out in $1 million yearly installments, was expected to spring for up to fourteen hundred demolitions. Mayor Kilpatrick, at a news conference in the backyard of an abandoned drug haven that was shortly razed to the cheers of neighbors, mumbled a familiar refrain about how the gift would "create a huge dent" in the number of homes needing to be knocked down.[72] The scene, however, was not without a bit of Sturm und Drang. "As a backhoe crashed through the hovel's roof, unleashing a vile odor, onlookers called out: 'Oh!' 'Pray!' 'Good night!'," said a report. "Only one person seemed disappointed, a woman who disappeared after running toward the doomed structure yelling, 'That's my . . . house!' "[73]

As for the coda to this passion play, Detroit's political and business honchos are rushing pell-mell "to remove or renovate about a dozen of downtown's most blighted and dangerous buildings in time for the 2006 Super Bowl." The prekickoff festivities included a $700,000 low-interest loan to tear down the vacant Madison-Lenox Hotel (a busted-windowed, cinder-blocked "eyesore" just two blocks from Ford Field, the Super Bowl site). And other nearby towers were being pondered for removal, including the twenty-five-story Statler-Hilton Hotel, which had sat vacant for more than twenty years (it was still decked out in awnings unfurled for delegates of the 1980 Republican National Convention). Officials said the structure could cost $5 million to safely dismantle. "If a viable plan can't be developed, they need to come down," said George Jackson, who headed the quasipublic Detroit Economic Growth Corp. "We need to move forward and show our best face to the rest of the world."[74]

Urban historian Camilo José Vergara has obsessively chronicled America's corroding inner cities for more than thirty years, and he has a few ideas about what sort of "best face" Detroit might think about putting on for posterity. Whatever the neighbors might say, Vergara thinks blight has its own kind of beauty. "I became so attached to derelict buildings," he once wrote, "that sadness came not from seeing them overgrown and deteriorating—this often rendered them more picturesque—but from their sudden and violent destruction, which often left a big gap in the urban fabric."[75] Demolition, he said, left us bereft of the past, however bitter and unlovely it might seem. Vergara had an idea, a riff on planned shrinkage, but without the wrecking. "I propose that as a tonic for our imagination, as a call for renewal, as a place within our national memory," he wrote, "a dozen city blocks of pre-Depression skyscrapers be stabilized and left standing as ruins: an American Acropolis."[76] Of course the very thought was repulsive to forward-moving city boosters and football fanatics, who would have dismissed it out of hand. But the prospect of pulling down those long-vacant Detroit hotels made others cringe as well. "The skyscraper, from a biblical perspective, may be as much an act of pride as the Tower of Babel," an Episcopal theologian, Bill Kellerman, commented. "They are huge projections, they have a life and history, they may even be synonymous with idolatry. If they level those skyscrapers, I can imagine the huge psychic toll that it would take on the city."[77]

Detroit has been dubbed "the Capital of the Twentieth Century" for its pioneering embrace of the not-always-so-savory future. What bold vision, asked Vergara, would the twenty-first-century city embrace? So far, he said, "most of the city center has been 'saved' by the lack of funds for demolition,"[78] a cost estimated to be in the neighborhood of $200 million to toast all of Detroit's troubled and vacant downtown buildings. So put the cash toward wrecking the really vile doghouses. The future of the shrinking American metropolis, said Vergara, downtown Detroit, would look something like this: Place a moratorium on the razing of skyscrapers, "our most sublime ruins." Then, to shore up the structures and avoid accidents from falling fragments, the entire urban core of nearly one hundred troubled

Blight has its own beauty: Camilo José Vergara captured this Victorian mansion in Detroit's Brush Park neighborhood, ripe with picturesque dereliction.

buildings could be transformed into "a grand national historic park of play and wonder, an urban Monument Valley."[79] Roaming through this wonderland on Detroit's People Mover, visitors would be confronted with a sublime vista: "Midwestern prairie would be allowed to invade from the north. Trees, vines, and wildflowers would grow on roofs and out of windows; goats and wild animals—squirrels, possum, bats, owls, ravens, snakes, and insects—would live in the empty behemoths, adding their calls, hoots, and screeches to the smell of rotten leaves and animal droppings."[80]

It was a beautiful dream. The half-ruined city, the American Acropolis. But in Detroit, as in America, demolition is more than a tool of public safety. It's a pragmatic philosophy, a whole state of mind. "Survival is more a matter of forgetting than remembering," offered Dan Hoffman, the architect, reflecting upon the city's wrecking travails. The images of bulldozed buildings and imploding skyscrapers are powerful totems of our romance with the new. This is, after all, the American way, Hoffman said. "There is no future in the past."[81]

[9]

RUBBLE AND REVELATION

O N SEPTEMBER 11, 2001, the fall of the World Trade
Center broke the heart of the world and unmoored a
whole city. Stripped from the skyline of lower Manhattan, where they anchored the island for twenty-eight years, the
Twin Towers touched off an unprecedented public dialogue on
the sudden death of buildings. Almost as soon as the structures
vanished into that acrid plume of dust, stunned New Yorkers
and metropolites the world over began parsing the fresh wound
in Manhattan's midst. "It looked like a demolition," a witness
gasped. The phrase echoed again and again as the looped videotape of the day's events seared the nation's psyche. White ash.
Billowing dust. Lattices of glass and steel. Empty space where a
hundred-ten-story tower had been. "Oh my God," someone else
said, "there's nothing there."[1] It was a maimed skyline, an
aching emptiness, an apotheosis of the towers in their very absence—the tropes grew thick on the shattered curbstones
around those still-scorching sixteen acres. This was no ordinary
act of demolition, although contractors and their excavators
would shortly arrive on the scene. Still, the world's most iconic

twinned buildings had been plundered on live television, and their demise on September 11 opened a decisive new chapter in the story of unbuilding.

Part carpet bombing, part demolition site, and part hallowed ground, lower Manhattan's swath of ruin made for uniquely bewildering terrain, and its story was not easily told. Some sought meaning in the history of the Twin Towers themselves, reading clues to the buildings' fate in their monumental hubris. Others looked to war-ravaged London and Dresden-like desolation as referents for New York's loss, both in the unfathomable destruction and in the discomfiting beauty of the ruins. Even atomized Hiroshima—the original Ground Zero—proved poignant as survivors grappled with the toll, a touchstone of tragedy and, later, rebirth. As months of painstaking cleanup work wore on, the scene recalled the stoic dismantling of World War II detritus. And in the public's fierce need to testify to the buildings' dwindling remains, one thought of the emotional unbuilding of the Berlin Wall. Even as the World Trade Center attack itself was spoken of as a "demolition," wrecking contractors who served there embodied a profound force of cleansing. New Yorkers knew they could never rebuild 2,749 lives. But scouring the site down to bedrock would help the city heal.

On that cloudless September morning, the imminent collapse was horribly apparent to veteran implosion experts like Mark Loizeaux. Watching the events unfold on television, Mark knew immediately that the towers would fall. "Within a nanosecond. I said, 'It's coming down. And the second tower will fall first, because it was hit lower down,' " he recalled. "I thought, Somebody's got to tell the fire department to get out of there. I picked up the phone, dialled 411, got the number, and tried it—busy. So I called the Mayor's Office of Emergency Management."[2] It was in 7 World Trade Center. He couldn't get through. Within days, however, Loizeaux and other demolition contractors would be rumbling toward Ground Zero to help mobilize the recovery and cleanup operation—an eight-month-long minuet of excavators and cranes that would steadily work away 1.6 million tons of debris. What wreckers found upon arrival, though, troubled even seasoned emergency-response crews. "We've been doing surgical demolition for 15 years at collapses and other disasters, but nothing compares with this," one contractor said. "Physically, it's tough work, but mentally, it's even tougher, seeing all the dead bodies."[3] It wasn't a demolition man but a firefighter who framed the effort most affectingly. Raking his way through the remains in search of a fallen comrade, he turned to explain the unearthly sensation. "We're gardeners," he said, "in the garden of the dead."[4]

Even mundane wrecking tasks went beyond the pale in this Manhattan moonscape. When an ordinary wrecking ball made an appearance on the scene, for instance, it caused such commotion you'd have thought it was a two-hundred-pound, acetylene-spitting iguana. "In Connecticut they still let us knock buildings down with balls and cranes," one contractor, Jon Manafort, later told an audience of demolition conventioneers. "They hadn't seen that in New York in twenty years." (When he told crane rental firms that he intended to repeatedly loose a ten-ton piece of steel onto the ruined buildings, he said, "They looked at me like I had two heads.") Indeed, some who perused the demolition plan for one of the Twin Towers' ravaged adjacent buildings were flummoxed at the notion of a skull cracker whanging away, since safety concerns in the tight urban grid had all but made the wrecking ball verboten. But the demolitionists were undaunted, even though, once smashing began, the plan hit a few snags. Wrecking balls kept getting swallowed up by the rubble, so contractors used lengths of steel columns instead, trimmed to size and weight as needed. This did the trick to mind-numbing effect. The engineer Donald Friedman described the monotonous assault of an old, battle-weary Manitowoc crane. The machine's arm rarely moved, straying only when the crane operator was seeking out new, crushable chunks of the building. The weight would be racked up to the top of the crane arm, and then dropped at free-fall speed onto the target. "If the weight hit into still-intact interior floor slabs, there would be a thud from the concrete and a small spray of dust. If it hit a steel beam, there was a dull clang." It was an unglamorous affair, almost absurd in its slow, thunking pace—and yet strangely defiant. It was, in other words, wrecking at its finest. "Watching the work," Friedman remarked, "I became convinced that the operator was one of the best on the site."[5]

Thus was dispatched, one solemn thud at a time, the last of the remaining structures at Ground Zero. Well before the final fifty-eight-ton steel column was wheeled out of the pit by flatbed truck on May 30, 2002, under ceremonial police escort, wreckers had grungily made what many around the site considered a far more profound transformation. More than even the torching away of that famous, fencelike shard of the Twin Towers' facade, the battering to the ground of these last bits of the World Trade Center complex "changed the appearance of the site from one of devastation to one that could pass for ordinary excavation and construction."[6]

Grinding away grim totems of disaster was, of course, a

wrecking industry forte by the time destructionists got to Ground Zero. But there would be plenty more memento-blotting contracts to be issued. As of 2005, at least five other buildings around the trade center site were slated to be destroyed, due to a mélange of structural, environmental, and bad-juju afflictions. A fifteen-story classroom building called Fiterman Hall, for instance, was gored by the collapsing 7 World Trade Center and ended up looming as a "ravaged ghost" and "dispiriting reminder" begging to be brought down. While some weren't exactly egging on the excavators (the architect who had just renovated the structure when it was mauled on September 11 likened the pending demolition to "a kick in the teeth"), wrecking was again the paradoxical path to salvation. "Through much of the ground zero precinct, hope is measured in the promise of construction," a reporter wrote. "At Fiterman Hall, hope will take the form of demolition."[7]

No building's destruction was called a brighter klieg light of hope than that of the stricken, forty-story Deutsche Bank tower at 130 Liberty Street. This stolid September 11 survivor was deemed irrecoverable, in the words of Governor George Pataki, "an ever-present reminder of the darkest moment in our past." The 536-foot-high building, directly south of Ground Zero, had been rent with a fifteen-story gash by falling pieces of 2 World Trade Center and lost seventeen hundred windows in the bargain. While Pataki was hefting the ceremonial sledgehammer, however, it became quickly apparent that demolition was not the slam dunk the governor wanted it to be. "Sentiment downtown was overwhelmingly in favor of repairing it if possible," a report said about the property, "the thought of another building coming down being too much for many people to bear."[8] While some engineers applauded the building's resilience and pined for its rehabilitation, Deutsche Bank deemed the structure infested with "a unique cocktail of highly hazardous substances" (asbestos, lead, mercury, dioxins, polynuclear aromatic hydrocarbons) that rendered the thirty-year-old tower a total loss. "Planning, psychology and politics also dictate demolition," a reporter wrote. "State officials call the building a blight and a grisly memento, an impediment to progress."[9] Plus, they wanted a new tower hewing to the trade center site's master plan by Studio Daniel Libeskind, including a new half-acre Liberty Park. The $45 million demolition contract eventually went to Gilbane Building Company of Providence, Rhode Island, but not before state officials began delicately referring to the job as a "deconstruction" to make clear that this would be no wig-flipping implosion.[10] No, siree, officials said: "For many reasons—the presence of contaminants, the nearness of other buildings and utility lines, and the trauma that would surely result from the sight of another dust plume downtown—there is no talk of imploding 130 Liberty Street."[11] And so the community girded for a year-long deconstruction of what was dubbed "one of the world's most contaminated buildings in one of the world's most densely populated neighborhoods"[12]—not by cathartic blasts of dynamite but by dust-suppressed debris chute. (Downtown residents, it turned out, would be waiting a little longer. Gilbane's contract was subsequently canceled after the project became mired in environmental disputes, and federal officials decided scaffolding would need to be erected around the entire structure to prevent the release of contaminants. The job was sent back out to bid.) To many, when the end did eventually come, it would be an appropriate demise. "The sense of this departure is that of a steamship slowly slipping away down the river," said Fredric M. Bell, executive director of the New York chapter of the American Institute of Architects. "Something eroding rather than being instantaneously removed is probably what's needed."[13]

The World Trade Center was deep-sixed with a horrid vengeance. No gently swaying vessel eased into the current of time, this was a first-class calamity, "the psychological equivalent of the sinking of the Titanic," one critic wrote, "an archetypal disaster" that wrecked our faith in forward-marching progress and invincible technology.[14] Everyone has a story about September 11, about the day the Twin Towers crumbled and everything changed. About laundry lists and naval brass and accelerated depreciation and how none of it was real. Or so we thought. Slowly—or quickly, as it seemed—the numbness receded, the markets reopened, the arbitrage commenced, and the acetylene flowed. But one thing did change with that walloping blow: The residue of the World Trade Center remains in the way we think about buildings, and the measure we take of their absence. "The image of the two towers collapsing shook our collective unconscious," architect Daniel Libeskind, who would design the master plan for the trade center site, later wrote. "We take it for granted that buildings this big, this heavy-footed and deeply grounded, will stand no matter what. After September 11, it seemed that all of our foundations, philosophical as well as physical, were under attack and might also collapse."[15]

The language of unbuilding has rarely been richer than it was in the wake of September 11. Erosion, erasure, meltingness—a whole new vocabulary welled up to speak of the Twin

Towers' absence. What was once bluntly "razed" was now given minutely graded emotional qualifiers. In one of the finest essays about Ground Zero, Verlyn Klinkenborg, a member of the *New York Times* editorial board, described the lost towers with astonishing nuance. "A great berg of the past simply broke off and drifted away," he wrote two months after the attacks. "That sudden crease in time will remain one of the critical psychological facts in our lives, a reminder of how illusory, how elliptical the sense of time really is. That was the day the World Trade Center plundered our imaginations." The shock that the towers had fallen, he said, rapidly turned to shock that they had ever stood there to fall. Almost moments after they were gone, you suddenly couldn't recall what they had looked like, where precisely they were planted. "Their presence was something New Yorkers took for granted," he went on, "and the depth of that grantedness—a measure of how long they had lurked in our eye—is the depth of the shock that came that morning." And so it was that the Twin Towers' ruins came to hold such an awesome attraction, over and above any human remains they might have harbored. While the wrecking crews thunked their way toward a broom-swept Ground Zero, the compulsion to touch the ruins only grew stronger. The garden of the dead was a last link to whoever we were before that chunk of time vanished from our lives, and when the final torqued beam or singed column was gone, Klinkenborg wrote, "we'll discover that it was the ruins that mattered to us, emotionally, and not the vacancy that remains or anything constructed afterward."[16]

Even before they were built, the Twin Towers were weirdly dogged by the imagery of destruction. Their enormity seemed to inspire apocalyptic turns of phrase from nearly every thoughtful writer who weighed in on the matter. "As presently designed, this fearful instrument of urbicide will be not only the tallest, but unquestionably one of the ugliest buildings in the world," wrote Wolf Von Eckardt in 1966, introducing the word *urbicide* to mean something like the assassination of the city. The "arrogant twins," he predicted in a zinger-filled tirade, "will woefully clobber Manhattan's beautiful skyline."[17] It was a searching time for cities in the throes of a new generation of super-tall buildings, and others, too, saw the World Trade Center as a killing floor of colossal proportions. "Who's afraid of the big, bad buildings?" Ada Louise Huxtable asked that same year. "Everyone, because there are so many things about gigantism that we just don't know." She added: "The Trade Center towers could be the start of a new skyscraper age or the biggest tombstones in the world."[18] The doom-mongers' dire appraisals were confirmed when, upon completion, the Twin Towers squashed the city around them—demolition by sheer Brobdingnagian bravado. "To anyone gawking from a car window during those last few grimy miles through New Jersey to the Holland Tunnel," a contemporary said, "it appears that there *is* no skyline any more; just those looming twin towers."[19] Unwittingly putting his finger on the eventual heart of the matter was seventy-six-year-old architecture critic Lewis Mumford, who kvetched that tall buildings were "outmoded concepts" and the stuff of "Victorian thinking." Such a non sequitur in the cityscape couldn't possibly keep standing; the wonky logic of their construction, their whole flawed raison d'être, their very Titanicness, would have to bring their fall. Mumford finally grumbled that "the Trade Center's fate is to be ripped down as nonsensical."[20]

That chilling prophecy would ultimately pay off in spades,

but there were still other wreckerly ironies heaping up around the still-rising behemoths. The Twin Towers would get a jump on urbicide when the authorities condemned a motley assortment of 164 buildings that had rudely been blocking the trade center site. Even then, it turned out, the destruction had a powerful allure, the ruins an instant magnetism. One writer visiting the work in progress stepped out of a cab on West Street and was dazzled by the remnants of an old ferry slip, which was being demolished to make way for excavated landfill in the Hudson River. "Only the façade was intact," she wrote, "with high Victorian windows and a handless clockface. At the sides, the steel and wood of the old walls were falling away, dripping down like lace, and the sun was reflected hotly in a second-floor window that still had glass in it. This dreamy remnant looked ready for instant collapse."[21] Beauty was in the eye of the rubble-drunk beholder.

Others quickly pointed out, in the wake of the disaster, that the Twin Towers were only the latest catastrophe du jour in a long-running conversation about the creative destruction of Gotham. The vocabulary might have been novel, but grimly searching scholars found that it had all been said before, again and again. Indeed, there were "fantasies, nightmares, and premonitions of New York's destruction that have pervaded New York and American culture for more than a century," wrote the historian Max Page. "Long before 2001," he continued, "American culture had returned repeatedly to the theme of New York's destruction almost as a leitmotif—a tic we couldn't stop. In movies and literature, painting and photography, software and advertising, New York has been destroyed, by fire, by bomb, by flood, by riot, by earthquake, by wrecking ball, and by monsters."[22] The aesthetics of destruction were so baroquely developed in the city, Page thought, that Gotham simply outclassed all others in the dubious genre of "disaster porn": "no place looks better destroyed than does New York."[23]

Pioneering this artful analysis of destruction was the eloquent Henry James, who in 1906 called New York "that concert of the expensively provisional,"[24] a place full of "the new landmarks crushing the old quite as violent children stamp on snails and caterpillars."[25] When you hear that such and such a house or whole block is getting flattened, you gasp, James writes, at "the strangeness of the moral so pointed. It rings out like the crack of that lash in the sky, the play of some mighty teamster's whip, which ends by affecting you as the poor New-Yorker's one association with the idea of 'powers above.' " This whip, James felt, was creative destruction personified, the sole defining fact about the city, and had he been writing a few decades later, he would doubtless have invoked the wrecking ball instead. For James, the battering of memory to the ground was no accident but a dread necessity in the land of the perpetually new. The minute we take for granted some structure—two towers, even— is the minute we get yanked through that sharp crease in time. As James concluded his parable of the whip: " 'No'—this is the tune to which the whip seems flourished—'there's no step at which you shall rest, no form, as I'm constantly showing you, to which, consistently with my interests, you *can*.' "[26]

The architectural historian Manfredo Tafuri summed up these apocalyptic yarns as the record of our struggle to figure out "how to come to terms with the anguish of urban dynamism."[27] One time-honored strategy, in the aftermath of September 11, was to look for loveliness in the wrenched-open city, to seek out tenderness in the still-hot cinders. "Is it unseemly now or ever to talk about the beauty of the World Trade Center's ruins?"[28] a reporter wondered eight months after the attack. It was an idle question at that late date, for many who roved among the rubble had been promptly thunderstruck by the site's sublime grandeur. As wrecking got under way, acetylene torches knifed through slabs of metal and left liquid slag dripping picturesquely from the cut. Great rivers of red and yellow sparks rained down upon the debris, at times so thickly they obscured the wreckage itself. "It was incredibly beautiful," Donald Friedman would write, "in exactly the same way a volcanic eruption can be beautiful: it was dangerous and represented enormous destruction, but the visual effect of that shower of sparks was the kind of thing that some artists spend their lives trying to create."[29] For others, the collapse of the towers became an instant ready-made. In an extraordinary aside, the writer Elizabeth Wurtzel told a Canadian journalist that the Twin Towers' collapse was a ravishing performance in its own right. "It was a most amazing sight in terms of sheer elegance," she said. "It fell like water. It just slid, like a turtleneck going over someone's head. It was just beautiful."[30] Many were offended by her comments and thought Wurtzel should be sent directly back to her padded cell, but that was nothing compared to the fury loosed upon seventy-three-year-old composer Karlheinz Stockhausen. Getting a bit carried away with himself, Stockhausen told a clutch of Hamburg journalists shortly after the attacks that the coordinated spectacle was "the greatest work of art that is possible in the whole cosmos,"[31] a sort of horrendous *Gesamtkunstwerk*—a feat encompassing all the various performing arts in one jaw-dropping fell swoop. The composer immediately clarified his rambling remarks, but by that time reporters had already rushed to phone in the sensational tidbit (ATTACKS CALLED GREAT ART was a typical take in the coming days), and the lynch-Stockhausen mob had soon gotten his scheduled performances ditched left and right.

There was beauty to be found in New York on that day, whether or not it was seemly, and not even the camera-confiscating National Guard could stamp it out. As any implosion junkie will confess, falling-down buildings inspire. Even the *Wall Street Journal* was pressed to admit that the September 11 spectacle made for "insidiously brilliant theater."[32] And having surveyed the smoldering ruins, no less an authority than Philippe de Montebello, director of the Metropolitan Museum of Art, would argue that the famous skeletal steel remnant of one of the towers was a potent, Piranesian landmark. "As a symbol of survival, it is already, in its own way, a masterpiece," he wrote, "and so it should remain."[33]

If many sought solace in the presence of the ruins—the life-affirming remnants certainly packed populist appeal—others followed Klinkenborg's tack, dipping into the deeper psychic eddies of the Twin Towers' absence. Some deemed the violent destruction an apotheosis for the trade center. Rather than blotting them from memory, the collapse rocketed them into posterity. "It is now stronger as a monument," said Allan Wexler, an architect and conceptual artist and admirer of the towers. "We'll never forget it. It will live in our memories. It's like the grassy knoll. It becomes a metaphysical structure at this point."[34] The sudden disappearance of those buildings showed New Yorkers like almost nothing before them how powerful, how present, even, absence could be. It was a hard lesson to absorb in a city with a well-known *horror vacui*. "We have a bias toward wanting to fill things back up, if indeed we notice that they're empty," said Richard Plunz, city planning professor at Columbia University. "You need a great urban design scheme for emptiness."[35]

The critic Herbert Muschamp built on this line of thinking when he soon began sighing contentedly over "the cultural value of the void itself."[36] The creative thing about destruction wasn't the blinding opportunity to build after you had sloughed off all the rubbish. It was the rubbish-free slate, period. And what's more, Muschamp said, voids of all sorts offered a bold new paradigm for reinventing the city. "Emptiness, obscurity, failure, bleakness, pallor—such noir terms are not found in the vocabulary of civic success with which urban revitalization programs are typically promoted," he wrote. "But these terms should be permissible wherever culture comes up." Is "failed space," he wondered, even more conducive to creativity than the tower-filled skyline? But of course. "Think of Goethe pondering Roman ruins. Postindustrial cities that are seeking to remake themselves as cultural centers might also benefit from pondering the success of failure: the glamour of their own collapse."[37] Suddenly, weed-choked lots, half-wrecked buildings, and picturesquely ruined plazas were brimming with opportunity. Such scenes of failure, and we can include the leveled World Trade Center among them, were redolent with what Goethe might have called the sublime: an uncanny sensation of fear, awe, vastness, infinitude, mystery, and the unknowable. Demolition was suddenly a profoundly generative act. Viewed from the far end of the looking glass, it was actually the builders who destroyed, and the destroyers who created. "Architecture, we forget at our peril, is inherently violent," Muschamp elsewhere wrote. "It invariably subtracts from the range of available possibilities, especially the perennially attractive option of building nothing at all. In this sense, construction sites are crime scenes."[38]

In the ruin-addled days after September 11, as busloads of camera-toting pilgrims converged upon lower Manhattan, there was no shortage of infinitude and mystery. Many of those who came to bear witness, though, didn't need a tutorial on "space noir" to help them parse the bleak panorama before them. Some had lived through it themselves, a half century earlier, during the ruin and decades-long reconstruction of Europe following World War II. As the excavators rumbled away beyond police barricades, Ground Zero summoned visions of the slow sifting of London; the implosion of half-blasted buildings all across Germany, like those I found so affectingly chronicled in *Detonation Deutschland*; and, decades later, the exuberant reunification of Berlin. Somehow, the memory of the war and its aftermath—that much greater tale of violence and resurrection—helped New Yorkers fathom their own moment in history.

In his poem "Little Gidding," T. S. Eliot alluded to the ravaging of wartime London as part of his meditation on time and mortality in the *Four Quartets*. Eliot saw the ruin of buildings as a full stop, a period inked in motes of brick and mortar. "Dust in the air suspended," he wrote, "Marks the place where a story ended."[39] The story for demolitionists, however, was just beginning. More than 16 million people saw their homes wrecked by bomb destruction during World War II, with more than 4.5 million housing units completely toasted. Just as in America sixty years hence, wreckers rose to the challenge. With London and Coventry knee-deep in rubble by the fall of 1940, a phalanx of

13,500 troops from the Royal Engineers got busy ripping down war-ravaged structures. And as in New York, the work could seem remarkably unsophisticated. Most of the ruins were yanked down with typical British no-nonsense: A large piece of timber was strapped across a window or door, with a steel rope lashed around the timber and then hooked to a waiting truck. The driver hit the petrol, and down went the wall. Thus was born the National Federation of Demolition Contractors, the British trade group, which frankly admits that when it was

The ruins of Coventry Cathedral, which was devastated by a German air raid in 1940, became perversely stirring monuments in their own right. They were preserved for posterity.

formed in 1941, "there was much amateurism in the world of demolition," with contractors "relying on brute strength rather than thought out procedures and special equipment." But brute strength they had in quantity, and the proof was in the rubble. So much of it had been carted away that it even became a highly sought-after export commodity. Around that same time, New York's FDR Drive was being constructed, which ran along the east side of Manhattan. "Much of the landfill on which it is constructed consists of the rubble of buildings destroyed during the Second World War by the Luftwaffe's blitz on London and Bristol," the historian Kenneth T. Jackson wrote. "Convoys of ships returning from Great Britain carried the broken masonry in their holds as ballast."[40]

Nor was debris removal the only contribution destructionists made to the war effort. In 1943, the United Kingdom was faced with a chronic shortage of heavy metal—at least a million tons was expected to be requisitioned for the good fight—and there was only one place to get it. "Much of this will come from steel girders in parts of buildings, structures, machinery, plant or articles which are not serving an immediate purpose," *Builder* magazine announced. "The necessity for this somewhat drastic move lies in the fact that the sources of metal, such as blitzed buildings and iron railings, have by now been largely depleted, if not actually exhausted." Grappling with this incredible state of affairs, *Builder* counseled readers that demolition of partly erected buildings and abandoned works would offer "the most readily available source" of metal, although it was conceded that property owners might have a few choice words to say about what exactly constituted material "suitable for scrap." Should the wrecker come calling, however, this was no time for nostalgia. "Constant supplies of metal for our war machine," the editors said sternly, "must be maintained."[41]

It was that same year, during the rebuilding of Britain's war-ravaged House of Commons, that Winston Churchill uttered his oft-quoted line about the special relationship between structures and souls. "We shape our buildings," he said, "and afterwards our buildings shape us."[42] To this truism has to be added the corollary: Our rubble shapes us, too. The nuanced reaction to the World Trade Center remains would have been unthinkable without the exhaustive debate touched off in ruin-ripe England. The astute chronicler of ruins Christopher Woodward, commenting just before September 11, wrote of "the perverse fertility of ruin, and of how genius germinates in architectural decay."[43] Woodward was summing up a long line of intensely observant British thinkers who had found in the war's architectural carnage a whole new realm of rubble artistry. At the height of the Blitz, the art historian Kenneth Clark declared that "bomb damage is in itself Picturesque." (As one scholar wryly commented: "This could only have been said in Britain."[44]) Like those eventually visited upon Manhattan, the ruins of World War II bombardment were fluorescent with meaning. Artists and intellectuals couldn't get enough of the stuff. The rubble, wrote one painter dispatched to document the destruction, "revealed new beauties in unexpected appositions."[45] Bomb damage was beautiful, and Londoners weren't shy about saying they wanted it to stay that way. "A ruin is more than a collection of debris," a group of artists and architects asserted shortly after the Blitz, fighting to preserve London's ruined churches as picturesque war memorials. "It is a place with its own individuality, charged with its own emotion and atmosphere and drama, of grandeur, of nobility, or of charm. These qualities must be preserved as carefully as the broken stones which are their physical embodiment."[46] The group pleaded, "Save us, then, some of our ruins."[47]

Nowhere was the saga of ruined buildings in Britain better told than in the writings of John Harris, who rambled through the English countryside as an aspiring architectural historian between 1946 and 1960. Harris visited more than two hundred houses, many of them suffering the delayed effects of the Blitz—some requisitioned by the military, others simply abandoned, their owners lacking the cash to fund exorbitant repairs. "In my nomadic travels," Harris wrote, "I discovered a situation that had no parallel elsewhere in Europe: a country of deserted country houses, many *in extremis,* most in a surreal limbo awaiting their fate." That fate, of course, was meted out by a familiar array of implements: "the sledgehammer, pick-axe and ball-and-chain, and frequently explosives."[48] Vast, once luxurious estates were put out of their misery to Harris's unending dismay. In 1952, Harewood Park in Herefordshire was "blown up by the local militia."[49] Willoughby Hall in Lincolnshire, too, met a fiery end. "The mode of Willoughby's demise was not uncommon: on 4 November 1964 the ruin was spectacularly blown up by 320 charges of dynamite, evoking a smug smile from its farming owner, and hurrahs from the assembled public and local reporters."[50]

By 1955, Harris wrote, one house was demolished every two and a half days. In that year, estates succumbed to incredible indignities. There was Fairford Park in Gloucestershire, for example, visited by Harris with his comrade the decorator Felix Harbord. Parts of the building dated to 1661 and included work by Sir John Soane. Tipped off to the demolition-in-progress, the two hastened to the mesmerizing scene. "Felix said the house was like a martyr who had had his tongue torn out, then his eyes pierced, before being half-strangled prior to burning at the stake," Harris recalled. The foreman gave them the all-clear, and the visitors clambered around the dying structure, boggled at the destruction—an unforgettable panorama of unbuilding. "The roof was off, the interiors were gutted, and the lovely Restoration doorway with its curly scrolled pediment joined to the window above was about to be removed. The Gibbsian façade stood precariously, without support at the back. Lying on the lawn were piles of Restoration panelling, some marbelised woodwork, and dismantled Soanic chimney-pieces. At the rear a bonfire burned acridly."[51] In the heat of such investigations, Harris owned to what he called "my morbid fascination with empty, derelict houses."[52] The unbuilding was intensely absorbing, a sensual and emotional thrill so potent it was a grave disappointment when the wreckers finished up their funereal work. "A house in process of dismemberment," Harris said, "is more affecting than one that is gone, leaving an empty site."[53]

The pièce de résistance in this respect was Burwell Park in Lincolnshire, an estate Harris visited in 1957. "It was now there occurred one of the oddest things I have ever experienced at any country house," he recounted. "Outside the place was deserted, but as I stood on the threshold I could hear shuffling inside." It was occupied, he concluded. He knocked and waited for the owner's tirade, but none came. There was just more shuffling. He knocked again and called out; to no avail. "I tried the door, it opened—and suddenly, as if caught up in a torrent, I was engulfed by a flock of sheep. They shot across the brambled lawn

and disappeared into a field."[54] Inside this makeshift barn—
other rooms contained "hundreds of sacks of potatoes and
mountainous heaps of grain"—Harris found rooms of Palladian
style laced with rococo decoration, all filled with "elegant balus-
ters," "superlative mahogany construction," and "plaster per-
fection." The structure, dating to 1760, was thought to be one
of the most perfect houses of its date in the nation. A year later,
alerted to Burwell Park's destruction, Harris hastened to the site.
It was another scene of exhilaration. "Silhouetted on the skyline
were three men with picks precariously hacking away at the rococo plasterwork and bricks. I just stood there watching plaster
decoration fall to the ground," Harris said. "On the lawn lay a
pile of chimney-piece overmantels, panelling, and the black-and-
white marble floor, which had been prised up. On a side terrace
a crackling bonfire consumed the sawn-up stairs and timber
beams."[55]

Clearly the lingering effects of the Blitz would haunt this
generation of architectural thinkers. Harris's field notes were
given fictional treatment in the English writer Graham Greene's
1954 story "The Destructors," a hauntingly resonant tale about
a young gang of boys in postwar England who meticulously take
to demolishing a two-hundred-year-old, war-damaged house by
the famed English architect Sir Christopher Wren. The house,
jagged and dark, supported by struts and leaning heavily between two bomb sites, had been narrowly saved from destruction, its fanlight miraculously unbroken by the blasts. It was
inhabited by a former builder and decorator, who served as the
site's benevolent caretaker. But the gang determines to do the
work the bomb had left undone, with unremitting attention to
detail. Parquet blocks are heaved up, dining-room skirting

boards chiseled out, and washbasins and china smashed with a sledgehammer. Then the plaster is cracked, joists sawn through, mortar worried out of the bricks, and even pillows and sheets torn up with a carving knife found in the kitchen—a surreal scene of destruction riddled with "the unfamiliar shadows of half things, broken things, former things."[56] The boys, intent upon their work, seemed to embody the torrential bouts of unbuilding that threatened to overwhelm the nation. As Greene wrote: "Streaks of light came in through the closed shutters where they worked with the seriousness of creators—and destruction after all is a form of creation. A kind of imagination had seen this house as it had now become."[57] Finally the remaining frame is yanked over by an unsuspecting lorry driver to whose truck the boys had fixed a rope. The driver stops at the commotion, gets out to survey the scene, and is convulsed with laughter as the house's owner, a gravely befuddled Mr. Thomas, looks on. "One moment the house had stood there with such dignity between the bomb-sites like a man in a top hat, and then, bang, crash, there wasn't anything left—not anything." The jolly driver says, "I'm sorry. I can't help it, Mr. Thomas. There's nothing personal, but you got to admit it's funny."[58]

Morbid hilarity was by then a practiced response to the nation's devastation. And laughter could have been the only rational rejoinder to Lewis Mumford, who weighed in to comment that, really, the Luftwaffe could have bothered to blow things up a little more thoroughly in England while they were at it. "There is a sense in which the demolition that is taking place through the war has not yet gone far enough," Mumford wrote, lamenting the dawn of a modern, mechanized world he thought was "confused, inefficient, depressing," just the empty shell of an "increasingly purposeless society." All the new high-rise "machines for living" must come down, Mumford declared. "We must therefore continue to do, in a more deliberate and rational fashion, what the bombs have done by brutal hit-or-miss, if we are to have space enough to live in and produce the proper means of living."[59]

If the Brits were fending off Mumford's postwar bulldozer strikes, their counterparts in Germany had no such worries. Rubble was so thick on the ground that, as writer W. G. Sebald recounted of a childhood trip to Munich, "few things were so clearly linked in my mind with the word 'city' as mounds of rubble, cracked walls, and empty windows through which you saw the empty air."[60] The ravaging of Germany in the Second World War was impressive even by Mumford's high standards. Three and a half million homes were destroyed; in more than forty German cities, the proportion of built-up area totally ruined exceeded 50 percent.[61] There were 31.1 cubic meters of rubble for every person in Cologne. The Dresden firestorm ravaged more than ninety-five thousand dwelling units and razed 85 percent of the city center; each citizen could claim fifty-six cubic yards of rubble (including the remains, it was noted with a dash of irony, of thirty-six insurance company buildings).[62] The statistics were staggering, Sebald writes, "but we do not grasp what it all actually meant. The destruction, on a scale without historical precedent, entered the annals of the nation, as it set about rebuilding itself, only in the form of vague generalizations." In short, "it never became an experience capable of public decipherment."[63]

A few artists and intellectuals did sift through the rubble and attempt to frame the new aesthetic. Beginning in 1945, for instance, Herbert List recorded "the beauty of the desolation that was once Munich: perfectly composed and lit, the remains of the buildings and sculptures appear frighteningly impressive."[64] But it wasn't until the symbolic finale—much later and by sledge-hammer—of this chapter in German history that the country would take full stock of its ruination. That was the rubbling of the Berlin Wall.

Bales of barbed wire littered the East German border on the night of November 11, 1989, heaped aside in one of the most politically charged demolition acts of our time. As hundreds of self-deputized rubble-rousers deliriously swung pickaxes and sledgehammers, a group took one of the first three-meter-tall bites out of the Berlin Wall. "From the East German side we

East German border guards gaze politely from above as a rubble-rouser takes a bite out of the Berlin Wall on November 11, 1989.

could hear the sound of heavy machines," recounted Andreas Ramos. "Every time a drill poked through, everyone cheered." Soldiers peered out from one narrow hole and then jubilantly reached through to shake hands. "Someone lent me a hammer and I knocked chunks of rubble from the wall, dropping several handfuls into my pocket," Ramos recalled. "The wall was made of cheap, brittle concrete: the Russians had used too much sand and water."[65] Predictably, perhaps, that night of rubble and revelry would culminate with the wall disappearing, all right—into the ever-fluid space of the commodity. "Most of the graffiti-covered concrete has been bulldozed, jack-hammered into rubble, sent to museums around the world, hoarded by collectors or sold as souvenirs."[66] One of those chunks, incidentally, went to Ronald Reagan, who in 1987 had glowered over the breach between East and West and delivered his famous "Tear down this wall" oration. "Like a modern-day Joshua at the battle of Jericho," an account said, Reagan would live to see the day, merrily writing about the demolition: "I never dreamed that in less than three years the wall would come down and a 6,000-pound section of it would be sent to me for my presidential library."[67]

Some weren't so tickled by the ordeal, however, particularly those who had suffered through life on the other side. As one woman from East Berlin haltingly recalled: "I did not go over there right away, I just was not able to go there. I was afraid of it all. I was afraid of it all, of the ravaging, of the opening, of all those people, of the bustle. For me it was a totally strange world, as if you suddenly were supposed to climb to the moon. I had anxiety attacks; I did not go."[68] Indeed, as the wall was coming down, German author Peter Schneider remarked that the mental metropolis would be difficult to destroy, no matter how many sledgehammer-happy citizens descended upon the physical barrier. "Demolishing the Wall in the head," he said, "will take longer than it will take for a demolition firm to do the same job."[69] Others noted that the frenzied destruction-seekers had done their job so thoroughly that almost not a shred of the wall was left to remind future generations what all the hubbub was about. "When the wall fell, there was a feeling of liberation and people wanted to tear it down as fast as they possibly could," a preservation director remarked. "It is understandable, but now there is an awareness that at least parts of the wall need to be preserved."[70]

Perversely, the fall of the wall has vastly accelerated the demolition of large swaths of German cities, particularly in eastern Germany, which has shrunk by 3.1 million residents since the barrier came down. All those seeking the good life left in their wake 1.3 million empty apartments (40 percent of which were Communist-era housing experiments gone awry, and the rest built after reunification as part of a disastrous government tax incentive plan to boost construction). In Germany's fastest-shrinking city, Hoyerswerda, which is about seventy-five miles southeast of Berlin, 39 percent of the residents have bailed out, and the city has been hard at work demolishing three thousand apartments, with five thousand more set to be razed by 2007.[71] Back in Berlin proper, moreover, the rubble is still flying high. "One of the issues confronting Berlin today is that it is repeating a form of destruction—urban erasure, if you will—that was prevalent from the late 1940s through 1970s," one commentator said. Only one-tenth of Berlin's buildings were left after World War II and its aftermath; 90 percent of the city had to be rebuilt. Now, the old palaces and their bitter memories were getting bulldozed by the dozen. "In the former West, but even more so in the former East, significant buildings that should have landmark status are being demolished because they are on the wrong side of the ideological fence."[72] The upshot is a city that perfectly illuminates the tetchy dynamic of destruction. "It is a landscape of exposed nerve-endings," said Berlin architect Wilfried Wang, "in a constant state of becoming."[73]

Speaking before September 11, World Trade Center chronicler Eric Darton called the Twin Towers "an icon of the world's skyline second only to the unforgettable mushroom cloud 'logo' of the hydrogen bomb."[74] At the time this must have seemed an unwarranted bit of braggadocio from a known trade center critic, but it would turn out to be all too close to the mark. The devastation of Japan in World War II would prove a final touchstone for the ruins in Manhattan—a reality check that both shed light on the traumatic destruction and offered a mute testimony to the power of rebirth.

It has been called "the largest and most spectacular demolition job ever undertaken by man."[75] The atomic devastation of Hiroshima savaged sixty-five thousand of the city's ninety thousand buildings, and nearly all the remaining structures sustained at least superficial blows. (And that was a drop in the bucket compared to the total 2.2 million buildings razed throughout the entire Japanese campaign—almost half of all structures in the sixty-six targeted cities. About 30 percent of the entire urban population of Japan lost their homes.[76]) The massive wrecking efficiency of the mushroom cloud is by now well known. According to the U.S. Strategic Bombing Survey, when the atomic bombs hit Hiroshima and Nagasaki, respectively, on August 6 and August 9, 1945, one hundred thousand people were killed. The bombs detonated with "a tremendous flash of blue-white light,"[77] then a blast of glare and heat. Following this came a powerful pressure wave and a rumbling explosion. The city's heavy clay roof tiles bubbled for up to a mile around; exposed granite blocks spalled; brick buildings were flattened; wood construction suffered total collapse; glass windows blew out at distances up to five miles; window frames, doors, and partitions were hurled at high velocity through any building that did not collapse.[78] There wasn't even any rubble, so to speak, due to the combustible nature of buildings in Japan. "All that remained were great expanses of scorched, flattened wasteland scored by the trace of street patterns and a moonlike scatter of bomb craters."[79]

Even amid this utter devastation, there were odd, touching signs in the wasteland. Radiation from the blast, it turned out, had hot-wired the underground organs of plants, setting off teeming flusters of botanic life all throughout the city. (This flourish of life, incidentally, was also reported after the Great Fire of 1666, where survivors were "flabbergasted by a spectacular and unexpected bloom of 'fire flowers,' the famous London Rocket."[80]) As John Hersey described the scene in Hiroshima in acutely observed prose in 1946:

> Over everything—up through the wreckage of the city, in gutters, along the riverbanks, tangled among tiles and tin roofing, climbing on charred tree trunks—was a blanket of fresh, vivid, lush, optimistic green; the verdancy rose even from the foundations of ruined houses. Weeds already hid the ashes, and wild flowers were in

bloom among the city's bones. The bomb had not only left the underground organs of plants intact; it had stimulated them. Everywhere were bluets and Spanish bayonets, goosefoot, morning glories and day lilies, the hairy-fruited bean, purslane and clotbur and sesame and panic grass and feverfew. Especially in a circle at the center, sickle senna grew in extraordinary regeneration, not only standing among the charred remnants of the same plant but pushing up in new places, among bricks and through cracks in the asphalt. It actually seemed as if a load of sickle-senna seed had been dropped along with the bomb.[81]

The World Trade Center couldn't top what happened in Japan in 1945. But the legacy of those mushroom clouds loomed large over the Twin Towers' remains. The trade center cleanup proceeded ahead of schedule and under budget, as reports duly noted, and yet somehow Verlyn Klinkenborg was right. There are no ruins downtown; rebirth comes in fits and starts; spectacular destruction brought no panic grass or feverfew. It will take time yet to understand the profound loss of that day.

It's a feeling intellectuals worrying over the city had already been getting used to. You can't compete with the bomb. "Beckett is the last writer to shape the way we think and see," Don DeLillo wrote in a 1991 novel. "After him, the major work involves midair explosions and crumbled buildings. This is the new tragic narrative."[82]

1 0

DEMOLITION DERBY

PEOPLE LOVE TO see things come down," Mark Loizeaux once said. "It's real, it's emotional, it's passion. It's adrenaline."[1] And over the last twenty years it's become an elaborate urban ritual whose pulse may have slackened after September 11 but shows no sign of stopping. For in America—and increasingly in cities everywhere—the public's penchant for "redecorating with dynamite" has spawned a new national pastime. Move over, NASCAR. As urban critic Mike Davis has observed, while Americans have long had a knack for laying waste to their downtowns, it's only in Las Vegas that demolition has reached its zenith as full-on public entertainment.

Las Vegas, Davis says, is "neon Babel."[2] Here, in this slot-machine-studded stretch of desert, the spectacle of modern demolition bloomed in full, Day-Glo flower. Fueled by a lust for cheap publicity, a building boom unseen in the history of the Vegas Strip, and a clutch of competing casino moguls locked in what one of them called "the most violent hand-to-hand commercial combat on the planet,"[3] blowing up buildings turned into epic entertainment. In the land of the new beginning, there was always another end, and preferably one involving large quantities of 60 percent nitroglycerin charges and roving NBC-TV correspondents. *Boom!* There goes the Sands, the Aladdin, the Hacienda, El Rancho, the Landmark, and the Desert Inn, all of them jauntily blasted away like some chorus line of high-kicking hotel towers. But the one that put Vegas on the front lines of wrecking fashion, that would "do for demolition what the Folies-Bergere did for legs,"[4] was the Dunes Hotel.

On October 27, 1993, a howling crowd of 250,000 Las Vegans spilled into the streets to bid adieu to the north tower of the Dunes, a twenty-two-story clunker being smacked down to make way for Vegas magnate Steve Wynn's $1.6 billion Bellagio Hotel, at the time the most expensive casino-resort ever built. Wynn's much-uttered motto in those days, "Anything worth doing is worth overdoing," was fully enforced in the barrage of preblast publicity. The downing of the Dunes gushed superlatives like the Clark County courthouse gushed wedding annulments. Wire reports trumpeted it as "the most spectacular show ever seen on the Las Vegas Strip"[5]; the *New York Times* called it "perhaps the most lavishly choreographed architectural blowup in United States history"[6]; it was said to be advertised as "the biggest nonnuclear explosion" ever detonated in the state of Nevada.[7] In the trade they call it "vanity blasting," and the Dunes was going to be the drop-dead belle of the ball. "It was a publicity stunt, a shameless, aggressive publicity stunt," Wynn later told the BBC, "and we gussied it up with all kinds of secondary pyrotechnic explosives so that the building looks like it was being blown up with all kinds of flashes and booms and bangs and commotion and tumult. It was wonderful. We even made a movie for television out of it."[8]

Surely no camera angle would be left unflamed. The implosion of the thirty-eight-year-old tower (decrepit by Las Vegas standards) led off with a fireworks show—yes, "the largest ever west of the Mississippi"—orchestrated by New York's Grucci family and featuring 46 firing batteries. Then there was the implosion itself, where 365 pounds of dynamite was gussied up by 300 special-effects charges and topped off with 460 gallons of aviation fuel. Stacey Loizeaux, having coordinated the pyrotechnics blitz for Wynn (a boss, as she later said, who "may quite possibly be the most demanding in terms of quality and performance on the face of the Earth"[9]), was in need of a few double martinis by the time someone finally pressed the launch button. The six-minute fireworks bonanza "was the longest six minutes of my life," she recalled. "I didn't know whether to go in a corner and throw up or what, but I was just smiling from ear to ear and going, 'Oh, this better work.' "[10] Her nausea was well warranted. The bill for the fifteen-second demolition was $1.6 million, and for that much dough, one contractor explained, Wynn wanted "the most spectacular demolition ever, one that would not be surpassed."[11]

And so at 10:12 P.M., with Wynn having addressed the masses from a loudspeaker and urged the faint-of-heart to repair to a non-cardiac-arrest zone, the tumult commenced with a ceremonial cannonball shot fired from the pirate frigate moored at Wynn's adjacent Treasure Island resort. The eighteen-story, minaret-topped Dunes Hotel sign, one of the most beloved on the Strip but deemed cheaper to convert into a flamethrower than to lug off to some museum, burst into a shower of sparks and hurled toward the hotel. Seconds later, blinding white strobes and a menacing curtain of flame flared through the full height of the tower and lashed fifty feet into the sky. Oil-black smoke billowed up in clouds as the pyrotechnics burned off, and then the charges kicked in, thumping the structure as the Dunes yawed back and finally succumbed to Steve Wynn's exacting specifications. As flames engulfed the hotel and the cameras rolled, former Dunes employees gazed on from nearby barstools, cheering the carnage as tears coursed down their cheeks. "What they were seeing was a place that they were attached to and had worked for many years being turned into a spectacle and destroyed," said art critic Ralph Rugoff, who had commiserated with the Vegas veterans. "But at the same time their showbiz instincts were so strong that they couldn't help but applaud their own destruction."[12]

After the choking dust had lifted from the streets and the empty beer cups were swept away (only thirteen arrests for minor disturbances, the police reported with obvious relief; they had apparently been expecting hordes of bug-eyed pyromaniacs rampaging down the Strip and trying to implode large Cadillacs with jugs of hundred-proof vodka), Wynn's celebratory press releases were faxed off and the accolades started pouring in. Media coverage ranged from the suitably agape to the droolingly delirious, but there was one dour note from the pocket-protector set over at *Engineering News-Record*. The journal had got its dander up over the evening's excesses and drubbed the implosion as "inappropriate entertainment," a respectable engineering feat tawdrily dressed up as "a dramatized event for the sake of a filmmaker." Citing the recent flying-debris death after a Glasgow implosion, editors slapped the blasters for being the life of the Vegas party. "It's absurd for construction firms to emphasize jobsite safety for workers, then invite everyone to the show when they blow something up," they scowled, adding that "inherently risky blasting should not be made into a staged event for the curious public."[13] Clearly, in this view, the Dunes had pushed demolition over to the dark side. Carpet-bomb all the buildings you like, but for Shiva's sake keep the kids at home. Others, too, sensed a dangerous turning point in the audacity of Wynn's plans. "Even at its most flamboyant, Las Vegas never before destroyed property just for the sake of showmanship," one architect complained. "Has America really become a country of such disparate values that a part of us does not recognize the decadence of the projected Las Vegas spectacle?"[14]

Steve Wynn, if he was alerted to these tirades, must have had

In Steve Wynn's Las Vegas, no one takes anything seriously. The Dunes Hotel was gussied up with large quantities of aviation fuel.

a good cackle. That the Strip should be decadent was precisely the point. Adrenaline-addled thrill-seekers piled into the Nevada desert from all points of the earth, belts of cash strapped to their bellies, for one reason only: to claim their slice of decadence. A falling-down building was just the icing on the cake. And really, guys. "This is Las Vegas," Wynn reminded television viewers before the blast. "We don't take anything seriously."[15]

With Wynn and others lording over the ceremonial plunger (and officials at the city's Convention and Visitors Authority writing dynamite into their "vision plan" for a frontal assault on wimpy resorts like Disneyland), over the next eleven years, Las Vegas would rebrand itself as the go-to town for tectonic performance art, never mind the city's cheeky promotional campaign about "What Happens in Vegas, Stays in Vegas." Quite obviously, what happens in Vegas gets booted from Vegas forever in a blazing fireball. That message was made loud and clear in 1996, the year two back-to-back implosions rocked the Strip and made Vegas destructo-tourism the envy of cities everywhere. First up was the Sands Hotel & Casino, a forty-four-year-old relic blasted to make way for the gondola-fronted Venetian Resort. Built as the city's first high-rise, the Sands was a circular tower topping out at a modest seventeen stories, easy prey by implosion standards. The once magnificent tower had turned into such a dump, said officials, there weren't even any ankle-chewing preservationists to fend off. But as preparations began, the Loizeaux crew found as-built drawings for the tower had vanished. (Wreckers are leery of working from blueprints, which are notoriously unreliable, given the changes made pell-mell to a building design over the course of its construction.) Meanwhile, the edifice had been off-limits due to asbestos abatement until a slim seventy-two hours before the blast. When crews finally hit the concrete and drilling for explosives began, a rude shock awaited: The structural system was groaning with heavy steel reinforcement from penthouse to boiler room. By the blast date, November 26, the team had rammed 278 pounds of explosives into the hotel—three times the amount originally planned—and on cue at 2:00 A.M., the Sands torqued and sagged into the annals of unbuilding. In the event, the blast was witnessed by a subdued crowd of stragglers (only "thousands" showed up), since its owner, Wynn rival Sheldon Adelson, was in no mood for glitz. (Adelson's marketing man claimed that they couldn't be bothered with fireworks and such, being much too busy plotting their Venice-themed project, what with all the gondoliers to be interviewed and the Piazza San Marco to be cloned.) The Sands, though it grabbed national media attention for the Loizeauxs— a fat cover story in *Harper's* profiling the family's flattening effect upon the American landscape[16]—was just an appetizer for the decadence to come.

Naked, drunken revelers roamed the Las Vegas Strip on New Year's Eve as hasta la vista hour arrived for the Hacienda Hotel. Surrounding luxury suites were booked solid for implosion parties; tourism officials were predicting a $55.9 million economic boost over the two-day bash; six hundred thousand onlookers descended upon the Strip to savor the Hacienda's final moments, a throng that police said was the largest crowd ever to watch anything in Vegas history. In a startling new development for Vegas promoters, the Hacienda's demise put the city into head-to-head combat with New York over which town would boast the nation's signature New Year's Eve spectacle. The blast was timed at

9:00 P.M. to coordinate with the East Coast's midnight hour; even Fox television had decamped from Times Square to broadcast the debauchery live. Goaded on by journalists smelling a good fight, Las Vegans touted their "brash flashiness" over Gotham's "stodgy traditionalism"; New Yorkers, on the defensive, muttered about their ball-dropping tradition, which had survived for so long in such a "pure form." Mark Loizeaux's comment on the subject—"Why drop a ball when you can drop a building, right?"—could have been the Las Vegas Chamber of Commerce's tagline for the evening. In the end, Vegas officials trumped everything by pointing out that they already had New York City on the Strip: the New York, New York casino hotel, that is, with its faux Gotham skyline, which was opening that very week.

When the Hacienda went down, it was all there: six minutes of fireworks, three thousand aerial shells, balls of fire, and a "waterfall of light." Fortunately for the many weddings to take place over the holiday, the hallowed Vegas hitching post known as the Little Church of the West (said to be the oldest existing structure on the Strip, having opened in 1942) had been moved, lock, stock, and garter belts, from its site on the hotel grounds. The forty-year-old Hacienda wasn't departing without a fight, however. When the dust had cleared, one stairwell was left standing, having only sunk two stories and swayed ten degrees to the south. The Loizeauxs blamed crews salvaging equipment from a boiler room, who removed load-bearing walls they shouldn't have; a crane and wrecking ball had to finish the job the next day. But as the confetti popped overhead and the hotel fountains filled up with wading sybarites, no one could be bothered. One die-hard reveler, in town for his twelfth New Year's Eve on the Strip, summed it all up: "This is a city that really enjoys itself," he said, "that really knows how to party."[17]

. . .

New Year's Eve paid off handsomely for Vegas wrecking, but there was still another card in the city's already loaded deck. A year earlier, the Loizeauxs were toiling to bring down the Landmark Hotel and Casino, a thirty-one-story structure that had for years been the tallest building in Nevada. At the time it was to be the tallest building in North America to be demolished by explosives. "And never before had anyone gone to such real lengths to show the 'power' of a Martian death ray."[18] That was thanks to director Tim Burton, who was grabbing footage of the blast for use in his film *Mars Attacks!* and helping to attract heady Hollywood interest in live-action exploding buildings. The Landmark had all the right plot elements. Work had begun on the five-hundred-room hotel in 1961, but it didn't open until 1969, after being acquired by its notoriously paranoiac owner, Howard Hughes. The cranky billionaire had apparently vaporized the original plans after installing his penthouse in the structure's mushroomlike cap—along with a hidden staircase running from the penthouse to a street-level exit, as the wrecking crew discovered. With four cameras rolling and actors prepped to bail out of harm's way, on November 7, 1995, at 5:37 A.M., the Martian death ray prevailed, and the building seemed to shear in half, then career over in fetching fashion. As a relieved Stacey Loizeaux put it, "We brought it over just like a tree."[19] Admirers of the tower weren't so thrilled by the alien invasion. They rued the day as one of the darkest ever for midcentury modern architecture, and not without justification—the hotel was leveled for a twenty-two-acre parking lot. But destructionists were ecstatic. "This was the Superbowl of wrecking," boasted John E. Weber, president of the general contracting firm overseeing the $3 million demolition. "It doesn't get any better."[20]

Though *Mars Attacks!* flopped, it showed that demolition vérité had become a bustling cottage industry, with wrecking firms turning cinematic implosions into a cash-positive sideline. Though Hollywood had long come calling for decadent film footage (*Atlantic City*'s implosion of the Traymore Hotel being a notable example), the implosion-packed 1990s had location scouts in a tizzy. Wreckers rolled out their own subsidiary scouting services, shooting made-to-order blasts for the likes of Sylvester Stallone (*Demolition Man,* of course) and Mel Gibson (*Boom!* There goes the Orlando City Hall). As producers fanned out across the nation to put dibs on the next big blast, cities

The Landmark Hotel à la director Tim Burton: Never had anyone gone to such lengths to show the fearsome effect of a Martian death ray.

began begging to be destroyed on the big screen. "Use and Destroy!" offered one *Hollywood Reporter* ad in 1995, touting the existential possibilities of the deserted Metro Center mall in Rockville, Maryland. Putting their white elephant's best foot forward, the copy writers beckoned: "Shopping Center. Urban, 70s, Bi-Level. 7 Acres—400,000 sq. ft." Just trying to be accommodating, explained the director of the Maryland Film Commission, which placed the ad. "We're always getting offers from [Hollywood] people who want to blow up a certain kind of building," he said, "and we can't find what they want."[21]

It was the same story over in Wichita, where city officials had a hunk of rotting real estate they'd love to see out with a bang. "For your next blow-'em-up-die-hard film production, the Allis Hotel in Wichita, Kansas, is at your disposal," read another ad in a Hollywood paper. Enterprising Wichitonians had hoped to avoid the estimated million-dollar demolition cost for its dilapidated, seventeen-story hotel. The structure did boast a certain appeal, having been handsome enough in its day to make the Kansas Register of Historic Places, but the hotel had been vacant for twenty-five years and was lousy with asbestos and pigeon droppings. Its immediate prospects were nil, save for violent destruction at the hands of, say, Quentin Tarantino. But film types were demurring. Only a few independent producers had nibbled, despite promises of a hassle-free, permit-ready wrecking opportunity. "To catch a drug dealer in Miami is a lot more exciting than to catch one in Wichita," a script-savvy veteran opined. The whole town was crestfallen as preparations went forward for a blast sans special effects. "It'd be a shame to do it without capturing it on film," the city manager moped. "It's not every day that we blow up a building."[22] In the event (following

Imploded in 1972, the Traymore Hotel took a star turn in cinematic history when director Louis Malle gave it top billing in the opening scenes of Atlantic City.

court challenges from preservationists still fighting to save the structure), Wichita's first-ever implosion and the biggest demolition project in the state of Kansas went off on December 22, 1996. The affair's money shot, as it turned out, was perhaps less sensational than officials had initially intended. Charity campaigners had vowed to send "a much sought-after 'Tickle Me, Elmo' doll" to its gruesome death with the hotel unless enough money was raised for the good cause. "But Elmo got a reprieve and is now in the arms of a young blind and deaf girl."[23]

It might be worth noting that film and demolition have had a boffo relationship since even before the Traymore Hotel. Early screenings of the Lumière brothers' 1896 film *Demolition of a Wall* were said to be a fantastic hit with viewers. "In the first part the wall collapsed in a cloud of dust; then the scene was projected in reverse," wrote Paul Virilio, "and the reconstitution of the wall introduced trick photography to the world of the cinema."[24] Little did the Lumières know that they'd spawn a whole genre of eye-popping deconstructions, nowadays nabbed by implosion junkies with their handi-cams and swapped on Internet chat forums. As Stacey Loizeaux explained the primal, cinematic appeal: "It's unsettling to see a manmade structure, something that you've been taught to trust since your very early years, literally melting before your eyes." That lovely, fluid aesthetic, of course, had good grounding in matters of physics. "We're not picking up this building and dropping it, creating a tremendous amount of vibration," Stacey went on, using one of her favorite metaphors of unbuilding. You could pick up a five-gallon bucket of sand, drop it to the ground, and make a big racket. "But what we're doing is rather pouring the sand out onto the ground. This building is coming down in tiny, tiny little pieces at all different increments in time. So basically the structure, as it's failing, is absorbing its own energy, so it's slowing itself down."[25] As wreckers racked up hours of footage of their work, moreover, the visual elegance of demolition became more than just a sign of a job well done. It was a point of pride. "The idea is to make a building fluid if you can," Doug Loizeaux once said. "When you watch someone else shoot a building, it'll stop, stop again, and then sort of lay over. When you watch one of our buildings collapse, there's an initial movement, then it just seems to dissolve."[26] Loizeaux's competitors naturally beg to differ with this comparison. But the sight of a well-melted building, preferably played back in slow motion and surround sound, remains one of the defining visions of our time.

You wouldn't necessarily hear this standing around the dynamite bin on a demolition site, but there are other reasons why the spectacle of implosion has so captivated the public imagination. Let's face it: Nothing sums up the postmodern world better than a fast-melting building. In 1982, a Frenchman named Jean Baudrillard, one of the maverick pundits of postmodernity, riffed on the subject of unbuilding. He was writing about a new Paris structure built atop the ruins of the Les Halles district—the Pompidou Center—but he pretty much nailed the nut of the issue for a worldwide epidemic of brazenly collapsing towers. The implosion, said Baudrillard, "openly declares that our age will no longer be one of duration, that our only temporal mode is that of the accelerated cycle and of recycling."[27] As everything from communications circuits to news cycles to fashion styles ratcheted up to a now well-known frenzy, implosion was a sign of the times. "Panic in slow motion," he called it.[28] And if you buy Baudrillard's train of thought, buildings are a lot like stars.

Stars, when they have burned themselves out, implode by a process that begins slowly and then speeds up to a fantastic pace. Under powerful gravitational forces, they suck up all the energy around them. And then they become black holes. Like an imploding star, a building takes a chunk of the universe with it when it goes. Panic in slow motion. It wouldn't make a bad motto for Las Vegas.

With demolition, of course, you're always headed back to earth, where metaphysical niceties are sometimes trampled by the industry's pragmatists. French philosophers aren't exactly a big draw at the annual conventions of the National Demolition Association, which often take place at Steve Wynn's former property on the Vegas Strip, the aptly named Mirage. In recent years, Baudrillard would have had a tough crowd, anyhow. When I visited the convention in 2002, it was clear that something had changed. "Demolition used to be fun," one contractor told me as I roved the exhibition hall amid large hulks of wrecking machinery and banners that said things like "American Pulverizer Company" and piles of must-read publications on the order of *Waste Handling Equipment News*. If you wanted to destroy something in America, you were in the right place. Concrete crackers? Check. "Scrape-dozers"? Come and get 'em. From the "Rammer" to the "Rubble Master," sales reps were standing by. The conference's keynote speaker was a violently excitable economist who delivered one of the most impassioned odes to the free market on record. Out in front of the hotel, the replica volcano discharged its lava and steam every quarter hour in an oblique tribute to the wreckers inside. But even in the heart of Las Vegas, in the bowels of the Mirage, there was a sense that the blow-up-and-build mentality was perhaps wearing thin, with some speaking up about "trophy blasting"—the use of explosive demolition merely to get your project in front of news cameras. September 11 in particular had crimped the lifestyle of the world's rowdy implosion junkies. Suddenly a frolicsome keg party just wasn't what it used to be. And implosionists were backing off in the face of tighter regulations all around. "The whole industry has changed," Doug Loizeaux said, citing authorities turning green at the thought of truckloads of explosives rumbling into town, as well as stricter environmental concerns. "I don't see implosion as the widely used method it was in the '70s and '80s and early '90s."

That was certainly the feeling in some quarters of Las Vegas in late 2001. "We're having the implosion, but it won't be a party," was the mantra at the time. Even Steve Wynn (who by that time had sold off his other resorts to focus on even more megalomaniacal visions, like the $2.7 billion Wynn Las Vegas) was putting hubris on hold. Wynn passed up the chance to throw another Strip-wide extravaganza when two towers of the Desert Inn were imploded in 2004 to make way for his newest property. Though the promotional possibilities were tempting— one tower was home to a penthouse pad where Howard Hughes holed up for four years; rumors of secret passageways were enticingly aired in the press—a spokeswoman said that the company would be skipping the added glitz "to focus on the future rather than the past."[29]

Gala festivities might have gone out the window for a time after September 11. But they're not gone for good. Perversely, perhaps, the gestalt of the last decade or two has only trended toward unbuilding as the primal attraction of our age. "Since the toppling of the Berlin Wall in 1989," wrote Herbert Muschamp, "no new building has so fully captured the public imagination as the growing list of wrecked, demolished, or exploding structures around the globe."[30] Well beyond Las Vegas, the spectacle of destruction continues to captivate. Ready or not, we're living in a demolition derby.

Cue the cameras once again. Location: Portsmouth, England. As strains of Tchaikovsky's *1812 Overture* wafted above the rubble, British wrecking crews bit into Portsmouth's Tricorn Centre, a shopping emporium Prince Charles once likened to a "mildewed lump of elephant droppings."[31] The shopping center, called "appealingly surly" even by its defenders, was beloved as a classic 1966 work of British "New Brutalist" architecture, a brand of assertively ugly yet flamboyant essays in concrete construction. "It was like having a depressive but not totally unlovable older brother who was always there," as one critic described the style, "inert, sullen, and communicating only a barely scrutable sarcasm."[32] Such lukewarm praise was no match for the outpouring of loathing heaped upon the shopping center, which eventually took top honors as "Britain's most hated building." And so it was that in 2004 the festivities kicked off. The Tricorn had been promoted in the 1960s as "an orchestration in reinforced concrete that is the equivalent of the *1812 Overture*" (hence the choice of tune to accompany the wreckers), and a winner of a local radio competition even got to start up the bulldozers.[33] It was all grimly amusing to the Tricorn's architect, seventy-five-year-old Owen Luder, no stranger to seeing his work merrily munched away. "There used to be a very exclusive club of architects who had had their buildings demolished during their lifetime," he chuckled as the center was about to be razed. "I joined that club within two years of being in practice."[34]

Location: Granby, Colorado. The American penchant for vigilante wrecking is still going strong. In June 2004, a muffler-shop owner, who apparently had a beef with the town over a zoning dispute, went on a bender and plowed into thirteen buildings in a fifty-three-ton homemade armored bulldozer. Residents of the mountain tourist town of twenty-two hundred described a bizarre scene as the bulldozer slowly crashed through buildings, trees, and lampposts, with dozens of officers walking ahead or behind it, firing into the machine and shouting at townspeople to flee.[35]

Jump-cut to Philadelphia Mayor John Street. In 2001, Street launched the city's massive Neighborhood Transformation Initiative, where, buoyed by $275 million in bonds and other financing, the city scooped up abandoned properties, razed the structures, and waited for developers to come calling. It was a bold move to keep Philadelphia from turning into a latter-day Detroit, and halfway into the five-year program, 6,885 buildings had been sacked or were under contract, well on the road to the program's aspiration of ten thousand demolitions. Street had established his impressive wrecking credentials from the get-go, having relished the job, during his first days in office, of clearing 32,852 abandoned cars from city streets. The sweep made him an instant hero among his constituents, and the house-wrecking program was the next logical step. It was quickly pointed out that towing cars and wrecking houses were not equivalent propositions, however. "The difference is, if you remove a car the problem is gone," one critic scolded. "Abandoned houses are not the cause of blight; they are its physical evidence. The causes run much deeper."[36]

Nevertheless, Mayor Street had now graduated to more boffo feats of urban erasure. It was time for a rousing, feel-good, constituent-pleasing implosion. On March 21, 2004, Street gave the ten-second countdown and yelped, "Fire! Fire!" at the grand finale of Veterans Stadium, the city's thirty-three-year-old concrete bowl imploded to make way for, yes, a colossal parking lot. The Vet had been reviled since opening day for its squirrelly sight lines—defects later trumped by crumbling concrete and roving rats—but as usual, impending doom had naysayers weeping nostalgically into their thermos-fulls of Jack Daniel's. ("It's amazing how emotional you can get about a giant slab of concrete," confessed one worked-up fan.[37]) The sixty-two-second blast—the longest ever for a single structure—sauntered leisurely around the stadium in a clockwise direction, clobbering column after column until each structural bay lumbered to the ground. Though some came spoiling for one last showdown (beery fans could be heard hoarsely yelling, "Stay up! Stay up!"), the Vet went straight to stadium Valhalla. "The sections fell like giants whose knees were buckling, one after the other," a sports reporter wrote. "Let it be said that the Vet was never elegant until yesterday, when it was erased from the landscape in an artistic bit of choreographed violence."[38]

The Vet's demise was engineered by implosion guru Steve Pettigrew, whose Tennessee firm, Demolition Dynamics, also crumpled the Atlanta-Fulton County Stadium in 1997, Jacksonville Coliseum in Florida, and Cinergy Field in Cincinnati. Stadiums and arenas, especially of the dowdy, multipurpose ilk, have driven the most recent uptick in high-profile implosions, with no fewer than nineteen major sports venues wrecked over the last decade. Civic leaders everywhere are resigning them-selves to team owners' and corporate clients' jones for junking beat-up ballparks and bowls, which are often bereft of skyboxes (those swanky, private-party bunkers that can clear $200,000 a season) and other plush amenities (like functional restrooms). The Seattle Kingdome, Pittsburgh's Three Rivers Stadium, and the U.S. Airways Arena in Maryland have all hit the dustbin, and others are poised to plummet: Busch Stadium, anyone? That St. Louis fixture was to topple in late 2005, while the Silver-dome's fate was being openly debated by itchy Detroiters. As for Houston's all-but-deserted Astrodome—crowned the "Eighth Wonder of the World" when the gates opened in 1965—the local paper was still rooting for an extended overtime. "Demoli-tion," an editorial carped, "would be the equivalent of Rome's pulling down the Colosseum because the gladiators moved on."[39] Despite the annoying picketers, the rage for arena razing and renewal has been such a bonanza for downtown boosters, it has its own genre (say "sports pork"), while the out-with-the-old routine is now axiomatic among big leaguers. "It's a cardinal rule in sports these days," one columnist dryly noted. "If you build something, you must destroy something."[40] Architects, toiling over their stadium blueprints, have grown philosophical on the matter. "You know, our Arizona stadium will be torn down in 30 years because it will be useless," Peter Eisenman said of his state-of-the-art abode for the Arizona Cardinals, set to open in 2006, replete with eighty-eight luxury suites on two lev-els. "All the great stadiums get torn down."[41]

Flashback to the about-to-be-blitzed St. Louis Arena in 1999. "You smell that?" Arnold Spirtas once said, feet planted in the shambles of the arena, nosing the air like a true connoisseur. "That plaster mixed with rain smell? The dust and the mildew?" As excavators gobbled away at bricks and showers of sparks from torches rained down, he grinned contentedly. "I can smell a building being wrecked from a mile away," Spirtas said. "I get a big thrill out of that aroma."[42] Given the fervid fan base, stadium blasting can bring out disturbing emotions in wreckers and fans alike. When Spirtas took down the seventy-year-old arena (the Loizeauxs did the blasting), fans were struggling to get a grip on the meaning of the event. "The spectacle was just heart-stopping," said fifty-two-year-old Norma Wheelehan. "I could feel the shots in my body. Just incredible."[43] But others weren't so wowed. One spectator said with a hint of disappointment, having scanned his videotape moments after the blast, "I guess I thought a building of that size would make a more dramatic mess."[44] Another was decidedly down on the whole scene. "I don't think it could be any sadder to watch someone executed. To have so many memories erased in seconds. In just seconds."[45] As the roof rolled over and the dust began to clear, still another positively pouted: "If I had known how it was going to feel, I wouldn't have come. I'm going home."[46]

The swashbuckling Spirtas was perhaps one of the proudest destructionists of his era. Chairman of Spirtas Wrecking Co., he claimed to have "popped" more than fifty thousand structures in a dozen or more states in the course of his four-decade career. "Pop 'em before they spread their disease," he would say. His youngest son, Eric, now runs much of the St. Louis company. Joel, his oldest, runs a firm specializing in asbestos removal. His middle son, Kevin, plays Dr. Craig Wesley—that's the "ruthless surgeon" and "resident bad boy doctor"—on the soap opera

Days of Our Lives. Spirtas's father was a junk collector (he owned a small scrap salvaging company). He's famous for hanging witty signs at his job sites such as "It's checkout time at Coral Courts—No more one night stands," and "Final surgery on this hospital by Arnold Spirtas Co. D.E. (Demolition Experts)." He once explained to a reporter, "I enjoy my job. I guess it shows."[47]

The wrecking business remains as bruisingly competitive as ever, and Spirtas made national media attention in 1999 when a competitor—Aalco Wrecking—agreed to pay a $760,000 settlement after Aalco's Myron Hochman "fessed up" to a "poison-pen letter campaign." The *Wall Street Journal* got hold of the story in a front-pager the following year (DEMOLITION DERBY: TWO GUYS, PLUS SLURS, LIES AND VIDEOTAPE, went the headline). "Myron Hochman and Arnold Spirtas, a couple of old-timers in the demolition business here, have taken the art of knocking things down to new heights," the report said. "Only they haven't been swinging their wrecking balls at buildings, but at each other."[48] Calling it "a strange, modern-day Hatfields-vs.-McCoys quarrel set against a backdrop of dusty rubble and twisted metal," the paper summed up the bizarre altercation. A lawsuit had alleged that Hochman had over ten years sent anonymous letters to unions, government regulators, the local media, and Spirtas customers deploring the company's work. One letter sent to the EPA, signed by "a Spirtas worker," reportedly said: "Spirtas buried asbestos at this jobsite. They were paid to remove it and they buried it!!"[49] Another letter, accusing Spirtas of not having insurance, landed at Anheuser-Busch. A letter alleging cost overruns went to Mercantile Bank. After having been confronted with evidence from handwriting experts and lawyers, Hochman admitted to sending forty letters, claiming to have used "a little poetic license."[50] Amid the troubling impressions the public was getting about the wrecking business, Spirtas wanted to make one thing clear: "We and the NADC are a class operation and do sensitive things in demolishing buildings, like surgeons," he said. "Don't judge wrecking contractors by what happened here."[51]

Destructionists seeking solace, take note. "Anybody can build a building," runs the industry truism. "It takes an expert to wreck one." And as is obvious by now, there's a bit of wrecker in all of us. Six hundred thousand Las Vegans can't all be wrong. "From the time when he first began to breathe and eat, up to the invention of atomic and thermonuclear devices, by way of the discovery of fire," wrote the social anthropologist Claude Lévi-Strauss, "what else has man done except blithely break down billions of structures and reduce them to a state in which they are no longer capable of integration?" Civilization, said Lévi-Strauss, tends to produce what physicists call *entropy*. Like the inevitable process of a star's implosion, entropy is the trend of all types of structures in the universe toward their own dismemberment. "Anthropology could with advantage be changed into 'entropology,' as the name of the discipline concerned with the study of the highest manifestations of this process of disintegration."[52] The wrecker as entropologist. It's a beautiful way of thinking about a long-maligned profession, the unsavory occupation.

But no one wrote more beautifully, heartbreakingly, about destruction than Walter Benjamin, the German thinker deeply engaged with notions of urban restlessness and regeneration. Benjamin spent a lifetime grappling with the after-images of our world. He "concerned himself with *space,* with discontinuities, with moments—fleeting or eternal," wrote the geographer Andy Merrifield. "His was a topographical imagination, passionately embracing *thingness,* seeing, hearing and feeling only buildings, fences, doorknobs, vistas, monuments, signboards, street names, all of which he allotted 'a brief, shadowy existence.' "[53] Benjamin, you might say, was a connoisseur of the entrances and exits of things. For a time he owned a 1920 ink-wash drawing by Paul Klee called *Angelus Novus,* depicting "a spindly abstract figure with a pair of wings and eyes glancing slightly over its own shoulder."[54] This became Benjamin's celebrated angel of history, who soars backward into the future. "Where a chain of events appears before *us, he* sees one single catastrophe, which keeps piling wreckage upon wreckage and hurls it at his feet." The angel would like to drop down into this wreckage, rouse the dead, and repair what has been smashed, Benjamin wrote. "But a storm is blowing from Paradise and has got caught in his wings; it is so strong that the angel can no longer close them. This storm drives him irresistibly into the future, to which his back is turned, while the pile of debris before him grows toward the sky. What we call progress is *this* storm."[55]

A storm blowing from Paradise: That's the permanent meteorological condition of Las Vegas—it's the weather pattern of our world.

As Benjamin elsewhere hinted, demolitionists are "destructive characters" par excellence, rustlers who alight on these debris-strewn plots of our cities. Well versed in matters of destruction, they are in some ways our rough-and-ready guides to the immaterial future. "The destructive character sees nothing permanent," Benjamin wrote in 1931. "But for this very reason he sees ways everywhere. Where others encounter walls or mountains, there, too, he sees a way. But because he sees a way everywhere, he has to clear things from it everywhere. Not always by brute force; sometimes by the most refined." This, Benjamin continued, constitutes a radical sort of freedom. You sensed it in Baron Haussmann; it was plain in the gusto of Jacob Volk; you feel it deeply in the attitude of Mark Loizeaux. It's the exhilaration of unbuilding. Because there are "ways everywhere," Benjamin said, the destructionist always stands at a crossroads. "No moment can know what the next will bring. What exists he reduces to rubble—not for the sake of the rubble, but for that of the way leading through it."[56]

The writer Salman Rushdie put it a little more plainly: "I mean, the world is not a naturalistic place," he said in a 2003 interview. "Buildings may fall down. The world is not like kitchen-sink drama; the world is this weird, operatic place."[57] Buildings may fall down. You've gotta be ready for anything.

NOTES

INTRODUCTION

1. Anthony Tung, *Preserving the World's Great Cities* (New York: Clarkson Potter, 2001), 1.

2. Edward W. Soja, *Postmodern Geographies* (London and New York: Verso, 1989), 158.

3. Mike Davis, *Dead Cities* (New York: The New Press, 2002), 346.

4. Matthias Winzen, "Steinle/Rosefeldt," trans. Pauline Cumbers, in *Deep Storage: Collecting, Storing, and Archiving in Art,* eds. Ingrid Schaffner and Matthias Winzen (Munich: Prestel, 1998), 260.

5. Roberta Smith, "In the Eye of the Collector," *New York Times,* 31 July 1998.

6. "Yea, Rah, Urban Renewal!" *Demolition Age,* 3, no. 6, June/July 1976, 27.

7. "The Las Vegas Dunes Is Demolished," *CBS This Morning* transcript, 28 October 1993.

8. Edmund Burke, *A Philosophical Enquiry,* ed. Adam Phillips (Oxford and New York: Oxford University Press, 1998), 123.

9. Andy Newman, "Last Days for Brooklyn's Giants," *New York Times,* 9 July 2001.

10. Scott Shifrel, "In Greenpoint, B'klyn, Folks Are Sad to See Them Go," *Daily News,* 16 July 2001.

11. Robert Polner, "Tanks for the Memories," *Newsday,* 16 July 2001.

12. Jean Poindexter Colby, *Tear Down to Build Up* (Eau Claire, Wis.: Cadmus, 1964), 35.

13. William Langewiesche, *American Ground* (New York: North Point Press, 2002), 181–82.

14. Rose Macaulay, *Pleasure of Ruins* (New York: Barnes & Noble, 1996), 1.

15. "The Earth, Subject to Cataclysms, Is a Cruel Master," interview in *Robert Smithson: The Collected Writings*, ed. Jack Flam (Berkeley: University of California Press, 1996), 256–57.

16. Sarah Boxer, "Even in a Moonscape of Tragedy, Beauty Is in the Eye," *New York Times*, 23 May 2002.

CHAPTER ONE

1. Christopher Reynolds, "Out with the Old: In L.A., There's More 'Erase-atecture' Than Preservation," *Los Angeles Times*, 29 December 2002.

2. Ibid.

3. Ibid.

4. Adrian Scott Fine and Jim Lindberg, *Protecting America's Historic Neighborhoods: Taming the Teardown Trend* (Washington, D.C.: National Trust for Historic Preservation, 2002), 1.

5. Peter Coy, "Should You Tear the Darn Thing Down?" *Business Week*, no. 3738, 25 June 2001, 112.

6. Candy J. Cooper, "The Tear-Down Wars," *Bergen Record*, 26 November 2000.

7. Fine and Lindberg, *Protecting America's Historic Neighborhoods*, 1.

8. Alison Leigh Cowan, "At a Whimsical, Turreted Suburban Castle, Condominiums Are at the Gate," *New York Times*, 28 September 2003.

9. Fine and Lindberg, *Protecting America's Historic Neighborhoods*, 17.

10. Cooper, "The Tear-Down Wars."

11. Patrick T. Reardon and Blair Kamin, "A Squandered Heritage Follow-Up: Paths of Destruction," *Chicago Tribune*, 24 April 2003.

12. Carole Paquette, "More Buyers Are Tearing Down Existing Homes," *New York Times*, 2 May 2004.

13. Ibid.

14. Lisa Prevost, "Teardowns, Trophies and Angry Neighbors," *New York Times,* 27 September 1998.

15. Mike Davis, *Dead Cities* (New York: The New Press, 2002), 166–67.

16. Michael Powell, "Knock-Down, Drag-Out Urban Renewal," *Washington Post,* 14 March 2003.

17. Blair Kamin and Patrick T. Reardon, "A Squandered Heritage: Research and Destroy," *Chicago Tribune,* 13 January 2003.

18. Patricia Leigh Brown, "In the City of Change, Is 'Las Vegas Landmark' an Oxymoron?" *New York Times,* 7 October 1993.

19. David Berson et al., *America's Home Forecast: The Next Decade for Housing and Mortgage Finance* (Washington, D.C.: The Homeownership Alliance, 2004), 19.

20. Robin Finn, "Man with a Mission: Saving Beauty, Saving Grace," *New York Times,* 22 August 2003.

21. George Ferguson, "Demolition Man," *Evening Standard* (London), 19 November 2003.

22. "Down with Eyesores," editorial, *Financial Times* (London), 7 August 2004.

23. Catherine Jones, "Ugly Showdown," *Liverpool Echo,* 18 August 2004.

24. Tom Leonard, "TV Viewers to Choose 'Most Vile Building,' " *Daily Telegraph* (London), 15 October 2004.

25. Marc Horne, "Rip It Up and Start Again," *Aberdeen Evening Express,* 18 October 2004.

26. Eric Gibson, "What's Falling Down Isn't London Bridge," *Wall Street Journal,* 29 October 2004.

27. Horne, "Rip It Up and Start Again."

28. Sherna Noah, "Viewers to Vote for Demolition of 'Most Vile' Building," Press Association (UK), 14 October 2004.

29. Ibid.

30. Tim Dowling, "Media: Smash Hits," *Guardian* (London), 18 October 2004.

31. Deyan Sudjic, "Celebratory Demolition? The Whole Idea Stinks," *Observer* (London), 2 January 2005.

32. Ibid.

33. Gibson, "What's Falling Down Isn't London Bridge."

34. Norman L. Koonce, FAIA, "Welcome to the AIA Journal of Architecture," *AIA/J: The AIA Journal of Architecture*, Spring 2003, 2.

35. Alan Hamilton and Sophie Kirkham, "Too Ugly to Live: The Award-Winning Town Begging to Be Put Out of Its Misery on TV," *Times* (London), 21 February 2005.

36. "Cedric Price: Enfant Terrible of the Architectural Profession Who Was Notable for Structures Which Were Never Actually Built," *Daily Telegraph* (London), 15 August 2003.

37. Robert Harbison, review of *Cedric Price: The Square Book*, in *Harvard Design Magazine*, no. 21, Fall/Winter 2004, 105.

38. "Cedric Price: Enfant Terrible of the Architectural Profession."

39. Office for Metropolitan Architecture, Rem Koolhaas, and Bruce Mau, *S,M,L,XL* (New York: Monacelli, 1995), 1099.

40. Ibid., 1128.

41. Frederick Gutheim, "The Philadelphia Saving Fund Society Building: A Re-Appraisal," *Architectural Record*, 106, no. 4, October 1949, 92.

42. Brian Libby, "A Glass of Green," *Metropolis*, 22, no. 10, June 2003, 40.

43. Brad Guy, "Demolition Industry Trends: Early Recovery," *Construction & Demolition Recycling*, 6, no. 4, July/August 2004, 46.

44. Joseph A. Schumpeter, *Capitalism, Socialism and Democracy* (New York: HarperPerennial, 1976), 84.

45. Ibid., 83. Emphasis in original.

46. Quoted in Edward W. Soja, *Postmodern Geographies* (London and New York: Verso, 1989), 102.

47. Karl Marx and Frederick Engels, *The Communist Manifesto* (London and New York: Verso, 1998), 38.

48. Marshall Berman, *All That Is Solid Melts into Air* (New York: Penguin, 1988), 47.

49. Peter Stockland, "Emotion Oddly Absent as the General Becomes Rubble," *Calgary Herald,* 5 October 1998.

50. Curtice K. Cultice, "Blasting a Path to World Markets," *Business America,* 118, no. 1/2, 11 January 1997, 42.

51. Lea Sitton, "Sears Demolition May Set a Record," *Philadelphia Inquirer,* 7 October 1994.

52. Patrick T. Reardon and Blair Kamin, "A Squandered Heritage: The City That Wrecks," *Chicago Tribune,* 14 January 2003.

53. Lawrence Downes, "Defacing the Skyline, a Heartless Act in the Heart of Chicago," *New York Times,* 30 October 2004.

54. Kamin and Reardon, "A Squandered Heritage: Research and Destroy."

55. Ibid.

56. Reardon and Kamin, "A Squandered Heritage: The City That Wrecks."

57. Ibid.

58. Chelsea Irving, "Construction Offers New View of IBM Building," CBS 2 Chicago transcript, 16 March 2005.

59. John Kenneth Galbraith, *The Affluent Society,* 2nd ed. (New York: Mentor, 1970), 200.

60. Louis Aragon, *Paris Peasant* [1926], trans. Simon Watson Taylor (Boston: Exact Change, 1994), 169.

CHAPTER TWO

1. Walter George Bell, *The Story of London's Great Fire* (London: John Lane, 1929), 114.

2. Ibid., 89.

3. Neil Hanson, *The Dreadful Judgement* (London: Doubleday, 2001), 137.

4. Claire Tomalin, *Samuel Pepys: The Unequalled Self* (New York: Knopf, 2002), 215.

5. Hanson, *The Dreadful Judgement,* 114–15.

6. Bell, *The Story of London's Great Fire,* 65.

7. Hanson, *The Dreadful Judgement,* 152.

8. Bell, *The Story of London's Great Fire,* 47–48.

9. Hanson, *The Dreadful Judgement,* 122.

10. Ibid., 138.

11. Tomalin, *Samuel Pepys: The Unequalled Self,* 222.

12. Bell, *The Story of London's Great Fire,* 153.

13. Ibid., 203.

14. Ibid., 204.

15. Herbert Asbury, "That Was New York: The Great Fire of 1835," *New Yorker,* 6, no. 24, 2 August 1930, 32.

16. Ibid., 35.

17. Ibid., 34.

18. Ibid., 36.

19. Horace White, "A Personal Experience of the Chicago Fire," *Cincinnati Commercial,* 18 October 1871.

20. Ross Miller, "Out of the Blue: The Great Chicago Fire of 1871," in *Out of Ground Zero: Case Studies in Urban Reinvention,* ed. Joan Ockman (Munich: Prestel, 2002), 50.

21. Frederick Funston, "How the Army Worked to Save San Francisco," *Cosmopolitan,* 41, no. 3, July 1906, 246.

22. Robert Shaplen, "Adventures of a Pacifist, Part Two," *New Yorker,* 34, no. 5, 22 March 1958, 41.

23. Robert Shaplen, "Adventures of a Pacifist, Part One," *New Yorker,* 34, no. 4, 15 March 1958, 49.

24. Ibid.

25. Shaplen, "Adventures of a Pacifist, Part Two," 50.

26. See Brent Blanchard, "The Birth of Explosive Demolition," www.implosionworld.com/history2.htm, accessed 14 October 2002.

27. Shaplen, "Adventures of a Pacifist, Part Two," 54.

28. Frederic Golden, "The Worst and the Brightest," *Time,* 156, no. 16, 16 October 2000, 100.

29. "Bought a House for $1.50," *New York Times,* 7 June 1895.

30. Patricia Volk, "A Family of Firsts," *New York Times Magazine,* 4 October 1987, 71.

31. "The Talk of the Town: Destructionist," *New Yorker,* 5, no. 5, 23 March 1929, 13.

32. "Jacob Volk," *Distinguished Jews of America* (Vol. 1), ed. J. Pfeffer (New York: Distinguished Jews of America Pub. Co., 1917), 465.

33. Ibid.

34. "The Talk of the Town: Destructionist," 13.

35. "Skyscraper Going; Higher One Coming," *New York Times,* 30 April 1910.

36. Ibid.

37. "Breaking Records in House-Wrecking," *New York Times,* 3 June 1910.

38. Ibid.

39. Jacob Volk, letter to the editor, *New York Times,* 18 August 1915.

40. Patricia Volk, *Stuffed: Adventures of a Restaurant Family* (New York: Knopf, 2001), 86.

41. Jesse F. Gelders, "Skyscrapers Torn Down from the Ground Up," *Popular Science,* 128, no. 1, January 1936, 15.

42. "The Talk of the Town: Destructionist," 13.

43. Quoted in Max Page, *The Creative Destruction of Manhattan, 1900–1940* (Chicago and London: University of Chicago Press, 1999), 238.

44. "Here's One Reader Who Likes Writing," *New York Times,* 4 October 1948.

45. " 'Hot Brick' Rushed for New Building," *New York Times,* 18 June 1928.

46. "Salvage Costs Rise in Building Trades," *New York Times,* 6 August 1928.

47. Daniel Schwarz, "New Wrecking Technique Speeds Up Building of Skyscrapers," *New York Times,* 5 July 1931.

48. "Salvage Costs Rise in Building Trades."

49. "Demo Contractors Reflect How Industry Has Evolved," *Demolition Age,* 16, no. 4, April 1988, 28.

50. "Wreckers Strike on 45 Buildings," *New York Times,* 2 April 1926.

51. Jack McFarland, unpublished paper, 24 December 1999.

52. "Demo Contractors Reflect," 28.

53. "Wreckers Busy on Wall Street," *New York Times*, 30 June 1929.

54. "Hotel Demolition Is a Costly Job," *New York Times*, 27 October 1929.

55. "Speed Adds to Cost of House Wrecking," *New York Times*, 10 February 1930.

56. "Hotel Demolition Is a Costly Job."

57. "City Urged to Curb Housewrecking Peril," *New York Times*, 17 February 1930.

58. "200 House Wreckers Strike for 'Safety,' " *New York Times*, 15 February 1930.

59. "Calls a Lock-Out of Housewreckers," *New York Times*, 16 February 1930.

60. Schwarz, "New Wrecking Technique."

61. Ibid.

62. "Albert A. Volk, 70, Tore Down Houses," *New York Times*, 9 September 1950.

63. Albert A. Volk, letter to the editor, *New York Times*, 22 June 1948.

64. "Here's One Reader Who Likes Writing."

65. Schwarz, "New Wrecking Technique."

66. Garrett Price, "All Right, Boys, Down She Comes," *New Yorker*, 6, no. 14, 24 May 1930, 21.

67. "The Talk of the Town: Notes and Comment," *New Yorker*, 6, no. 10, 26 April 1930, 7.

68. "The Talk of the Town: Wrecker's Reminiscences," *New Yorker*, 6, no. 51, 7 February 1931, 12.

69. Quoted in Matthew A. Postal, "Williamsburg Houses," *New York City Landmarks Preservation Commission Designation Report*, 24 June 2003.

70. Jean Poindexter Colby, *Tear Down to Build Up* (Eau Claire, Wis.: Cadmus, 1964), 16.

71. "Columbus Circle Loses Landmark," *New York Times*, 15 June 1954.

72. "Garment District Resists Wrecker," *New York Times*, 19 August 1962.

73. "Demolition Boss Plays Swan Song for Center Theatre," *New York Times,* 30 July 1954.

74. Theodore Strongin, "Wreckers Begin Demolishing Met," *New York Times,* 18 January 1967.

75. Jean Poindexter Colby, *Building Wrecking* (New York: Hastings House, 1972), 21.

76. Sam Blum, "What Goes Up Must Come Down," *New York Times Magazine,* 27 December 1964, 14.

77. Ibid.

78. Red Smith, "World's Greatest Saloonkeeper," *New York Times,* 24 December 1976.

79. Robert Lipsyte, "Ball Park Well Built and 'Could Have Lasted Forever,' " *New York Times,* 31 May 1964.

80. "Helicopter with Steel Ball Used to Demolish Rail Pier on Hudson," *New York Times,* 23 September 1962.

81. Blum, "What Goes Up Must Come Down," 18.

82. "The Lipsett Brothers: Biggest Wreckers in the Building World," *Architectural Forum,* 120, no. 1, January 1964, 77.

83. Blum, "What Goes Up Must Come Down," 18.

84. "Witnesses Paint Brindell as Despot, Ruling and Ruining Labor and Capital," *New York Times,* 29 October 1920.

85. Ibid.

86. "Labor Clues Fade in Wall St. Blast," *New York Times,* 13 November 1920.

87. "Granddaddy of 'Em All," *Demolition Age,* 4, no. 1, October/November 1976, 22.

88. Colby, *Tear Down to Build Up,* 54.

89. Blum, "What Goes Up Must Come Down," 18.

90. Jane Cobb, "Living and Leisure: El Razing," *New York Times,* 1 December 1940.

91. Edgar A. Guest, *Living the Years* (Chicago: Reilly & Lee, 1949), 89.

CHAPTER THREE

1. Jim Lynch, "Landmark's Rise and Fall," *Oregonian,* 23 March 2000.

2. Tom Yarbrough, "Expert's Aim: Bring Pruitt-Igoe to Knees," *St. Louis Post-Dispatch,* 24 February 1972.

3. Doug Stewart, "These Architects in Reverse Make Demolition an Art," *Smithsonian,* 17, no. 9, December 1986, 99.

4. Michael Ryan, "The Good Guys Who Blow Up Buildings," *Parade Magazine,* 28 April 1996, 5.

5. Janet Naylor, "Demolition Maestros Choreograph Hudson's Demise," *Detroit News,* 23 October 1998.

6. Robert L. Jamieson Jr., "Kingdome Blast Is Team Effort for This Family," *Seattle Post-Intelligencer,* 24 March 2000.

7. Lynch, "Landmark's Rise and Fall."

8. Art Thiel, "Dome Saver," *Seattle Post-Intelligencer,* 27 May 1997.

9. Ibid.

10. Lynch, "Landmark's Rise and Fall."

11. Stephen H. Daniels, "Dome Drop Is Flat-Out Fabulous," *Engineering News-Record,* 244, no. 13, 3 April 2000, 12.

12. Douglas Gantenbein, "Bringing Down the House," *New York Times Magazine,* 19 March 2000, 26.

13. "Mark Loizeaux of Controlled Demolition, Incorporated, Talks About the Planned Implosion of Seattle Kingdome," NBC News transcript, 24 March 2000.

14. Jamieson, "Kingdome Blast Is Team Effort."

15. Jim Lynch, "Kingdome Crumples Without a Hitch," *Oregonian,* 27 March 2000.

16. Daniels, "Dome Drop Is Flat-Out Fabulous."

17. Jeff Hodson, "Ready for Fall, Good or Bad," *Seattle Times,* 24 March 2000.

18. Sid Moody, Associated Press, 22 November 1981.

19. William Flannery, "Tearing Down Builds Up Business," *St. Louis Post-Dispatch,* 5 February 1996.

20. Moody, Associated Press.

21. Ryan, "The Good Guys," 5.

22. Richard Rhodes, "Strung Out on Blast," *Playboy,* 21, no. 2, February 1974, 142.

23. Ibid.

24. "Monumental Dullness," *Time,* 69, no. 2, 14 January 1957, 82.

25. "Explosives Drop Concrete Buildings in Neat Piles," *Engineering News-Record,* 159, no. 10, 5 September 1957, 58–59.

26. "The Loizeaux Family Blasts Its Way to the Top," *Engineering News-Record,* 189, no. 6, 10 August 1972, 24.

27. Elaine Woo, "Jack Loizeaux, Pioneer in Razing Buildings by Implosion," *Los Angeles Times,* 7 December 2000.

28. Jamieson, "Kingdome Blast Is Team Effort."

29. David Samuels, "Bringing Down the House," *Harper's,* 295, no. 1766, July 1997, 44.

30. Frederick N. Rasmussen, "John D. 'Jack' Loizeaux, 85, Expert in Use of Explosives in Demolition," *Baltimore Sun,* 30 November 2000.

31. Rhodes, "Strung Out on Blast," 142, 196.

32. Robert Dvorchak, "Church Asks God to Guard the Glass," *Pittsburgh Post-Gazette,* 23 May 1997.

33. Robert Dvorchak, "500 Wood St. Building, Razed Yesterday, Now Pittsburgh Memory," *Pittsburgh Post-Gazette,* 26 May 1997.

34. "Controlled Demolition Brings Pittsburgh Building Down," CNN transcript, 26 May 1997.

35. Mackenzie Carpenter, "Building's Rubble Attracts Onlookers," *Pittsburgh Post-Gazette,* 27 May 1997.

36. Ibid.

37. Samuels, "Bringing Down the House," 39.

38. Dvorchak, "500 Wood St. Building."

39. "Controlled Demolition Brings Pittsburgh Building Down."

40. Hal Hellman, "The Demolition Family: Bringing Down the House," *Geo,* 1, no. 6, October 1979, 87.

41. Linell Smith, "The Explosive Story Behind the Downfall of Useless Buildings," *Los Angeles Times,* 25 December 1989.

42. Ibid.

43. Yarbrough, "Expert's Aim: Bring Pruitt-Igoe to Knees."

44. Sue Anne Pressley, "Dust and Tears Attend the Fall of a Tragic Symbol," *Washington Post,* 24 May 1995.

45. Dan Thanh Dang, "Purging a Reminder of Tragedy," *Baltimore Sun,* 22 May 1995.

46. Ibid.

47. Jesse Katz, "Oklahoma City's Symbol of Terror Is Brought Down," *Los Angeles Times,* 24 May 1995.

48. W. D. Turck, "Dynamite Cuts Wrecking Costs," *Explosives Engineer,* 1, no. 5, July 1923, 136.

49. "Dynamite—A Constructor of Civilization," editorial, *Explosives Engineer,* 1, no. 2, April 1923, 32.

50. Rhodes, "Strung Out on Blast," 141.

51. Ibid., 141–42.

52. John Arlidge, "Death Mars Tower Blocks Demolition," *Independent* (London), 13 September 1993.

53. Carl Gordon, Keith Sinclair, and Calum Macdonald, "Woman Dies in Demolition Blast," *Herald* (Glasgow), 13 September 1993.

54. Andrew Collier, "Tower Block Firm Insists Fatal Blast Was a Success," *Times* (London), 14 September 1993.

55. J. Mark Loizeaux and Douglas K. Loizeaux, "Demolition by Implosion," *Scientific American,* 273, no. 4, October 1995, 148.

56. Ibid.

57. Bill Hewitt and Amanda J. Crawford, "Sudden Impact," *People,* 50, no. 17, 9 November 1998, 139.

58. Jack McFarland, unpublished paper, 24 December 1999.

59. Smith, "The Explosive Story."

60. Yarbrough, "Expert's Aim: Bring Pruitt-Igoe to Knees."

61. Samuels, "Bringing Down the House," 43.

62. Rhodes, "Strung Out on Blast," 141.

63. Ayn Rand, *The Fountainhead* (New York: Signet, 1971), 617.

64. Ibid., 676.

65. "The Loizeaux Family Blasts Its Way to the Top," 25.

66. Ibid.

67. Ellen Weiss, *Odd Jobs* (New York: Aladdin, 2000), 17.

68. Ibid., 18.

69. Jennifer Hile, "Imploding the Male Monopoly of Demolition Business," *National Geographic News,* 15 June 2004.

70. Ibid.

71. "Fun, Fearless Females," *Cosmopolitan,* 226, no. 3, March 1999, 32.

72. Robert Dvorchak, "Company Specializes in Bringing Down the Past," *Pittsburgh Post-Gazette,* 22 May 1997.

73. Wolfgang Saxon, "Thomas R. Ottenstein, 70: Built Belittled Tower at Gettysburg," *New York Times,* 5 August 2000.

74. George Strawley, "Tower Demolition to Highlight Re-Enactment," Associated Press, 27 June 2000.

75. "Much-Derided Gettysburg Observation Tower Is Felled," *New York Times,* 4 July 2000.

76. "Judge's Ruling Allows Company to Topple Tower at Gettysburg," Associated Press, 7 June 2000.

77. Michael A. Fletcher, "Last Casualty of Gettysburg," *Washington Post,* 7 June 2000.

78. John M. R. Bull, "Gettysburg Regains Its Civil War–Era Battle Vista," *Pittsburgh Post-Gazette,* 4 July 2000.

79. Ibid.

80. Maria Blackburn, "The Nuts and Bolts of Park Memorabilia," *Baltimore Sun,* 20 July 2000.

81. "Statement by Richard Moe on Gettysburg Tower Demolition," National Trust for Historic Preservation, 1 July 2000.

82. Bradford McKee, "When Preservation Equals Demolition," *New York Times,* 31 March 2005.

83. Mary Jo Putney, *The Burning Point* (New York: Berkley, 2000), 2.

84. Ibid., 29.

85. Ibid., 248.

86. Ibid., 11.

87. Ibid., 74.

88. Ibid., 295.

CHAPTER FOUR

1. Le Corbusier, *The Radiant City* (New York: Orion, 1967), 210.

2. Walter Benjamin, *The Arcades Project,* trans. Howard Eiland and Kevin McLaughlin (Cambridge, Mass., and London: Belknap, 1999), 128.

3. Robert Moses, "What Happened to Haussmann," *Architectural Forum,* 77, no. 1, July 1942, 57.

4. Peter Hall, *Cities in Civilization* (London: Weidenfeld and Nicolson, 1998), 706.

5. Michel Carmona, *Haussmann: His Life and Times, and the Making of Modern Paris,* trans. Patrick Camiller (Chicago: Ivan R. Dee, 2002), 6.

6. Ibid., 8–9.

7. Anthony Vidler, "The Scenes of the Street," in *On Streets,* ed. Stanford Anderson (Cambridge, Mass., and London: MIT Press, 1986), 37.

8. Louis Chevalier, *The Assassination of Paris* (Chicago and London: University of Chicago Press, 1994), 183.

9. Carmona, *Haussmann,* 123.

10. Willet Weeks, *The Man Who Made Paris Paris* (London: London House, 1999), 33.

11. Carmona, *Haussmann,* 10.

12. Ibid., 404.

13. Vidler, "The Scenes of the Street," 68.

14. Carmona, *Haussmann*, 270.

15. Ibid., 115.

16. Vidler, "The Scenes of the Street," 68.

17. Ibid., 91.

18. T. J. Clark, *The Painting of Modern Life*, rev. ed. (Princeton: Princeton University Press, 1999), 39.

19. Carmona, *Haussmann*, 150.

20. Le Corbusier, *The Radiant City*, 120.

21. Carmona, *Haussmann*, 222.

22. Ibid., 223.

23. Ibid., 231.

24. Ibid., 286.

25. Le Corbusier, *The Radiant City*, 210.

26. David H. Pinkney, *Napoleon III and the Rebuilding of Paris* (Princeton: Princeton University Press, 1958), 157.

27. Carmona, *Haussmann*, 171.

28. Pinkney, *Napoleon III and the Rebuilding of Paris*, 37.

29. Chevalier, *The Assassination of Paris*, 236.

30. Carmona, *Haussmann*, 159.

31. Ibid., 160.

32. Ibid., 434.

33. Benjamin, *The Arcades Project*, 122–23.

34. Sigfried Giedion, *Space, Time & Architecture*, 5th ed. (Cambridge, Mass.: Harvard University Press, 1967), 767.

35. Clark, *The Painting of Modern Life*, 33.

36. Carmona, *Haussmann*, 289.

37. Ibid., 290.

38. Ibid., 291.

39. Pinkney, *Napoleon III and the Rebuilding of Paris*, unpaginated folio.

40. Le Corbusier, *The Radiant City*, 210.

41. Edmond and Jules de Goncourt, *The Goncourt Journals, 1851–1870*, ed.

and trans. Lewis Galantière (Garden City, N.Y.: Doubleday Anchor, 1958), 92.

42. Norma Evenson, *Paris: A Century of Change, 1878–1978* (New Haven: Yale University Press, 1979), 324.

43. Victor Hugo, *Notre-Dame of Paris,* trans. John Sturrock (London: Penguin, 1978), 135.

44. Clark, *The Painting of Modern Life,* 37.

45. Evenson, *Paris: A Century of Change,* 6.

46. Benjamin, *The Arcades Project,* 95.

47. Clark, *The Painting of Modern Life,* 274, n. 24.

48. Philip Hofer, introduction to Giovanni Battista Piranesi, *The Prisons* (New York: Dover, 1973), xii.

49. Emile Zola, *The Kill,* trans. Arthur Goldhammer (New York: Modern Library, 2004), x.

50. David Harvey, *Paris, Capital of Modernity* (New York and London: Routledge, 2003), 261.

51. Zola, *The Kill,* 74.

52. Ibid., 74–75.

53. Ibid., 275.

54. Ibid., 276.

55. Ibid., 277.

56. Ibid., 277–78.

57. Carmona, *Haussmann,* 433.

58. Hugo, *Notre-Dame of Paris,* 28.

59. Ibid.

60. Ibid., 123.

61. Ibid., 126–27.

62. Ibid., 195.

63. Ibid., 189.

64. Ibid., 199.

65. Ibid., 149–50.

66. Quoted in Vidler, "The Scenes of the Street," 99.

67. Harvey, *Paris, Capital of Modernity*, 152.

68. Weeks, *The Man Who Made Paris Paris*, 142.

69. Hall, *Cities in Civilization*, 739.

70. Le Corbusier, *The Radiant City*, 211.

71. Evenson, *Paris: A Century of Change*, 265.

72. Ibid., 287.

73. Ibid., 22.

74. Le Corbusier, *The City of Tomorrow and Its Planning* [*Urbanisme*, 1929], trans. Frederick Etchells (New York: Dover, 1987), 281.

75. Ibid., 287.

76. Clark, *The Painting of Modern Life*, 35.

77. Le Corbusier, *The City of Tomorrow and Its Planning*, 10.

78. Ibid., 12.

79. Le Corbusier, *The Radiant City*, 96.

80. Mindy Thompson Fullilove, MD, *Root Shock* (New York: One World/Ballantine, 2004), 70.

81. Carmona, *Haussmann*, 8.

82. Jane Kramer, "A Reporter in Europe: Paris," *New Yorker*, 54, no. 18, 19 June 1978, 76.

83. Ibid., 77.

84. Chevalier, *The Assassination of Paris*, 260.

85. Ibid., 211.

86. Ibid., 260.

87. Ibid., 215.

88. Ibid., 245.

89. Richard Cobb, "The Assassination of Paris," *New York Review of Books*, 27, no. 1, 7 February 1980, 18.

90. Pamela M. Lee, "On the Holes of History: Gordon Matta-Clark's Work in Paris," *October*, no. 85, Summer 1998, 80.

91. Chevalier, *The Assassination of Paris*, 84.

92. Cobb, "The Assassination of Paris," 18.

93. Evenson, *Paris: A Century of Change,* 307.

94. Chevalier, *The Assassination of Paris,* 240.

95. Walter Benjamin, "The Paris of the Second Empire in Baudelaire," trans. Harry Zohn, in *Selected Writings Volume 4: 1938–1940,* eds. Howard Eiland and Michael W. Jennings (Cambridge, Mass., and London: Belknap, 2003), 52.

CHAPTER FIVE

1. Ada Louise Huxtable, foreword to Lorraine B. Diehl, *The Late, Great Pennsylvania Station* (New York and London: Four Walls Eight Windows, 1996), 10.

2. David Samuels, "Bringing Down the House," *Harper's,* 295, no. 1766, July 1997, 37.

3. "Penn Station to Give Way to Madison Square Garden," *Progressive Architecture,* 42, no. 9, September 1961, 65.

4. Farnsworth Fowle, "84 Penn Station Doric Columns May Be Moved to Flushing Park," *New York Times,* 20 February 1962.

5. Charles G. Bennett, "City Acts to Save Historical Sites," *New York Times,* 22 April 1962.

6. "Farewell to Penn Station," editorial, *New York Times,* 30 October 1963.

7. "Penn Station's Perils," editorial, *New York Times,* 29 September 1962.

8. "Long Island's New Era About to Begin," *New York Times,* 4 September 1910.

9. "Eve of a New Era," *New York Times,* 4 September 1910.

10. Tony Hiss, "The Death and Life of Preservation," *New York Times,* 26 October 2003.

11. Hilary Ballon, *New York's Pennsylvania Stations* (New York and London: W. W. Norton, 2002), 37.

12. Martin Tolchin, "Doom Advances on Penn Station," *New York Times,* 25 January 1964.

13. Diehl, *Pennsylvania Station,* 25.

14. Robert A. M. Stern, Thomas Mellins, and David Fishman, *New York 1960,* 2nd ed. (New York: Monacelli, 1997), 1114.

15. "Penn Station's Perils."

16. Tolchin, "Doom Advances on Penn Station."

17. Diehl, *Pennsylvania Station,* 145.

18. Ibid., 144.

19. Huxtable, foreword to Diehl, *Pennsylvania Station,* 8.

20. "Save Our City," advertisement, *New York Times,* 2 August 1962.

21. "Penn Pals," *Time,* 80, no. 6, 10 August 1962, 42.

22. Quoted in Ballon, *New York's Pennsylvania Stations,* 105.

23. Quoted in Stern, Mellins, and Fishman, *New York 1960,* 1139.

24. Diehl, *Pennsylvania Station,* 29.

25. Ibid., 19.

26. Martin Tolchin, "Demolition Starts at Penn Station; Architects Picket," *New York Times,* 29 October 1963.

27. James Merrill, *Water Street* (New York: Atheneum, 1962), 3.

28. "Kill Him, but Save the Scalp," editorial, *New York Times,* 21 March 1962.

29. Andrés Duany, interview in "Nine Questions About the Present and Future of Design," *Harvard Design Magazine,* no. 20, Spring/Summer 2004, 37.

30. "City Honor Given to Eisenhower," *New York Times,* 28 September 1963.

31. Charles G. Bennett, "City Acts to Save Historical Sites," *New York Times,* 22 April 1962.

32. Harold F. Smith, "To Save Penn Station," letter to the editor, *New York Times,* 24 July 1962.

33. "Reactions to Pennsylvania Station Demolition," *Progressive Architecture,* 42, no. 9, September 1961, 82.

34. "Penn Station's Perils."

35. Ada Louise Huxtable, "Architecture: How to Kill a City," *New York Times,* 5 May 1963.

36. Tolchin, "Demolition Starts at Penn Station."

37. Diehl, *Pennsylvania Station,* 29.

38. Ibid., 16.

39. "Penn Station Columns Dumped in Jersey," *New York Times,* 9 October 1964.

40. Diehl, *Pennsylvania Station,* 18.

41. Vincent Scully, *American Architecture and Urbanism,* new revised ed. (New York: Henry Holt, 1988), 143.

42. "Farewell to Penn Station."

43. Robert D. McFadden, "Morris Lipsett, Razing Expert Who Tore Down Penn Station," *New York Times,* 27 January 1985.

44. "The Lipsett Brothers: Biggest Wreckers in the Building World," *Architectural Forum,* 120, no. 1, January 1964, 77.

45. Ibid., 76.

46. Ibid.

47. "Set to Scrap Normandie," *New York Times,* 30 November 1946.

48. "The Lipsett Brothers," 76.

49. Charles G. Bennett, "Wrecker Offers $330,665 for 'El' in Surprise Bid," *New York Times,* 9 July 1955.

50. Max Frankel, "Third Ave. Holds a Lively Wake to Mark El's Passing," *New York Times,* 2 August 1955.

51. Ibid.

52. Milton Bracker, "Drama of Cranes Enchants 3d Ave.," *New York Times,* 7 November 1955.

53. Meyer Berger, "About New York: Wreckers on Third Avenue El Do Their Work Under a Strict Order of Precedence," *New York Times,* 31 August 1955.

54. "The Lipsett Brothers," 77.

55. Meyer Berger, "About New York: Brothers Lipsett, Who Will Tear Down Third Avenue El, Prefer to Build Things," *New York Times,* 15 July 1955.

56. Tolchin, "Demolition Starts at Penn Station."

57. "Reactions to Pennsylvania Station Demolition," 78.

58. Anne Matthews, "End of an Error," *Preservation*, 51, no. 2, March/April 1999, 50.

59. *The Destruction of Penn Station: Photographs by Peter Moore,* ed. Barbara Moore (New York: D.A.P., 2000), 27.

60. Richard Cahan, *They All Fall Down* (Washington, D.C.: Preservation Press, 1994), 13.

61. Ibid., 12.

62. Ibid., 92.

63. Ibid., 107.

64. Ibid., 117.

65. Ibid., 161.

66. Steven Holl, "Idea, Phenomenon, and Material," in *The State of Architecture at the Beginning of the 21st Century,* eds. Bernard Tschumi and Irene Cheng (New York: Monacelli, 2003), 27.

67. Cahan, *They All Fall Down,* 199.

68. Ada Louise Huxtable, "The Architecture of Destruction," *New York Times,* 26 May 1968.

69. David W. Dunlap, "Reclaiming 'Day' and 'Night,' Memories in Marble," *New York Times,* 9 February 1998.

70. David W. Dunlap, "Piece of Penn Station's Past Is Found in Salvage," *New York Times,* 25 March 1998.

71. David W. Dunlap, "A Quest for Fragments of the Past," *New York Times,* 16 August 1998.

72. Robert Sullivan, *The Meadowlands* (New York: Scribner, 1998), 161–62.

73. Dunlap, "Reclaiming 'Day' and 'Night.' "

74. Rita Reif, "Razing a Building Raises Decorators' Spirits, Too," *New York Times,* 8 February 1958.

75. "Wrecking Companies—New Source for Home Decorations," *Better Homes & Gardens,* 39, no. 9, September 1961, 26.

76. Deborah Baldwin, "The Look of Age, Without the Wait," *New York Times,* 15 August 2002.

77. Maureen McDonald, "Missing Treasures," *Detroit News,* 17 April 2002.

78. "The Gargoyle Snatchers," *Time,* 85, no. 10, 5 March 1965, 74.

79. Ada Louise Huxtable, "Arts Group Saves Bits of Landmark," *New York Times,* 6 October 1964.

80. "City Fragments," *New Yorker,* 42, no. 16, 11 June 1966, 29.

81. Ibid.

CHAPTER SIX

1. "You Haven't Seen the Last of Him," *Demolition Age,* 2, no. 5, April/May 1975, 6.

2. "Featured NADC Speakers," *Demolition Age,* 2, no. 5, April/May 1975, 18.

3. "Dear Friends," *Demolition Age,* 2, no. 5, April/May 1975, 2.

4. "A President Retires," *Demolition Age,* 2, no. 5, April/May 1975, 11.

5. Sam Blum, "What Goes Up Must Come Down," *New York Times Magazine,* 27 December 1964, 10.

6. A. W. Irwin and W. R. L. Bain, "Planned Obsolescence and Demolition of Tall Buildings," *Build International,* 7, no. 6, November/December 1974, 549.

7. Ibid., 560.

8. Ibid., 553.

9. Ibid.

10. Ibid., 560.

11. David M. Pledger, *A Complete Guide to Demolition* (Lancaster, England: Construction Press, 1977), 7.

12. Ibid., 12.

13. "Featured NADC Speakers," 15.

14. Pledger, *A Complete Guide to Demolition,* 17.

15. Ibid., 27.

16. Larry Trojak, "Demolition Is All About the Reach," *Demolition,* 32, no. 5, September/October 2004, 12.

17. Dennis C. Poziviak, "There's a Right Way and Wrong Way," *Demolition Age,* 2, no. 6, June/July 1975, 20.

18. Joshua 6:20.

19. Judges 16:30.

20. Philip Hastings, "The Role of the Structural Engineer in Demolition," *Demolition Age,* 15, no. 3, March 1987, 20.

21. Jean Poindexter Colby, *Building Wrecking* (New York: Hastings House, 1972), 88.

22. Robert A. Wilson, letter to the editor, *New York Times,* 25 October 1987.

23. Richard Cahan, *They All Fall Down* (Washington D.C.: Preservation Press, 1994), 219.

24. "Blast Your Troubles Away," *Demolition Age,* 3, no. 3, December/January 1976, 16.

25. "Who Spoke?" *Demolition Age,* 3, no. 5, April/May 1976, 17.

26. "Demolition Becoming Specialized," *Demolition Age,* 3, no. 4, February/March 1976, 35.

27. Mary Louise Mason, "O.S. to Review City's Policies on Demolitions," *Sun Herald* (Biloxi), 7 April 2004.

28. Dee Wedemeyer, "Destroyers of Buildings, Too, Look for an End to the Lean Years," *New York Times,* 5 March 1978.

29. Joseph P. Fried, "End of Skyscraper: Daring in '08, Obscure in '68," *New York Times,* 27 March 1968.

30. Ada Louise Huxtable, "A Matter of Urban Delight," *New York Times,* 28 January 1968.

31. "Tallest," *New Yorker,* 43, no. 29, 9 September 1967, 38.

32. Ibid., 37.

33. Ibid., 38.

34. Wedemeyer, "Destroyers of Buildings."

35. Ibid.

36. "Yes, You Can Raze an Occupied Building," *Demolition Age,* 10, no. 8, August 1982, 8.

37. John A. Jakle and David Wilson, *Derelict Landscapes* (Savage, Md.: Rowman and Littlefield, 1992), 22–23.

38. Ibid., 23.

39. "Bulldozer Lifts Roof of Florida Family at Dinner," Associated Press, 30 August 2002.

40. Hannah Sampson, "Bulldozer Plows into Wrong Home," *Miami Herald,* 30 August 2002.

41. "House Demolished by Mistake," *Demolition Age,* 17, no. 6, June 1989, 16.

42. Colby, *Building Wrecking,* 46.

43. U.S. Supreme Court, *Adamo Wrecking Co. v. United States,* 434 U.S. 275 (1978), decided January 10, 1978.

44. "The Demolition Industry: Meeting the Challenges of the Nineties," *Engineering News-Record,* 229, no. 4, 27 July 1992, D5.

45. Michael R. Taylor, "Editor's Notes," *Demolition Age,* 19, no. 8, August 1991, 4.

46. Gregory A. Mahin, "Demolition for Progress," quoted in Richard J. Burns, "NADC President's Corner," *Demolition Age,* 16, no. 4, April 1988, 3.

47. Richard J. Burns, introduction to special advertising section, *Demolition Age,* 17, no. 2, February 1989, D3.

48. National Association of Demolition Contractors, "Demolition Contractors Can Strengthen First Response Team Efforts," January 2004, 5.

49. "National Demolition Association: A New Logo, a New Identity," *Demolition,* 33, no. 2, March/April 2005, 7.

50. National Association of Demolition Contractors, "Demolition Contractors," 9.

51. Hans Halberstadt, *Demolition Equipment* (Osceola, Wis.: Motorbooks, 1996), 13.

52. Jennifer Lowe, "Analyzing Demolition Contractors," *Journal of Lending & Credit Risk Management,* 81, no. 6, 1 February 1999, 53.

53. "Demo Contractors Reflect How Industry Has Evolved," *Demolition Age,* 16, no. 4, April 1988, 29.

54. "NADC: Broadening Its Scope, Expanding Its Identity?" *Demolition,* 32, no.1, January/February 2004, 13.

55. Gary J. Tulacz and Mary B. Powers, "Uncertainties Abound," *Engineering News-Record,* 253, no. 15, 18 October 2004, 38.

56. Ralph Blumenthal, "Waste Lumber Is Piling Up at Construction Sites," *New York Times,* 17 January 1966.

57. National Association of Demolition Contractors, "Demolition Industry Promotes C&D Recycling," January 2004, 5.

58. Andrew Pollack and Keith Bradsher, "China's Need for Metal Keeps U.S. Scrap Dealers Scrounging," *New York Times,* 13 March 2004.

59. Ibid.

60. Neil Seidman, "Deconstruction Shifts from Philosophy to Business," *BioCycle,* 41, no. 7, July 2000, 34.

61. National Association of Demolition Contractors, "Demolition . . . the First Step of Reconstruction," November 1999, 5.

62. William Turley, "Careful Handling," *Construction & Demolition Recycling,* 6, no. 3, May/June 2004, 19.

63. Michael R. Taylor, "From the Editor," *Demolition,* 32, no. 6, November/December 2004, 4.

64. Michael R. Taylor, "President Bush Signs Massive Transportation Bill," *Demolition Age,* 20, no. 2, February 1992, 12.

65. Lisa Schreibman, "On a Tear," *Planning,* 67, no. 1, January 2001, 11.

66. Ibid., 13.

67. John J. Fialka, "U.S. Cleanup of Nuclear Sites Will Soon Face First Big Test," *Wall Street Journal,* 3 February 2003.

68. "Leonard Cherry Becomes NADC's 16th President," *Demolition,* 29, no. 3, May/June 2001, 7.

69. D. St. J. Fox and A. J. Kispal, "A Knowledge Based Safety Advisor for the

Demolition Industry," in *Decommissioning and Demolition: Proceedings of the Third International Conference on Decommissioning Offshore, Onshore Demolition and Nuclear Works,* ed. I. L. Whyte (London: T. Telford, 1992), 9.

70. I. L. Whyte, "Demolition: A Review for Civil Engineers," ibid., 133.

71. Susan Klitzman, DrPH, et al., *Health Hazards to Construction Workers During the Demolition of Two Tenement Buildings,* report published by the Center to Protect Workers' Rights, November 1994.

72. "Crushing and Fall Hazards at Lawrence, Mass., Demolition Site Lead to $258,300 in Fines for Pawtucket, R.I., Contractor," OSHA Regional News Release, 18 June 2003.

73. Tim Barlass, "Deadly Rain," *Daily Telegraph* (Sydney), 15 July 1997.

74. "Death and the Media Event," *Engineering News-Record,* 239, no. 3, 21 July 1997, 106.

75. "The Loizeaux Family Blasts Its Way to the Top," *Engineering News-Record,* 189, no. 6, 10 August 1972, 25.

76. Jay Apperson, "Kevin Campbell Auchter, 22, Demolition Worker, Drummer," *Baltimore Sun,* 27 February 2000.

CHAPTER SEVEN

1. Charles Jencks, *The Language of Post-Modern Architecture* (New York: Rizzoli, 1977), 9.

2. "Slum Surgery in St. Louis," *Architectural Forum,* 94, no. 4, April 1951, 129–30.

3. Lee Rainwater, "The Lessons of Pruitt-Igoe," *Public Interest,* no. 8, Summer 1967, 116.

4. Sylvester Brown Jr., "Great-Niece of Igoe Says It's Time to Restore Good Name of 'Uncle Will,' " *St. Louis Post-Dispatch,* 30 January 2005.

5. Andrew B. Wilson, "Demolition Marks Ultimate Failure of Pruitt-Igoe Project," *Washington Post,* 27 August 1973.

6. James Bailey, "The Case History of a Failure," *Architectural Forum,* 123, no. 5, December 1965, 24.

7. "Slum Surgery in St. Louis," 129.

8. Jane Holtz Kay, "Architecture," *Nation*, 217, no. 9, 24 September 1973, 284.

9. "Four Vast Housing Projects for St. Louis," *Architectural Record*, 120, no. 2, August 1956, 186.

10. "Slum Surgery in St. Louis," 130.

11. "CityLife: St. Louis Project Razing Points Up Public Housing Woes," *New York Times*, 16 December 1973.

12. Katharine G. Bristol, "The Pruitt-Igoe Myth," *Journal of Architectural Education*, 44, no. 3, May 1991, 168.

13. Eugene J. Meehan, *The Quality of Federal Policymaking: Programmed Failure in Public Housing* (Columbia: University of Missouri Press, 1979), 73.

14. Bristol, "The Pruitt-Igoe Myth," 165.

15. Peter Hall, *Cities of Tomorrow*, 3rd ed. (Malden, Mass.: Blackwell, 2002), 260–61.

16. Wilson, "Demolition Marks Ultimate Failure."

17. Frances A. Koestler, "Pruitt-Igoe: Survival in a Concrete Ghetto," *Social Work*, 12, no. 4, October 1967, 7.

18. Hall, *Cities of Tomorrow*, 258.

19. Koestler, "Survival in a Concrete Ghetto," 9, 11.

20. Ibid., 9.

21. John Herbers, "The Case History of a Housing Failure," *New York Times*, 2 November 1970.

22. Koestler, "Survival in a Concrete Ghetto," 4.

23. Bristol, "The Pruitt-Igoe Myth," 168.

24. Sara Rimer, "Minoru Yamasaki, Architect of World Trade Center, Dies," *New York Times*, 9 February 1986.

25. "Most of $36-Million Housing Project Faces Razing." *Engineering News-Record*, 188, no. 13, 30 March 1972, 9.

26. "CityLife: St. Louis Project Razing."

27. Tom Yarbrough, "High-Rise Laid Low by Blast," *St. Louis Post-Dispatch*, 17 March 1972.

28. Tom Yarbrough, "Expert's Aim: Bring Pruitt-Igoe to Knees," *St. Louis Post-Dispatch,* 24 February 1972.

29. Theodore P. Wagner, "Pruitt-Igoe Building Crumbles in Seconds," *St. Louis Post-Dispatch,* 22 April 1972.

30. Richard Rhodes, "Strung Out on Blast," *Playboy,* 21, no. 2, February 1974, 198.

31. "The Beat of Life: Instant Demolition in a St. Louis Slum," *Life,* 72, no. 17, 5 May 1972, 10–11.

32. Hall, *Cities of Tomorrow,* 256.

33. "CityLife: St. Louis Project Razing."

34. Sylvester Brown Jr., "Former Conservation Commissioner Views Plan for Fishing Lake as Lost Opportunity," *St. Louis Post-Dispatch,* 27 February 2005.

35. Wilson, "Demolition Marks Ultimate Failure."

36. Ellen Sweets, "The Late, Great LaClede Town," *St. Louis Post-Dispatch,* 30 November 1997.

37. Wilson, "Demolition Marks Ultimate Failure."

38. Kay, "Architecture," 284.

39. William Flannery, "Tearing Down Builds Up Business," *St. Louis Post-Dispatch,* 5 February 1996.

40. Jencks, *Language of Post-Modern Architecture,* 9.

41. Sylvester Brown Jr., "Monument to Failure Lies Fallow amid Ghosts of Danger and Decay," *St. Louis Post-Dispatch,* 2 January 2005.

42. Ada Louise Huxtable, "He Adds Elegance to Modern Architecture," *New York Times Magazine,* 24 May 1964, 18.

43. Camilo José Vergara, *The New American Ghetto* (New Brunswick, N.J.: Rutgers University Press, 1995), 61.

44. Camilo José Vergara, "Blowing Up Projects Doesn't Solve Problems of Housing," *New York Times* (New Jersey Weekly section), 14 June 1987.

45. Clifford J. Levy, "4 High-Rises Torn Down by Newark," *New York Times,* 7 March 1994.

46. Deb Riechmann, "Dynamite Topples Public Housing Development," Associated Press, 1 March 1987.

47. Larry Keating and Carol A. Flores, "Sixty and Out: Techwood Homes Transformed by Enemies and Friends," *Journal of Urban History*, 26, no. 3, March 2000, 304.

48. Ibid., 287.

49. Susan J. Popkin et al., *A Decade of HOPE VI: Research Findings and Policy Challenges*, report published by the Urban Institute, May 2004, 1.

50. Henry Cisneros and Bruce Katz, "Keep HOPE (VI) Alive," *MetroView* (The Brookings Institution), 17 May 2004.

51. Kellie Lunney, "Dashed Hopes," *National Journal*, 37, no. 5, 29 January 2005, 274.

52. Alexander Garvin, *The American City*, 2nd ed. (New York: McGraw-Hill, 2002), 154.

53. Jewel Bellush and Murray Hausknecht, "Urban Renewal: An Historical Overview," in *Urban Renewal: People, Politics, and Planning*, eds. Jewel Bellush and Murray Hausknecht (Garden City, N.Y.: Doubleday Anchor, 1967), 9.

54. Herbert J. Gans, "The Failure of Urban Renewal: A Critique and Some Proposals," in *Urban Renewal: People, Politics, and Planning*, 465.

55. Bellush and Hausknecht, "Urban Renewal," 14.

56. Harrison Salisbury, "The Shook-Up Generation," in *Urban Renewal: People, Politics, and Planning*, 429–30.

57. John A. Jakle and David Wilson, *Derelict Landscapes* (Savage, Md.: Rowman and Littlefield, 1992), 176.

58. Nathan Silver, *Lost New York*, expanded and updated ed. (Boston and New York: Mariner, 2000), xiv.

59. Robert Caro, "The City-Shaper," *New Yorker*, 73, no. 41, 5 January 1998, 49.

60. Ibid.

61. Quoted in Robert Caro, *The Power Broker* (New York: Vintage, 1975), 849.

62. Mindy Thompson Fullilove, MD, *Root Shock* (New York: One World/Ballantine, 2004), 89.

63. Lee Dembart, "Carter Takes 'Sobering' Trip to South Bronx," *New York Times,* 6 October 1977.

64. Ibid.

65. Richard Severo, "Bronx a Symbol of America's Woes," *New York Times,* 6 October 1977.

66. Herbert E. Meyer, "How Government Helped Ruin the South Bronx," *Fortune,* 92, no. 5, November 1975, 140.

67. Jakle and Wilson, *Derelict Landscapes,* 177.

68. S. Terry Atlas, "Torches for Sale," *Newsweek,* 90, no. 11, 12 September 1977, 89.

69. Jerry Herron, "Throw-Away Cities," www.shrinkingcities.com/fileadmin/shrink/downloads/pdfs/Herron_eng_.pdf, accessed 14 November 2003.

CHAPTER EIGHT

1. Ron French, "Razing Paves Way for Renewal," *Detroit News and Free Press,* 25 October 1998.

2. Kristin Palm, "One Building's Struggle," *Metropolis,* 17, no. 9, June 1998, 39.

3. Nadine M. Post, "Record-Breaking Implosion Unprecedented in Complexity," *Engineering News-Record,* 241, no. 17, 2 November 1998, 19.

4. Ibid.

5. Judy DeHaven, "Today, We Say Goodbye to Years of Frustration," *Detroit News and Free Press,* 25 October 1998.

6. Lisa Jackson and Mark Puls, "Partygoers Revel as Building Drops," *Detroit News and Free Press,* 25 October 1998.

7. "People Mover Will Remain Closed Longer Than Expected," Associated Press, 27 October 1998.

8. French, "Razing Paves Way for Renewal."

9. Wayne Woolley, "Nostalgia Lures Crowd to Experience Drama," *Detroit News and Free Press,* 25 October 1998.

10. Santiago Esparza, "Dust Clouds Swallow Downtown," *Detroit News and Free Press,* 25 October 1998.

11. Blair J. McGowan, letter to the editor, *Detroit News,* 6 November 1998.

12. Janet Naylor, "Few Invited to See Hudson's Blow Out," *Detroit News,* 15 October 1998.

13. Kevin Lynch, "Hudson's Implosion Dust Safe, Tests Find," *Detroit News,* 30 October 1998.

14. Jennifer Dixon, "State to Probe Implosion for Safety of Workers," *Detroit News and Free Press,* 31 October 1998.

15. Ibid.

16. Martha A. Churchill, "TV Slant on Implosion Plays to Hysteria," *Detroit News,* 3 November 1998.

17. Janet Naylor, "Hudson's Rubble Turns to Charities' Treasure," *Detroit News,* 4 November 1998.

18. Gregory D. Watson, letter to the editor, *Detroit News,* 29 October 1998.

19. Iver Peterson, "Downtown Detroit Shops for a Future, but Not at Once-Grand Hudson's," *New York Times,* 23 December 1979.

20. Dan Hoffman, "Erasing Detroit," in *Architecture Studio: Cranbrook Academy of Art, 1986–1993* (New York: Rizzoli, 1994), 28.

21. See Allen C. Goodman, "Detroit Housing Rebound Needs Safe Streets, Good Schools," *Detroit News,* 10 March 2004.

22. "Facts," in *Stalking Detroit,* eds. Georgia Daskalakis, Charles Waldheim, and Jason Young (Barcelona: Actar, 2001), 14.

23. Jeff Long, Patrick T. Reardon, and Blair Kamin, "A Squandered Heritage: The Alternatives," *Chicago Tribune,* 15 January 2003.

24. Cameron McWhirter and Darren A. Nichols, "City Council's Blunders Speed Detroit's Decline," *Detroit News,* 28 October 2001.

25. Cameron McWhirter, "Wrecking Homes Standard Practice," *Detroit News,* 19 June 2001.

26. Jodi Wilgoren, "Shrinking, Detroit Faces Fiscal Nightmare," *New York Times,* 2 February 2005.

27. Cameron McWhirter, "3-Day Arson Spree Hurt City's Image," *Detroit News,* 20 June 2001.

28. "Detroit Mayor Dennis W. Archer Thanks Thousands for Their Help in Shaping a Successful Angels' Night Career," City of Detroit press release, 2 November 2001.

29. Charles Waldheim and Marili Santos-Munné, "Decamping Detroit," in *Stalking Detroit,* 107.

30. Dennis Byrne, "Downsizing Cities Has an Up Side," *Chicago Sun-Times,* 4 May 1993.

31. David Usborne, "Motor City Fights Against Fulfilling a Death Wish," *Independent* (London), 31 May 1993.

32. Nancy Costello, "Detroit Official Proposes Turning Blighted Neighborhoods into Pastures," Associated Press, 5 May 1993.

33. "Day of the Bulldozer," *Economist,* 327, no. 7810, 8 May 1993, 33.

34. "Clearance Sale for Detroit?" editorial, *Detroit News,* 30 April 1993.

35. Costello, "Detroit Official Proposes."

36. Kim Trent, "Official's Plan Would Put Detroit's Slums out to Pasture," *Detroit News,* 27 April 1993.

37. Usborne, "Motor City Fights."

38. Scott Bowles, "Some Rooted in Decaying Blocks Vow They'll Stay," *Detroit News,* 30 April 1993.

39. Michael Betzold, "Vacant Lots Cast Blight on Neighborhoods," *Detroit Free Press,* 13 August 1990.

40. Detroit City Planning Commission, "Survey and Recommendations Regarding Vacant Land in the City," 24 August 1990.

41. Waldheim and Santos-Munné, "Decamping Detroit," 105.

42. Joseph P. Fried, "City's Housing Administrator Proposes 'Planned Shrinkage' of Some Slums," *New York Times,* 3 February 1976.

43. Roger Starr, "Making New York Smaller," *New York Times Magazine,* 14 November 1976, 105.

44. Ibid.

45. Witold Rybczynski, "The Zero-Density Neighborhood," *Detroit Free Press Sunday Magazine,* 29 October 1995, 17.

46. Kate Stohr, "Shrinking City Syndrome," *New York Times,* 5 February 2004.

47. Patricia Montemurri, Zachare Ball, and Roger Chesley, "15,215 Buildings Stand Empty," *Detroit Free Press,* 9 July 1989.

48. Georgia Daskalakis, Charles Waldheim, and Jason Young, "Introduction: Committee Work," in *Stalking Detroit,* 13.

49. Peter Gavrilovich, "Rubble Sits . . . and Sits . . . and Sits . . . ," *Detroit Free Press,* 13 July 1989.

50. Zachare Ball and Dori J. Maynard, "Neighborhood 'House-Busters' Strike Again," *Detroit Free Press,* 2 July 1989.

51. Mike Williams, "Neighbors Keep Up Demolition," *Detroit Free Press,* 3 July 1989.

52. Anne Kim, "Fists Fly as House Debris Blocks Chatham," *Detroit Free Press,* 7 July 1989.

53. Michael Betzold, "Don't Do It Yourself, Demolition Expert Says," *Detroit Free Press,* 4 July 1989.

54. Constance Prater, "Have Patience with Vacant Houses, Council Pleads," *Detroit Free Press,* 6 July 1989.

55. "Soundoff: Should Residents Tear Down Abandoned Dwellings?" *Detroit Free Press,* 4 July 1989.

56. Anne Kim, "City Gets Tough on House-Busting Neighbors," *Detroit Free Press,* 8 July 1989.

57. Anne Kim, "House-Busters Say They Feel No Regrets, May Wreck Again," *Detroit Free Press,* 9 July 1989.

58. Darci McConnell, "Council Suspects Politics Is Driving Demolition Plan," *Detroit Free Press,* 21 October 1997; Robert Ankeny, "Archer Seeks $50M to Raze Buildings," *Crain's Detroit Business,* 1 September 1997.

59. Alyssa Katz, "Dismantling the Motor City," *Metropolis,* 17, no. 9, June 1998, 33.

60. Jennifer Dixon and Darci McConnell, "HUD Hands Detroit a $160-Million Gift Days Before Election," *Detroit Free Press,* 29 October 1997.

61. Katz, "Dismantling the Motor City," 37.

62. "Demolishing the City," editorial, *Detroit News,* 11 November 1998.

63. "Abandoned Housing Misery," editorial, *Detroit News,* 24 September 2000.

64. Cameron McWhirter and Brian Harmon, "Derelict Buildings Haunt School, Kids," *Detroit News,* 24 September 2000.

65. Cameron McWhirter, "Detroit Seeks to Increase Condemnations," *Detroit News,* 2 November 2000.

66. McWhirter and Nichols, "City Council's Blunders."

67. Sarah Karush, "Detroit Gets New Weapon Against Urban Decay: Blight Court," Associated Press, 30 December 2004.

68. Cameron McWhirter, "Detroit Destroys Vacant Buildings," *Detroit News,* 1 November 2000.

69. Cameron McWhirter, "Bureaucracy Chokes Detroit," *Detroit News,* 29 October 2001.

70. Jodi S. Cohen, "Schools Ignore Vacant Houses," *Detroit News,* 25 November 2001.

71. Cameron McWhirter and Darci McConnell, "Kilpatrick Gets Ready to Start Demolitions," *Detroit News,* 29 January 2002.

72. Darren A. Nichols, "$10 Million Gift to Raze Detroit Eyesores," *Detroit News,* 7 May 2003.

73. M. L. Elrick, "Big Donor's $10 Million Will Raze City's Eyesores," *Detroit Free Press,* 7 May 2003.

74. R. J. King, "Detroit's Eyesores Slated for Cleanup," *Detroit News,* 9 August 2002.

75. Camilo José Vergara, *American Ruins* (New York: Monacelli, 1999), 23.

76. Camilo José Vergara, "Downtown Detroit," *Metropolis,* 14, no. 8, April 1995, 33.

77. Ibid., 35.

78. Ibid., 36.

79. Ibid.

80. Ibid., 37.

81. Dan Hoffman, "The Best the World Has to Offer," in *Stalking Detroit*, 43.

CHAPTER NINE

1. N. R. Kleinfield, "U.S. Attacked: Hijacked Jets Destroy Twin Towers and Hit Pentagon in Day of Terror," *New York Times*, 12 September 2001.

2. John Seabrook, "The Tower Builder," *New Yorker*, 77, no. 36, 19 November 2001, 71.

3. Debra K. Rubin et al., "Crews Mobilize to Remove Debris but Painstaking Work Takes Toll," *Engineering News-Record*, 247, no. 13, 24 September 2001, 14.

4. Sarah Boxer, "Even in a Moonscape of Tragedy, Beauty Is in the Eye," *New York Times*, 23 May 2002.

5. Donald Friedman, *After 9-11* (Philadelphia: Xlibris, 2002), 171.

6. Ibid., 172.

7. David W. Dunlap, "Erasing a Skeletal Reminder of 9/11," *New York Times*, 11 February 2004.

8. Edward Wyatt and Charles V. Bagli, "Last Days for a Survivor of Sept. 11," *New York Times*, 20 June 2003.

9. David W. Dunlap, "A Survivor Faces a Slow Death, Piece by Piece," *New York Times*, 16 April 2004.

10. David W. Dunlap, "Architectural Team Is Chosen for Trade Center Memorial," *New York Times*, 14 April 2004.

11. Dunlap, "A Survivor Faces a Slow Death."

12. Miriam Hill, "Demolition Plan Stirs Concern," *Philadelphia Inquirer*, 14 January 2005.

13. Dunlap, "A Survivor Faces a Slow Death."

14. Martin Filler, "Dividing Reality and Myth in the Fate of the Towers," *New York Times*, 10 December 2003.

15. Daniel Libeskind, *Breaking Ground* (New York: Riverhead, 2004), 274.

16. Verlyn Klinkenborg, "Touching Ground Zero," *Mother Jones,* 27, no. 1, 1 January 2002, 48.

17. Wolf Von Eckardt, "New York's Trade Center: World's Tallest Fiasco," *Harper's,* 232, no. 1392, May 1966, 94.

18. Ada Louise Huxtable, "Who's Afraid of the Big Bad Bldgs?" *New York Times,* 29 May 1966.

19. Glenn Collins, "Notes on a Revolutionary Dinosaur," *New York Times Magazine,* 6 August 1972, 13.

20. Ibid., 20.

21. Edith Iglauer, "The Biggest Foundation," *New Yorker,* 48, no. 37, 4 November 1972, 143–44.

22. Max Page, "Creatively Destroying New York: Fantasies, Premonitions, and Realities in the Provisional City," in *Out of Ground Zero: Case Studies in Urban Reinvention,* ed. Joan Ockman (Munich: Prestel, 2002), 168–69.

23. Ibid., 171.

24. Henry James, *New York Revisited* (New York: Franklin Square, 1994), 35.

25. Ibid., 41.

26. Ibid., 88–89.

27. Quoted in Jonathan Crary, "J. G. Ballard and the Promiscuity of Forms," in *Zone 1/2,* eds. Jonathan Crary, Michel Feher, Hal Foster, and Sanford Kwinter (New York: Urzone, 1986), 163.

28. Boxer, "Even in a Moonscape of Tragedy."

29. Friedman, *After 9-11,* 165.

30. Jan Wong, "That's Enough About Me, Now, What Do You Think of Me?" *Globe and Mail* (Toronto), 16 February 2002.

31. "Comment: But Was It Art?" *Wall Street Journal,* 11 October 2001.

32. Ibid.

33. Philippe de Montebello, "The Iconic Power of an Artifact," *New York Times,* 25 September 2001.

34. Tara Bahrampour, "An Artist's Inspiration Lives On in His Mind," *New York Times,* 30 September 2001.

35. Richard Plunz, panel discussion, New York City, 5 April 2002.

36. Herbert Muschamp, "The New Ground Zero: With a Dubious Idea of 'Freedom,' " *New York Times,* 31 August 2003.

37. Herbert Muschamp, "Public Space or Private, a Compulsion to Fill It," *New York Times,* 27 August 2000.

38. Herbert Muschamp, "A Handsome Hunk of a Glass Tower," *New York Times,* 2 June 2002.

39. T. S. Eliot, *Collected Poems 1909–1962* (San Diego: Harcourt Brace Jovanovich, 1970), 202.

40. Kenneth T. Jackson, "FDR Drive," *The Encyclopedia of New York City* (New Haven and London: Yale University Press, 1995), 393.

41. "Demolition for Salvage," *Builder,* 164, no. 5218, 5 February 1943, 138.

42. Robert Rhodes James, ed., *Winston S. Churchill: His Complete Speeches, 1897–1963,* vol. 7 (New York: Chelsea House, 1974), 6869.

43. Christopher Woodward, *In Ruins* (London: Chatto and Windus, 2001), 239.

44. Ibid., 212.

45. Ibid., 221.

46. Ibid., 214–15.

47. Ibid., 214.

48. John Harris, *No Voice from the Hall* (London: John Murray, 1998), 1.

49. Ibid., 13.

50. Ibid., 202.

51. Ibid., 135.

52. Ibid., 24.

53. Ibid., 95.

54. Ibid., 180.

55. Ibid., 182.

56. Graham Greene, "The Destructors," in *21 Stories* (New York: Viking, 1962), 236.

57. Ibid., 235.

58. Ibid., 245.

59. Lewis Mumford, *City Development: Studies in Disintegration and Renewal* (London: Secker and Warburg, 1947), 131.

60. W. G. Sebald, *On the Natural History of Destruction,* trans. Anthea Bell (New York: Random House, 2003), 74.

61. Mike Davis, *Dead Cities* (New York: The New Press, 2002), 383.

62. Kenneth Hewitt, "Place Annihilation: Area Bombing and the Fate of Urban Places," *Annals of the Association of American Geographers,* 73, no. 2, June 1983, 272–73.

63. Sebald, *Natural History of Destruction,* 3–4.

64. Midas Dekkers, *The Way of All Flesh,* trans. Sherry Marx-Macdonald (New York: Farrar, Straus and Giroux, 2000), 36.

65. Andreas Ramos, "A Personal Account of the Fall of the Berlin Wall," at www.andreas.com/berlin.html, accessed 3 March 2001.

66. Edmund L. Andrews, "The Wall Berlin Couldn't Quite Demolish," *New York Times,* 13 August 2001.

67. Marilyn Berger, "Ronald Reagan Dies at 93," *New York Times,* 6 June 2004.

68. Véronique Héon-Klin, MD, MPH, Erika Sieber, MD, Julia Huebner, AB, and Mindy Thompson Fullilove, MD, "The Influence of Geopolitical Change on the Well-Being of a Population: The Berlin Wall," *American Journal of Public Health,* 91, no. 3, March 2001, 372.

69. Quoted in Greg Goldin, "Mutually Assured Destruction? The RAND Building Comes out of the Cold," *Los Angeles,* 1 April 2003, 117.

70. Andrews, "The Wall Berlin Couldn't Quite Demolish."

71. Kevin J. O'Brien, "Last Out, Please Turn Off the Lights: Poor Economy Is Driving East Germans from Home," *New York Times,* 28 May 2004.

72. Ralph Stern, interview in Hubertus Siegert and Ralph Stern, "Berlin: Film and the Representation of Urban Reconstruction Since the Fall of the Wall," in *Out of Ground Zero,* 128.

73. Christopher Hume, "Lucky Berlin: A City and a Province," *Toronto Star,* 27 September 2004.

74. "Divided We Stand: A Conversation with Eric Darton," *City*, 5, no. 3, November 2001, 429.

75. "The End of the Manhattan Project," *Demolition*, 29, no. 4, July 2001, 19.

76. United States Strategic Bombing Survey: Summary Report (Pacific War), July 1, 1946, 17.

77. Ibid., 22.

78. Ibid., 23.

79. Hewitt, "Place Annihilation," 267.

80. Davis, *Dead Cities*, 380.

81. John Hersey, *Hiroshima* (New York: Vintage, 1989), 69–70.

82. Don DeLillo, *Mao II* (New York: Penguin, 1992), 157.

CHAPTER TEN

1. Linell Smith, "The Explosive Story Behind the Downfall of Useless Buildings," *Los Angeles Times*, 25 December 1989.

2. Mike Davis, *Dead Cities* (New York: The New Press, 2002), 93.

3. Howard Stutz, "Wynn Las Vegas: The Unveiling," *Las Vegas Review-Journal*, 24 April 2005.

4. Patricia Leigh Brown, "In the City of Change, Is 'Las Vegas Landmark' an Oxymoron?" *New York Times*, 7 October 1993.

5. Tim Dahlberg, "Vegas Resort Implodes in Spectacular Demolition," Associated Press, 28 October 1993.

6. Brown, "Is 'Las Vegas Landmark' an Oxymoron?"

7. Davis, *Dead Cities*, 85.

8. *Virtually Las Vegas*, BBC video documentary, 1995.

9. "Doug and Stacey Loizeaux Discuss Their Family's Demolition Business and Various Buildings They Have Imploded," *Fresh Air* transcript, 20 August 2001.

10. Ellen Weiss, *Odd Jobs* (New York: Aladdin, 2000), 17.

11. "Implosion Entertains on Las Vegas Strip," *Engineering News-Record*, 231, no. 19, 8 November 1993, 9.

12. *Virtually Las Vegas,* 1995.

13. "Inappropriate Entertainment," editorial, *Engineering News-Record,* 231, no. 21, 22 November 1993, 98.

14. Eugene Wukasch, "Blowing Up the Dunes," letter to the editor, *New York Times,* 21 October 1993.

15. "The Las Vegas Dunes Is Demolished," *CBS This Morning* transcript, 28 October 1993.

16. David Samuels, "Bringing Down the House," *Harper's,* 295, no. 1766, July 1997, 37.

17. Tom Gorman, "Las Vegas Has a New Year's Blast—Literally," *Los Angeles Times,* 1 January 1997.

18. William J. Angelo, "Down and Out in Las Vegas," *Engineering News-Record,* 234, no. 21, 20 November 1995, 19.

19. Ibid.

20. Ibid.

21. Karl Vick, "Will Rockville Bust Go Boom?" *Washington Post,* 27 January 1995.

22. Louise Lee, "When the Allis Hotel Blows Up, Don't Expect to See Bruce Willis," *Wall Street Journal,* 7 September 1994.

23. "Controlled Explosion of 66-Year-Old Allis Hotel," Associated Press, 22 December 1996.

24. Paul Virilio, *War and Cinema,* trans. Patrick Camiller (London and New York: Verso, 1989), 14.

25. "Doug and Stacey Loizeaux Discuss Their Family's Demolition Business."

26. Doug Stewart, "These Architects in Reverse Make Demolition an Art," *Smithsonian,* 17, no. 9, December 1986, 102.

27. Jean Baudrillard, "The Beaubourg-Effect: Implosion and Deterrence," trans. Rosalind Krauss and Annette Michelson, *October,* no. 20, Spring 1982, 5.

28. Ibid., 10.

29. Rod Smith, "Wynn to Complete $400 Million Stock Offering," *Las Vegas Review-Journal,* 9 November 2004.

30. Herbert Muschamp, "Filling the Void: A Chance to Soar," *New York Times,* 30 September 2001.

31. Alan Cowell, "Britain: Eyesore Meets the Wrecking Ball," *New York Times,* 25 March 2004.

32. Stuart Jeffries, "The Joy of Concrete," *Guardian* (London), 15 March 2004.

33. Ben Mitchell, "Eyesore Shopping Centre to Be Demolished," Press Association (UK), 24 March 2004.

34. Jonathan Gornall, "Brutal Way to Go," *Times* (London), 23 March 2004.

35. P. Solomon Banda, "Man in Bulldozer Rampage Dead, Authorities Say," Associated Press, 6 June 2004.

36. Gregory Heller, "We Want a Victory for Philadelphia!" *Next American City,* no. 5, July 2004, 22.

37. Patrick Walters, "Veterans Stadium Reduced to Rubble," Associated Press, 22 March 2004.

38. Phil Sheridan, "The Scene: You'd Think It Was the Fourth of July," *Philadelphia Inquirer,* 22 March 2004.

39. "Eighth Wonder," editorial, *Houston Chronicle,* 27 September 2004.

40. Dan Daly, "It's Time to Turn RFK into Rubble," *Washington Times,* 23 March 2004.

41. Hugo Lindgren, "A Little Fascist Architecture Goes a Long Way," *New York Times,* 12 October 2003.

42. Paul Hampel, "I Can Smell a Building Being Wrecked from a Mile Away," *St. Louis Post-Dispatch,* 21 February 1999.

43. Tim O'Neil, "The Spectacle Was Just Heart-Stopping," *St. Louis Post-Dispatch,* 28 February 1999.

44. Ibid.

45. Lorraine Kee, "Thousands Gather to Watch Last Moments of an Institution," *St. Louis Post-Dispatch,* 28 February 1999.

46. Ibid.

47. Hampel, "I Can Smell a Building Being Wrecked."

48. Barbara Martinez, "Demolition Derby: Two Guys, Plus Slurs, Lies and Videotape," *Wall Street Journal,* 21 July 2000.

49. Richard Korman, "Settlement of $760,000 Ends Poison-Pen Letter Campaign," *Engineering News-Record,* 244, no. 2, 17 January 2000, 13.

50. Ibid.

51. Ibid.

52. Claude Lévi-Strauss, *Tristes Tropiques,* trans. John and Doreen Weightman (New York: Modern Library, 1997), 505–06.

53. Andy Merrifield, *Metromarxism* (New York and London: Routledge, 2002), 49–50.

54. Ibid.

55. Walter Benjamin, "On the Concept of History," trans. Harry Zohn in *Selected Writings Volume 4: 1938–1940,* eds. Howard Eiland and Michael W. Jennings (Cambridge, Mass., and London: Belknap, 2003), 392.

56. Walter Benjamin, "The Destructive Character," trans. Edmund Jephcott in *Selected Writings Volume 2: 1927–1934,* eds. Michael W. Jennings, Howard Eiland, and Gary Smith (Cambridge, Mass., and London: Belknap, 1999), 542.

57. "Salman Rushdie Talks with Terry Gilliam," interview in *Believer,* 1, no. 1, March 2003, 106.

INDEX

ABOUT THE AUTHOR

JEFF BYLES has written about architecture, urbanism, and culture for the *New York Times, Village Voice, Metropolis, Cabinet, The Believer,* and other publications. He studied English literature at the University of California at Berkeley, and holds a MFA in creative nonfiction from the University of Alaska at Anchorage. A native of Portland, Oregon, he lives in New York City.